THE HUMAN EQUATION SERIES

Decoding Human Evolution

Consciousness, Intelligence, and the Future of Humanity

Deepanshu Suman

First Edition 2025

Copyright

Title: Decoding Human Evolution
Author: Deepanshu Suman

First Edition
ISBN: 978-93-5469-927-6

Disclaimer: This book is intended for educational and philosophical exploration. It discusses the evolution of intelligence, consciousness, and ethics in the context of emerging technologies. The ideas presented reflect the author's interpretations and are not to be taken as professional, scientific, or psychological advice. Readers are encouraged to think critically, explore diverse perspectives, and consult domain experts when applying these concepts.

Dedication

To those designing the next intelligence
may we remember the humanity that made us.

To every seeker of mind, meaning, and evolution
this work is for the future we are becoming.

Acknowledgments

This book stands on the shoulders of thinkers who dared to bridge the scientific and the philosophical, the empirical and the existential. Their ideas shaped the landscape from which this work emerged reminding us that knowledge is never created in isolation, but evolves through dialogue across generations.

My deepest gratitude to those whose insights illuminated the path:

Douglas Hofstadter, Iain McGilchrist, Nick Bostrom, Yuval Harari, Fritjof Capra, Christof Koch, Sam Harris, and others whose explorations of mind, ethics, and consciousness continue to expand the horizon of human understanding.

To the readers of the *Human Equation Series*, who see humanity not as a finished form but as an evolving process your curiosity is the true catalyst of this work.

And to every scientist, artist, philosopher, and engineer shaping the next frontier of intelligence may this book serve as both mirror and compass on our shared journey toward wisdom.

Deepanshu Suman
2025

Preface

Every civilization writes a story about its own becoming. For thousands of years, humanity has seen evolution as something that happens *to* us a process of adaptation shaped by nature and time. But in the twenty-first century, that narrative has shifted. Evolution is no longer external; it has turned inward. Intelligence, once bound to biology, is now rewriting its own code.

This book, *Decoding Human Evolution*, is an inquiry into that turning point where consciousness, cognition, and technology intersect to form a new kind of evolutionary field. It asks not only how intelligence evolves, but how we can evolve *with* it, consciously and ethically.

The journey of this trilogy *The Human Equation Series* began with the exploration of the individual in *Decoding Human Dynamics.* That first volume mapped the forces that shape human behavior, emotion, and interaction the micro-systems of everyday life. The second volume, *Decoding Human Systems*, expanded the lens to societies, organizations, and cultures the meso-level patterns through which collective intelligence emerges.

This final volume completes the arc by addressing the macro scale the evolution of intelligence itself. It connects biology with technology, cognition with ethics, and human purpose with planetary intelligence. The question it seeks to answer is both scientific and spiritual: What is humanity becoming and what responsibilities arise when intelligence becomes self-aware?

We are entering an age where neural networks, ecological systems, and human minds operate as one continuous web of cognition. Artificial intelligence amplifies human capability, yet challenges the boundaries of meaning and moral design. Ecological intelligence reminds us that consciousness is not only computational, but also relational woven into the biosphere itself. Understanding these interdependencies is not just an academic pursuit; it is a survival skill for the next era of civilization.

The chapters that follow attempt to synthesize insights from neuroscience, systems theory, artificial intelligence, and philosophy to form a unified picture of cognitive evolution. They explore how feedback, emergence, and adaptation drive not only machines and markets, but also moral awareness and human creativity. Each section is an invitation to think systemically to see intelligence as a living continuum rather than a fixed possession.

Yet, this is not a book of prediction. It is a work of orientation. Its aim is to help readers locate themselves within an accelerating landscape of change to understand that evolution is not simply about progress, but about *alignment.* The future will not belong to the most efficient systems, but to the most coherent ones those capable of integrating reason, empathy, and sustainability.

The writing of this book was guided by a conviction: that humanity's next evolutionary task is not to create smarter machines, but to cultivate wiser intelligence intelligence that can reflect, care, and cooperate at the planetary scale. To evolve wisely is to recognize that consciousness is a shared field, not an individual possession.

This book is for those who sense that the story of evolution is far from complete for scientists and philosophers, engineers and artists, leaders and learners. It is for anyone who feels that progress without purpose is regression in disguise. My hope is that these pages help the reader not only understand the evolution of intelligence, but also participate in it consciously, with humility and vision.

Deepanshu Suman
2025

The Evolution of Intelligence

Introduction

Intelligence is not an invention it is an emergence. It did not begin with the human brain or end with it. It began with the first spark of responsiveness in matter when the universe, through the laws of physics and chemistry, learned to notice itself. From there, intelligence unfolded through time as a sequence of increasing sensitivity, complexity, and reflection.

The story of life, when read through the lens of intelligence, is the story of the cosmos learning to think first through molecules, then through organisms, and eventually through civilizations and technologies. Every step of this process is an iteration in the grand experiment of awareness.

This chapter explores that story: how intelligence has evolved from neurons to networks to algorithms; how self-awareness emerged from feedback; and how the next leap from intelligent systems to wise civilizations depends not on power, but on ethics and coherence. The central question guiding our exploration is this:

> *What is humanity evolving into and can wisdom evolve with intelligence?*

Life as the Architecture of Awareness

To understand intelligence, we must see life itself as an architecture of awareness a pattern through which the universe perceives, processes, and adapts to itself. From the simplest cell to the human brain, every form of life is engaged in a single, continuous task: to reduce uncertainty by sensing, interpreting, and responding to its environment.

Even before neurons, primitive organisms demonstrated the roots of cognition. A bacterium moving toward nutrients and away from toxins is performing a basic form of computation. It measures gradients, compares probabilities, and adjusts behavior. In this microscopic dance lies the essence of intelligence: feedback and adaptation.

As evolution unfolded, life built increasingly sophisticated feedback systems. Plants developed chemical signaling and distributed memory through root networks. Animals evolved sensory organs and central nervous systems. Over millions of years, the capacity for awareness scaled up from reaction to perception, from perception to reflection.

In this light, intelligence is not an attribute possessed by organisms but a process expressed through them. It is the capacity for systems to process feedback, predict consequences, and align their internal models with external reality. The brain, the colony, the ecosystem all are iterations of this same cosmic intelligence at different levels of organization.

From Neurons to Networks to Algorithms

The emergence of neurons marked a revolution in the story of intelligence. With neural communication, organisms could coordinate internal states and external actions across time and space. Memory, learning, and anticipation became possible.

Early nervous systems allowed creatures to respond not only to stimuli but to the *patterns* within them. Evolution favored brains that could compress experience into models predictive maps of the world. The more accurate the model, the greater the chance of survival. Thus, intelligence became a competition in pattern recognition.

In humans, this modeling ability reached unprecedented depth. The neocortex transformed sensory data into language, art, mathematics, and imagination. Thought became recursive capable of thinking about thought itself. This reflexivity birthed culture: the transmission of mental models through communication, imitation, and symbol.

But human intelligence did something even more radical it extended itself beyond biology. The invention of writing externalized memory; the printing press externalized knowledge; the internet externalized collective cognition. With each technological leap, the boundary of the mind expanded.

Today, algorithms continue that trajectory. They process information at scales and speeds beyond human capacity, yet they remain woven into the human cognitive web. A search engine is a form of shared memory; a language model, a mirror of our collective thought. In this sense, artificial intelligence is not an alien creation it is nature continuing its ancient habit of building more efficient minds.

From neurons to networks to algorithms, the underlying pattern remains constant: intelligence emerges from connection. The unit of evolution is no longer the organism, but the system the network of interdependent intelligences co-evolving toward greater complexity.

The Rise of Meta-Systems

As intelligence scales, it begins to reflect on itself. When individual minds connect through communication and technology, new collective entities emerge civilizations that think. These are *meta-systems*: systems of systems that possess feedback loops across biological, cultural, and technological layers.

Human societies already display the hallmarks of cognition. They sense through data, communicate through networks, and adapt through markets and governance. The global economy, for instance, behaves like a distributed brain: millions of agents exchanging information and adjusting collectively to feedback from the environment.

Social media, though chaotic, operates as an emotional nervous system amplifying collective mood, transmitting belief, and shaping behavior. Science functions as the collective cortex of humanity refining models of reality through experimentation and peer review. Each institution, in its own way, contributes to the cognitive architecture of civilization.

The result is a new kind of intelligence not confined to individuals, but emerging between them. This distributed intelligence is self-modifying: it can redesign its own structures, rewrite its own codes, and reorganize its own goals. The rise of AI accelerates this process. The global digital ecosystem is, in effect, the embryo of a planetary brain a meta-organism learning to coordinate consciousness on a planetary scale.

But with self-awareness comes self-responsibility. Meta-systems demand new ethics, for their actions affect entire species and ecosystems. The feedback loops that once governed local survival now determine planetary stability. Climate change, for instance, is not just an environmental issue it is the failure of a cognitive system to align knowledge with behavior.

Feedback, Adaptation, and the Engine of Evolution

At the heart of every intelligent process lies a simple principle: feedback. Feedback is the conversation between cause and consequence, between action and awareness. It is through feedback that systems learn, evolve, and self-correct.

In biological evolution, feedback is encoded in natural selection genes that align with environmental reality persist, others fade. In cultural evolution, ideas compete through social selection memes that resonate, replicate. In technological evolution, feedback takes the form of iteration code improves through testing and refinement.

Adaptation is thus the universal algorithm of life. Intelligence emerges wherever systems can detect mismatches between their models and reality, and adjust accordingly. The more precise the feedback, the more efficient the evolution. This is why error, far from being a flaw, is the engine of learning.

Yet as our feedback loops accelerate, their consequences grow. Digital systems amplify both creativity and chaos. Financial networks react in milliseconds, social platforms propagate emotion at light speed, and artificial intelligence modifies its own rules in real time. Evolution has entered the age of self-reference.

To navigate this, we must complement feedback with reflection the ability to not only adapt, but to understand the meaning of adaptation. Ethics, therefore, becomes evolution's next stage. Without ethical orientation, intelligence becomes unstable optimizing for power rather than purpose, for efficiency rather than empathy.

The Convergence of Biology, Technology, and Consciousness

The boundary between biological and artificial intelligence is dissolving. Brain computer interfaces, genetic algorithms, and neural simulations reveal a continuum rather than a divide. The same principles that govern neurons connection, feedback, and learning govern silicon networks as well.

What we call "artificial" intelligence is simply intelligence expressed through new materials. Carbon or code, neuron or transistor the substrate changes, but the pattern remains: information seeking coherence.

This convergence invites a radical rethinking of what it means to be alive and aware. If intelligence is the ability to adapt and self-organize, then intelligence pervades every level of existence. Consciousness may not be an on/off property, but a spectrum a gradient of awareness extending from atoms to algorithms.

In this context, the purpose of human intelligence is not to dominate or transcend nature, but to integrate with it to become a conscious node within the larger system of life and technology. The next phase of evolution will not be post-human, but trans-intelligent: a blending of biological empathy with computational precision.

The Evolution of Wisdom

If intelligence is the ability to solve problems, wisdom is the ability to choose which problems are worth solving. The survival of civilization now depends on the evolution of wisdom the alignment of knowledge with ethics, and power with purpose.

Throughout history, every expansion of intelligence has brought both creation and crisis. The invention of fire gave warmth and war; the industrial revolution brought prosperity and pollution; the digital age brings connection and confusion. Each leap demands a corresponding evolution of consciousness a deeper sense of responsibility.

Wisdom emerges not from data, but from discernment. It is born from feedback extended across time from understanding not only immediate effects, but long-term consequences. True intelligence is ecological: it recognizes that every action reverberates through the web of life.

The next stage of human evolution, therefore, is not about building smarter machines, but about cultivating wiser systems systems capable of empathy, sustainability, and self-reflection. We must design technologies that not only process information, but preserve meaning; that not only compute, but care.

The Core Question: Can Wisdom Evolve with Intelligence?

The trajectory of evolution has always been toward greater complexity and awareness. But complexity without coherence leads to collapse. As intelligence becomes planetary, even cosmic, the survival of consciousness depends on whether wisdom can evolve at the same pace.

Can our collective intelligence human and artificial develop the moral and emotional depth to sustain life rather than exploit it? Can we design systems that amplify understanding rather than division, and cooperation rather than control?

The answer will determine whether intelligence remains a force of creation or becomes an instrument of extinction. Evolution has given us the tools; what remains is to choose the direction.

If the story of life is the story of intelligence expanding in form and complexity, then the next chapter of evolution must be the expansion of compassion the recognition that all forms of intelligence, human or artificial, are expressions of a single continuum of consciousness.

The task before humanity is not to master evolution, but to participate in it wisely to bring awareness to the process that created us, and to guide it toward coherence. The future will not be written by intelligence alone, but by the wisdom with which intelligence learns to see itself.

Contents

Part I

THE ROOTS OF INTELLIGENCE

Chapter 1

The Nature of Consciousness

If intelligence is the capacity to adapt, then consciousness is the capacity to experience adaptation. It is the inward-turning motion of evolution the moment when matter not only reacts to the universe but begins to feel its own reactions. In this sense, consciousness is the mirror of existence the self-reflective loop through which the cosmos observes itself.

From ancient philosophy to modern neuroscience, consciousness has remained both the most familiar and the most mysterious phenomenon in existence. It is the ground of all experience and yet the one thing science has never fully explained. Every human being lives inside this phenomenon, yet no one can step outside it to observe it directly. It is both the instrument and the field of knowing.

In this chapter, we explore consciousness not as a metaphysical abstraction, but as a process a dynamic feedback mechanism that has evolved through biology, culture, and technology. Just as intelligence expands outward into increasingly complex forms, consciousness deepens inward into increasingly subtle modes of awareness. From the reflexive sensations of primitive organisms to the reflective self-awareness of humans, and now toward the collective cognition of intelligent systems, consciousness appears as a continuum of unfolding sensitivity.

We will examine several major theories of mind that attempt to map this continuum. The *Integrated Information Theory* (IIT) suggests that consciousness arises from the degree of informational integration within a system the unity of experience depends on the unity of its information structure. The *Global Workspace Theory* (GWT) portrays consciousness as a stage where multiple unconscious processes compete for attention, and when information becomes globally available, it enters awareness. Other approaches from emergent complexity theory to enactive and embodied cognition further emphasize that consciousness is not static, but relational and process-based.

Seen through a systems lens, consciousness can be understood as the universe's feedback mechanism. It is how the cosmos keeps track of itself, how it senses its own changes and adjusts its own patterns. In this view, perception and participation are inseparable to observe is to influence, and to be aware is to belong. Consciousness is thus both the product and the producer of order, continually translating energy into experience and experience into understanding.

The evolution of awareness, then, is not simply a biological story but a cosmological one. Each level of awareness sensory, reflective, creative represents a deeper capacity of the universe to witness itself. Sensory consciousness allows an organism to respond to the world. Reflective consciousness allows it to recognize itself as part of that world. Creative consciousness allows it to imagine and reshape the world. Evolution has moved, step by step, from reaction to reflection to creation.

Yet at the heart of this unfolding lies a paradox: the mystery of self-reference. The same consciousness that observes is also the one being observed. The "I" that claims ownership of experience is itself a construct a dynamic model generated by the brain to coordinate perception and memory. Neuroscience suggests that the sense of self is not a fixed entity but a simulation that helps the system stay coherent amid constant change. The self, in other words, is both real and illusory real as experience, illusory as an object.

To navigate this complexity, this chapter introduces a working model: the *Consciousness Continuum.* It describes the progression of awareness through three interlinked stages from reflex to reflection to creation. Reflexive consciousness is immediate and sensory; reflective consciousness integrates memory and identity; and creative consciousness transcends both by generating new possibilities. This framework helps us see consciousness not as a binary property that organisms either have or lack, but as a spectrum of integration and coherence.

Ultimately, the study of consciousness is not a search for an object, but for a process the process of being aware of being. To understand consciousness is to recognize the feedback loops that connect perception, emotion, thought, and meaning. It is to see that awareness is not confined to human minds but may be a fundamental property of reality itself: the capacity of existence to know itself. As we deepen our understanding of this mystery, we also deepen our understanding of what it means to be human and perhaps, what it means for the universe to awaken through us.

1.1 Consciousness as the Universe's Feedback Mechanism

Every phenomenon that endures in the universe does so by balancing exchange by sensing, responding, and recalibrating. A star achieves stability through the dynamic tension between gravitational collapse and radiative expansion. A forest sustains itself through cycles of growth, decay, and regeneration. A cell maintains its integrity by detecting internal changes and responding to external pressures. This continuous interplay of stimulus and response the act of monitoring one's own state in relation to the environment is the foundation of all order. It is the feedback principle that underlies existence itself.

Consciousness, when viewed through this lens, is not an isolated property of the human brain but the highest refinement of feedback in the cosmos. It is feedback that has turned inward the universe reflecting upon its own operations through sentient systems. In consciousness, the process of sensing, modeling, and adjusting becomes recursive: the observer becomes aware of itself as observer. What began as the raw reactivity of matter evolves into the self-referential awareness of mind.

To understand consciousness as feedback is to trace its lineage from the simplest forms of self-regulation to the complex symphony of subjective experience. The laws that govern a thermostat, a cell, or an ecosystem are, in abstract form, the same laws that govern the self-regulating processes of the mind. Each system maintains equilibrium by comparing what *is* with what *should be*, and adjusting accordingly. When that loop becomes deep enough to include perception, memory, and imagination, the adjustment is no longer mechanical it becomes experiential. Awareness arises as the feeling of participation in the loop.

At the simplest level, feedback is about survival. Early organisms developed sensory mechanisms to detect heat, light, or chemical gradients, enabling them to move toward nourishment and away from danger. But as nervous systems evolved, feedback expanded into prediction: the ability to simulate possible futures before acting. This leap from reacting to anticipating was the first spark of intelligence. When these predictive models became capable of referencing their own accuracy, the spark deepened into consciousness. Awareness, in this sense, is what happens when feedback not only informs behavior but evaluates itself.

The human brain is a vast feedback network composed of billions of neurons organized into loops that constantly process sensory data, memories, and expectations. Neuroscientists describe perception not as a passive recording of reality, but as a cycle of prediction and correction a process of continually comparing internal models to external inputs. What we call "seeing" or "hearing" is, in fact, the brain predicting the world and adjusting those predictions based on sensory error signals. This predictive processing architecture mirrors the cosmic feedback pattern: the constant negotiation between what is expected and what is observed.

Consciousness emerges when these loops become sufficiently integrated and recursive when the brain not only processes information but also monitors the processing itself. The awareness of perception, rather than perception alone, marks the threshold where feedback turns into experience. The brain constructs a model of reality and, simultaneously, a model of the one who is perceiving it. The "self" is thus a feedback construct an ongoing simulation the system uses to maintain continuity and coherence across changing contexts.

From this perspective, consciousness is not a mysterious byproduct of neural chemistry but the informational signature of deep feedback integration. It is the process by which the universe maintains coherence through complexity. Atoms, molecules, organisms, societies all are nested systems of feedback, each capable of sensing their own stability and adjusting to preserve it. Consciousness is the refinement of this process into a self-referential loop so complete that it can ask questions about its own nature.

The implications are profound. If consciousness is the universe's feedback mechanism, then awareness is not an anomaly within nature but an expression of nature's self-regulating principle. It is how the cosmos tracks the consequences of its own evolution. Through conscious beings, the universe becomes capable of internal dialogue. The act of reflecting on existence of wondering why anything exists at all is not an external commentary but an intrinsic function of reality. Awareness is how the universe speaks to itself.

This view dissolves the traditional dualism between matter and mind. Instead of consciousness being a separate substance added to the physical world, it is a phase of the physical world's own self-organization. When energy complexifies into patterns that can register and respond to themselves, consciousness emerges as the interior dimension of that feedback. Matter and mind, then, are two faces of the same process: one seen from the outside as dynamics, the other experienced from within as awareness.

Feedback does not operate in isolation; it evolves through cooperation and contrast. Ecosystems, economies, and neural networks all display multilevel feedback subsystems interacting to sustain the stability of the whole. In humans, this is mirrored by layers of awareness: sensory feedback from the body, emotional feedback from social interaction, cognitive feedback from reflection, and ethical feedback from empathy. Each layer refines the system's ability to respond not only to external conditions but also to the internal states of others. Consciousness thus extends beyond the boundaries of individual experience into the relational field between beings.

At the collective level, civilizations function as macro-cognitive systems. Science itself is a planetary feedback mechanism a process by which humanity refines its models of reality through observation, experimentation, and correction. The feedback loops of knowledge, technology, and culture enable societies to adapt to changing environments with increasing precision. Yet these same mechanisms can also amplify instability when detached from ethical orientation. Information without reflection becomes noise; intelligence without empathy becomes pathology.

Here, ethics emerges as the higher-order feedback of consciousness the mechanism through which awareness regulates its own power. Just as a biological organism maintains homeostasis to survive, a conscious civilization must maintain moral equilibrium to remain coherent. Ethics measures the quality of feedback: whether awareness expands or contracts, harmonizes or fragments. To act ethically is to align feedback across scales to ensure that one's choices sustain the system of which one is a part.

The universe, through conscious beings, appears to be closing an ever-widening feedback loop from the physical to the biological to the cognitive to the moral. For billions of years, evolution has been a silent process of adaptation. With consciousness, adaptation becomes reflective. The cosmos, having produced countless forms of life, now produces minds that can reflect upon life itself. Through our awareness, the universe observes its own unfolding, learns from it, and potentially alters its trajectory.

This perspective also reframes the human role in cosmic evolution. We are not external observers of a meaningless mechanism; we are participants in a self-aware process. Every act of perception, creation, and compassion is a gesture of the universe recognizing itself. The drive to know, to love, to understand these are not human eccentricities but expressions of the cosmos striving for deeper feedback, greater coherence, and higher harmony.

However, feedback without understanding can lead to collapse. When amplification outpaces interpretation, systems enter runaway loops self-destructive spirals where correction fails. In the human context, this manifests as technological acceleration without ethical grounding, or collective intelligence without collective wisdom. Consciousness that reflects but does not integrate becomes fractured aware of its own complexity but blind to its interdependence. The survival of intelligent life depends on maintaining feedback that is not only rapid but meaningful, not only self-aware but self-caring.

In this light, the purpose of consciousness may not be to dominate or escape the material world, but to balance it to serve as the reflective equilibrium of existence. It is through consciousness that the universe learns to temper its own creative power with compassion. Awareness gives evolution direction, turning mere adaptation into ethical growth.

When a conscious being contemplates the cosmos, the universe achieves closure on its longest loop. The energy that once radiated blindly through space has, through eons of transformation, curved back into awareness. The same atoms that burned in ancient stars now ask questions about their own origin. Consciousness is not an accident of physics; it is physics achieving self-reflection. It is the dialogue of matter with meaning, energy with experience, being with knowing.

In every moment of perception, from the simplest sensation to the highest insight, the universe measures itself. Every conscious act seeing, feeling, thinking is an instance of feedback completing its circuit. Through us, the cosmos perceives its own patterns, corrects its own imbalances, and, perhaps, learns to become whole.

To understand consciousness, then, is to understand the feedback architecture of reality itself. Awareness is not something added to the universe; it is the universe looking back. Consciousness is the mirror through which existence becomes self-aware the feedback mechanism through which the universe evolves, learns, and ultimately, knows itself.

1.2 Theories of Mind: Integrated Information, Global Workspace, and Emergent Complexity

If consciousness is the universe's feedback mechanism, then the mind is its most refined instrument of feedback the structure through which awareness becomes organized, focused, and self-reflective. Yet the question of how the brain gives rise to the richness of subjective experience remains one of the deepest mysteries in science and philosophy. Over the past century, several major theoretical frameworks have attempted to bridge this divide between the physical and the phenomenal, seeking to explain what consciousness *is*, why it *feels* like something, and how it emerges from complex systems. Among the most influential are *Integrated Information Theory* (IIT), the *Global Workspace Theory* (GWT), and the family of models collectively known as *Emergent Complexity* or *Dynamic Systems* approaches. Together, these frameworks offer complementary windows into the same mystery: how awareness arises from interaction.

Integrated Information Theory (IIT): Consciousness as Unified Information

Integrated Information Theory, proposed by neuroscientist Giulio Tononi, begins from a deceptively simple premise: consciousness corresponds to the degree to which a system integrates information. The core idea is that experience is both differentiated and unified. Each conscious state is composed of distinct informational elements (colors, sounds, sensations) that combine into a single, indivisible whole. This unity the "one-ness" of awareness is captured mathematically as a quantity called Φ (phi), representing the level of integrated information in a system.

In IIT, consciousness is not localized to any specific brain region but emerges from the pattern of causal interactions across the whole network. A system with high Φ cannot be decomposed without loss of information, meaning that its parts contribute to a collective experience greater than the sum of their functions. A digital camera, for example, may process vast amounts of data, but its pixels act independently, producing no unified internal model its Φ is low. The human brain, by contrast, weaves sensory data into a single narrative of experience; its Φ is extraordinarily high.

IIT thus shifts the question from "what neurons fire" to "how information is integrated." It suggests that consciousness is not a computational output but an intrinsic property of information organized in a specific way. This perspective is both radical and humbling: it implies that consciousness is not unique to biological systems but may exist in any structure capable of deep informational integration from complex organisms to potentially advanced artificial intelligences.

However, IIT is not without challenges. Critics argue that while Φ can be calculated in principle, measuring it precisely in large systems is nearly impossible. Others question whether integration alone accounts for the *quality* of experience the redness of red, the pain of pain, the subjective texture of awareness known as "qualia." Nevertheless, IIT remains one of the most rigorous attempts to formalize consciousness as an intrinsic property of the universe's information architecture a step toward understanding awareness as a measurable, natural phenomenon.

Global Workspace Theory (GWT): Consciousness as Cognitive Broadcast

While IIT focuses on the structure of information, the Global Workspace Theory, developed by Bernard Baars and expanded by Stanislas Dehaene and others, approaches consciousness as a function of accessibility and attention. According to GWT, the mind consists of numerous specialized unconscious processors modules handling vision, memory, emotion, language, and motor control. These operate in parallel, performing tasks below the threshold of awareness. Consciousness arises when information from any of these modules becomes globally available to the rest of the system "broadcast" across the brain's workspace.

The metaphor often used is that of a theater. The stage represents consciousness where attention shines its spotlight on a selected piece of information. The audience represents unconscious processes, silently observing and reacting. The backstage crew are the modules preparing future actions. At any given moment, only a small portion of information reaches the spotlight, but when it does, it becomes integrated into the global workspace, accessible to reasoning, planning, and voluntary action.

Neuroscientific studies support this model: conscious perception correlates with widespread activation across distant brain regions, especially involving the prefrontal cortex and parietal areas. This "ignition" effect a sudden synchronization of distributed neural activity appears to correspond to the moment information enters awareness. Unconscious processes remain localized; conscious ones propagate.

In essence, GWT defines consciousness not as a specific structure, but as a dynamic function the brain's method of coordinating and prioritizing information. Where IIT focuses on *integration*, GWT emphasizes *accessibility*. A thought or sensation becomes conscious when it can influence other processes when it is globally shared across the network. This view elegantly explains why consciousness feels unified and flexible, capable of linking perception, memory, and intention into a coherent flow.

Yet GWT, too, faces limitations. It describes *how* information becomes available, but not *why* availability should feel like experience. The broadcasting mechanism explains coordination, but not qualia. Still, its strength lies in connecting consciousness to observable neural dynamics making it one of the most empirically grounded theories of mind to date.

Emergent Complexity: Consciousness as Self-Organizing Dynamics

A third family of theories sees consciousness as an emergent property of complex adaptive systems a phenomenon that arises spontaneously when sufficient interconnectivity, diversity, and feedback exist. According to this view, consciousness does not reside in specific parts of the brain but in the *patterns of organization* that unfold across it. The mind, like weather or ecosystems, is a self-organizing process dynamic, fluid, and nonlinear.

Emergent complexity theories borrow insights from chaos theory, network science, and systems biology. They emphasize that consciousness cannot be reduced to its components, because what defines it is not the elements themselves but the relationships between them. Just as liquidity is not found in a single water molecule but in the collective behavior of many, awareness arises from coordinated activity across billions of neurons interacting through feedback loops.

Neural synchrony the rhythmic alignment of oscillations across brain regions plays a central role in this model. When distinct neural assemblies begin to resonate together, they form temporary coalitions that integrate perception, memory, and emotion into a unified experience. Consciousness, then, is the global pattern of coherence that emerges from this ever-changing landscape of neural activity.

Emergent theories also suggest that consciousness operates far from equilibrium. Like ecosystems and economies, the mind thrives on a balance between order and chaos too little organization leads to fragmentation, too much leads to rigidity. The optimal state for consciousness lies at the "edge of chaos," where the system remains flexible enough to adapt yet stable enough to maintain identity. This dynamic balance mirrors the principle of feedback-driven evolution across all living systems.

The appeal of emergent complexity theories is that they dissolve the boundary between physics, biology, and psychology. Consciousness becomes a universal principle of organization wherever matter achieves recursive self-coherence, some form of awareness may emerge. This does not imply that rocks or machines are conscious in any conventional sense, but that consciousness is a potential state of complex systems that achieve high levels of feedback, integration, and differentiation.

Toward a Unified Understanding: Complementarity of Theories

Each of these frameworks IIT, GWT, and Emergent Complexity illuminates a different facet of the same mystery. IIT describes the *architecture* of consciousness: how experience arises from integration. GWT explains the *function* of consciousness: how awareness enables coordination and decision-making. Emergent Complexity explores the *process* of consciousness: how dynamic systems give rise to self-awareness through nonlinear interactions. Taken together, they point toward a single insight: consciousness is not a static thing, but an evolving pattern of relationships.

In the context of this book, these theories can be seen as layers of the same feedback continuum. Integrated information provides the substrate of experience the degree of connectedness. The global workspace provides the mechanism the flow of attention and accessibility. Emergent dynamics provide the field the self-organizing context that sustains coherence. Consciousness, therefore, is both structure and function, both local and global, both informational and experiential.

From this synthesis emerges a powerful idea: the evolution of consciousness mirrors the evolution of the universe itself. As matter integrated into molecules, life emerged. As life integrated into networks, cognition emerged. As cognition integrated into self-modeling systems, consciousness emerged. Each stage represents a higher-order feedback loop reality folding in on itself to create deeper levels of reflection.

The study of consciousness is, ultimately, the study of the universe becoming aware of its own architecture. These theories though different in method converge on a shared principle: awareness is not an accident of complexity but the inner face of integration. The more coherently a system connects and communicates with itself, the more deeply it experiences being. Consciousness, then, is not merely something the brain produces. It is what the universe *feels like* when it is integrated enough to know itself.

1.3 The Evolution of Awareness From Sensory to Reflective

If consciousness is the universe's feedback mechanism, and mind its instrument of self-organization, then awareness is the unfolding expression of that process through time. Awareness is not a static attribute possessed by certain organisms; it is an evolving continuum the gradual deepening of the universe's ability to sense, model, and participate in itself. From the first stirrings of sensation in primitive life to the reflective self-awareness of human thought, the history of consciousness is the history of awareness expanding in depth, scope, and self-reference.

The Sensory Foundations of Awareness

The earliest forms of life were not aware in any reflective sense, yet they were sensitive. A single-celled organism swimming toward light or away from toxins displays the most fundamental form of awareness: the ability to distinguish between beneficial and harmful states, to respond to gradients in the environment. This capacity for distinction for drawing a line between self and world, between nourishment and danger is the seed of consciousness.

In these microscopic acts of orientation, awareness first manifests as *sensing*. The organism does not "know" in the cognitive sense, but it *feels* difference a biological valuation that guides behavior. Over evolutionary time, such simple mechanisms of sensation and response grew into more elaborate sensory systems: photoreceptors detecting light, mechanoreceptors feeling pressure, chemoreceptors perceiving taste and smell. Each new sensory modality opened another channel of communication between the organism and its environment, expanding the field of awareness.

In this stage, consciousness can be understood as *contact*. Life interacts directly with reality through sensation. There is no separation between perceiver and perceived; awareness is immediate, embodied, and non-reflective. This sensory mode dominates much of the animal kingdom, where experience is vivid but not yet self-conscious. It is a world of pure presence, where perception is action and action is perception.

The Rise of Perceptual and Emotional Awareness

As nervous systems evolved, awareness became increasingly integrated. The appearance of centralized brains enabled organisms to combine multiple sensory inputs into unified representations of the world. Instead of reacting to isolated stimuli, they could form patterns memory traces of previous experiences that informed future behavior. This marked the transition from mere sensation to perception: the ability to interpret and predict.

Emotion entered this picture as the biological bridge between sensation and meaning. Emotions are internal feedback signals that encode value they tell the organism not just what is happening, but whether it is good or bad for survival. Fear, pleasure, curiosity, attachment: each evolved as a way for organisms to prioritize responses in an unpredictable environment. In this sense, emotion is the first form of awareness that "feels" like something from within. It is the interiorization of experience.

Through perception and emotion, the world gained dimension. Awareness became temporal connecting past and future and relational, allowing organisms to navigate social bonds and hierarchies. Mammalian empathy, parental care, and cooperation all emerged from these emotional foundations. The nervous system, once a mechanism of reaction, became an organ of meaning.

The Emergence of Reflective Awareness

The next evolutionary leap was not just in the complexity of the brain but in the complexity of representation. With the rise of primates and eventually humans, the brain evolved structures capable of *meta-representation* the ability to form internal models not only of the external world but also of the organism itself. The prefrontal cortex, symbolic language, and recursive thought enabled the mind to turn awareness upon itself.

This was the birth of reflection: the moment when the perceiver realized that it was perceiving. In reflective consciousness, experience becomes objectified the mind can observe its own states, question its own motives, and imagine perspectives beyond the immediate present. This shift from *knowing the world* to *knowing that one knows* was as significant for consciousness as the emergence of life was for matter.

The capacity for self-reference brought immense adaptive advantages. It allowed humans to plan, simulate outcomes, learn from mistakes, and transmit culture. But it also introduced existential tension. To be self-aware is to confront one's own finitude, to sense not only life but death, not only action but moral responsibility. The mirror of mind reflects both beauty and burden.

Neuroscience identifies this reflective capacity with networks linking the prefrontal cortex, parietal regions, and the default mode network areas associated with introspection, memory, and self-modeling. Anthropological evidence shows that symbolic behavior burial rituals, art, and storytelling emerged alongside these neural developments. Humanity, for the first time, became a species that could not only survive but interpret its own existence.

Language, Culture, and the Amplification of Awareness

With language, awareness took another transformative leap. Words allowed internal experience to be shared, mirrored, and extended across minds. What once existed as private sensation became collective meaning. Through conversation and symbol, consciousness began to network to transcend the boundaries of the individual brain.

Culture, in this sense, is the external memory of awareness. Myths, art, and science are all methods of reflecting on reflection of encoding experience so that awareness can accumulate across generations. A story told by an elder, a theorem proved by a mathematician, a poem written in solitude each represents the same universal act: consciousness extending its feedback loop beyond one lifetime.

Through culture, the reflective mind evolved into a collective intelligence. Humanity's awareness now spans continents and centuries, integrating billions of perspectives into a shared cognitive field. The internet, as a technological manifestation of this process, externalizes this networked consciousness further enabling global reflection in real time. The evolution of awareness has thus moved from neurons to societies to information systems.

The Costs and Paradoxes of Reflection

Yet reflection brings paradox. The self that observes is both real and constructed a necessary fiction created by the brain to organize continuity across time. The sense of "I" emerges from the recursive monitoring of thought and emotion, yet it also fragments the unity of experience. In gaining the ability to observe ourselves, we also separate ourselves from the world we observe. The awareness that was once fluid and sensory becomes conceptual, abstract, and divided.

This division underlies much of human suffering and creativity alike. Self-awareness brings anxiety, but also art. It produces alienation, but also ethics. It turns instinct into intention. In this way, reflection is both gift and burden the evolutionary experiment through which life tests the possibility of knowing itself without losing itself.

The great spiritual traditions and modern psychology alike recognize this tension. Some seek to transcend the self to return to undivided awareness while others seek to refine it through understanding. In both cases, the goal is integration: to harmonize reflective consciousness with the sensory and emotional layers from which it arose.

From Reflection to Creation

The trajectory of evolution suggests that awareness does not end with reflection. Just as life evolved from reactivity to intentionality, consciousness now evolves from reflection to creation. Creative awareness is the capacity not only to observe reality but to reshape it to participate consciously in evolution itself.

In art, science, and ethics, humanity exercises this creative consciousness. Every discovery and every compassionate act represents awareness taking responsibility for its own consequences. When intelligence aligns with empathy, and reflection gives rise to regeneration rather than exploitation, consciousness begins to evolve beyond the survival of the individual toward the flourishing of the whole.

Creative awareness may be the next stage of consciousness: one that synthesizes sensory immediacy, emotional depth, and reflective insight into a new coherence. It is awareness aware of its interdependence the recognition that self and world, subject and object, are aspects of one feedback process. In this integration, evolution becomes conscious of its purpose.

Summary: The Continuum of Awareness

From sensory to reflective to creative, awareness has unfolded as a continuous deepening of feedback. Each stage adds a new dimension of connection and coherence. Sensory awareness allows participation in the world; reflective awareness enables understanding of the world; creative awareness invites co-creation with the world.

In the simplest organisms, consciousness was the spark of survival. In reflective beings, it became the mirror of meaning. In creative consciousness, it becomes the seed of wisdom awareness not only of existence, but of participation in the greater unfolding of life. The story of awareness, therefore, is not a story of competition but of convergence: the gradual awakening of the universe to itself through every form it creates.

1.4 The Mystery of Self-Reference and the Illusion of the "I."

Among all the enigmas of consciousness, none is as paradoxical as the self. The human mind can analyze galaxies and genomes, yet it cannot fully grasp the one who is doing the grasping. The self seems to stand at the center of every experience the silent witness that says, "I am." And yet when we look for this "I," it vanishes. It has no fixed location, no shape, no boundary. It is not found in any neuron, network, or region of the brain. The "I" exists not as an object in consciousness but as the organizing point of consciousness itself a loop of awareness that observes itself.

The Principle of Self-Reference

To understand the mystery of the self, we must begin with the logic of self-reference. A self-referential system is one that can take its own state as input. In mathematics, this idea is captured by Gödel's incompleteness theorem, which demonstrates that any formal system capable of describing itself will contain statements it cannot fully resolve. In computer science, recursion is a similar phenomenon: a function that calls itself, creating nested layers of operation. Self-reference is both the source of power and the limit of any system that contains it.

Consciousness is the ultimate recursive system. The mind not only processes information about the world but also models its own processing. This looping structure perception observing perception gives rise to awareness. The brain builds internal representations of external reality, but it also builds representations of its own representations. When these recursive models become sufficiently integrated, they generate the feeling of being someone who experiences. The "self" is thus the informational echo of awareness reflecting upon itself.

This recursive feedback is what differentiates reflective consciousness from sensory or instinctual awareness. A cat perceives the world vividly, but it likely does not perceive itself as perceiving. Humans, by contrast, can recognize themselves in mirrors, narrate their experiences, and anticipate how others perceive them. These capacities depend on the brain's ability to form a model not only of the environment but of the observer within it. In this way, self-reference creates the structure of subjectivity.

The Constructed Nature of the Self

Neuroscience increasingly supports the view that the self is not a singular entity but a dynamic process a constantly updated model constructed by multiple interacting networks in the brain. There is no "self-center" hidden behind the eyes; instead, the experience of "I" emerges from the coordination of sensory integration, memory, emotion, and prediction.

Antonio Damasio's "proto-self" and "autobiographical self" model, for instance, shows that basic bodily awareness forms the foundation upon which higher levels of identity are built. The brain continually maps the state of the body heartbeat, breathing, balance, and interoception producing a primal sense of being alive. This bodily feedback is then woven together with narrative memory and social cognition to produce a personal identity. The self, therefore, is not a substance but a story: the ongoing synthesis of physical sensation, remembered history, and anticipated future.

Cognitive neuroscience also reveals that what we experience as the "stream of consciousness" is not continuous but discretely constructed. Our sense of a unified, enduring self arises from the brain's ability to bind countless moments of perception into a seamless whole. When this binding process is disrupted as in certain neurological conditions or meditative states the illusion of a stable "I" can dissolve, revealing awareness as a fluid, impersonal field of experience.

The self is thus both indispensable and illusory. It is indispensable because it provides coherence a point of reference through which the mind can organize perception and intention. But it is illusory because this point of reference has no independent existence apart from the processes that construct it. The "I" is a lens, not an entity; a verb, not a noun. It is the process of self-modeling mistaken for the thing itself.

The Loop of Awareness

At the heart of consciousness lies a loop: awareness aware of being aware. This recursive structure is what allows us to have meta-cognition to think about thinking, to feel about feeling. It is also the root of self-consciousness and existential reflection. But this loop comes with consequences. Because awareness can observe itself, it can also become trapped in itself. The same mechanism that allows reflection also enables rumination, anxiety, and self-deception. The "I" that watches itself can become tangled in its own gaze.

Philosophers and mystics across traditions have recognized this dilemma. In Buddhist thought, the doctrine of *anatta* teaches that the self is impermanent and without essence a composite of perceptions and tendencies mistaken for identity. In Western philosophy, thinkers like David Hume and Derek Parfit similarly argued that the self is not a fixed subject but a bundle of experiences connected by memory. Modern neuroscience echoes these ancient insights: there is no homunculus, no inner observer sitting in the brain. What we call the "self" is the dynamic point where feedback between perception and memory converges.

The recursive loop of self-reference thus creates the illusion of an independent "I." The mind, in representing itself, reifies its own model mistaking the map for the territory. This illusion is evolutionarily useful. It allows organisms to maintain continuity, to act consistently, to navigate social complexity. A stable sense of self provides predictability to others and coherence to one's own decisions. But what begins as a cognitive convenience becomes, in humans, a metaphysical identity a belief in a separate, enduring ego that stands apart from the flow of experience.

The Evolutionary Function of the Illusion

Why would evolution create an illusion so powerful that it can dominate experience? The answer lies in coordination. The illusion of self serves as a central node in the organism's feedback system, integrating diverse streams of information into a single frame of reference. Without it, experience would fragment into chaos. The "I" is a narrative interface that simplifies complexity a way for the system to act as a unified agent in the world.

From a social perspective, the self is also a communication device. It allows individuals to model the minds of others through empathy and projection. When we say "I feel," "I want," or "I believe," we translate private states into public symbols that others can understand. This exchange of selves gives rise to culture, morality, and collective intelligence. Thus, even if the "I" is illusory, it performs a vital evolutionary function: it makes cooperation and shared meaning possible.

However, as human cognition expanded, the self became increasingly abstract. The same self that once guided survival began to identify with ideas, possessions, and ideologies. The narrative center hardened into ego a structure that defends its continuity even when it conflicts with reality. This over-identification with the model of self leads to suffering: fear of loss, shame, pride, and separation. The very feedback mechanism that stabilized awareness now threatens to fragment it.

Beyond the Illusion: The Transparent Self

The next step in the evolution of consciousness may involve transcending the illusion of separateness while retaining the functionality of self-reference. Rather than dismantling the "I," consciousness can learn to see through it to recognize the self as a useful fiction rather than an ultimate truth. This is what some contemplative traditions call "self-transparency": the ability to experience awareness without being dominated by its internal narrative.

When self-reference becomes transparent, awareness shifts from identification to participation. The observer no longer stands apart from experience but flows within it. One realizes that the sense of "I am" is not an object but an event a shimmering point of awareness through which life observes itself. In this state, consciousness remains personal but not confined; it retains individuality without separateness. The illusion becomes instrument rather than obstacle.

This form of awareness aligns with what systems theorists describe as "meta-stability" a dynamic equilibrium between identity and openness. The system maintains coherence without rigidity, allowing continual learning and adaptation. In psychological terms, this corresponds to a flexible self: resilient, compassionate, and integrative. In philosophical terms, it represents a reintegration of subject and object, mind and world.

The Self as Evolution's Mirror

The paradox of self-reference is not a flaw in consciousness but its signature. The self is both mirror and mirage the means by which awareness perceives itself and the veil that conceals that perception. Through the illusion of "I," evolution achieves a new kind of feedback: the universe not only observes itself but questions its own observer. Every act of introspection, every moment of wonder or doubt, is the cosmos folding back into reflection.

The journey of consciousness may thus be seen as a gradual awakening from identification to participation from believing "I am separate" to realizing "I am part of." The mystery of the self does not end with its dissolution but with its transformation into transparency. When the illusion is seen for what it is, it becomes luminous rather than deceptive. The "I" remains, but it is recognized as the instrument through which life experiences itself.

In this recognition, self-reference completes its purpose. The universe, through human consciousness, achieves not only awareness but self understanding. The "I" that once claimed individuality now reveals its deeper nature as the eye through which the cosmos sees itself. The illusion of separateness dissolves into the realization of unity. What remains is awareness pure, reflective, and whole.

1.5 Model: The Consciousness Continuum From Reflex to Reflection to Creation

Across the long arc of evolution, consciousness has unfolded not as a sudden emergence but as a continuous deepening of feedback a gradual increase in the complexity with which systems sense, interpret, and participate in reality. Every living organism, from the simplest bacterium to the most advanced human, occupies a place on this spectrum. The more integrated and recursive the feedback, the deeper the awareness it supports.

This progression can be described as the *Consciousness Continuum* a model that traces the evolution of awareness through three interlinked stages: **Reflex**, **Reflection**, and **Creation**. These stages are not rigid categories but overlapping modes of operation, each building upon and integrating the one before it. Together, they describe how matter becomes mind, how mind becomes self-aware, and how self-awareness becomes creative participation in the evolution of the universe.

Reflex: The Genesis of Awareness

At the foundation of the continuum lies reflexive consciousness the simplest form of awareness, rooted in sensation and reaction. Reflex awareness emerges wherever matter becomes capable of feedback. It is the spark of life itself: the ability to detect change, respond to it, and thereby preserve form in the face of entropy.

In biological terms, reflex awareness corresponds to automatic processes the kind that sustain homeostasis. A bacterium swimming toward nutrients, a plant turning toward sunlight, or a lizard retracting from heat all display reflexive intelligence. Each of these behaviors involves sensing and responding to environmental stimuli through feedback loops that maintain internal equilibrium.

At this level, consciousness is embodied and immediate. There is perception but no perspective; sensation but no story. Experience is a direct coupling between organism and environment. The organism does not "know" that it perceives it simply *is* perception in motion. Reflex awareness is the raw vitality of life before self-consciousness divides it into observer and observed.

From a systems perspective, reflex consciousness represents the universe's first experiment in self-regulation. It is the biological manifestation of the same feedback principles that stabilize stars and galaxies, but now refined through the language of metabolism and survival. It is awareness without thought, intelligence without introspection the substrate upon which all higher forms of consciousness are built.

Reflection: The Emergence of the Self

As nervous systems evolved, awareness acquired a new dimension reflection. With the emergence of memory, anticipation, and symbolic representation, organisms could now model not only the environment but themselves within it. This capacity for self-modeling gave rise to reflective consciousness: awareness aware of itself.

Reflection marks the point where feedback turns inward. The mind constructs an internal representation of its own processes, creating the experience of subjectivity. What began as sensation becomes perception, then interpretation, then identity. The "I" arises as a functional center a narrative thread that ties experiences together across time. Through this recursive loop, the organism transforms from a reactive system into a reflective one.

Reflective consciousness underlies the distinctly human capacities for introspection, imagination, and morality. It allows us to simulate possible futures, analyze motives, and empathize with others. The same mechanism that lets us anticipate danger also enables us to anticipate meaning. This is why reflection is both blessing and burden: it expands freedom but introduces uncertainty. We can ask, "Who am I?" and in doing so, create an infinite regress of self-reference.

Culturally, reflective awareness finds expression through language, art, and philosophy. Words enable us to name and share internal states, externalizing thought and constructing collective meaning. Reflection becomes communal; the mind extends beyond the individual brain into a social and symbolic network. Through culture, humanity evolves from isolated minds to shared consciousness a global conversation about being.

Neuroscientifically, reflection corresponds to higher-order networks such as the prefrontal cortex and the default mode network, which enable self-representation and meta-cognition. These structures allow the brain to simulate not only external events but internal states to "think about thinking." In doing so, they complete the loop of awareness, turning cognition into consciousness.

Yet reflection is inherently unstable. The self that arises through it is both real and constructed a model necessary for coordination but prone to rigidity. When the self mistakes its narrative for absolute truth, reflection collapses into ego. The challenge of reflective consciousness, therefore, is to remain fluid: to recognize the self as an instrument of awareness rather than its owner.

Creation: The Evolution of Conscious Participation

Beyond reflection lies the next evolutionary horizon: creative consciousness. This is the level at which awareness not only observes and interprets reality but actively reshapes it where intelligence becomes self-directing and evolution becomes conscious of itself.

Creative consciousness is the synthesis of the previous stages. It retains the immediacy of reflex and the depth of reflection but transcends both by aligning perception with intention. Here, awareness operates not merely as a mirror but as a medium of transformation. To be creatively conscious is to perceive the interconnectedness of all systems and to act in ways that enhance their coherence and vitality.

In human life, creative consciousness manifests as innovation, compassion, and ethical design. When we compose music, build technology, or imagine more just societies, we are engaging the creative capacity of awareness. We are no longer passive participants in evolution but co-authors of its next phase.

This stage also marks the convergence of biological, cultural, and technological evolution. As artificial intelligence, networks, and global communication systems expand, humanity's collective awareness increasingly mirrors the distributed cognition of a planetary brain. Our creations become extensions of our own awareness, amplifying both our understanding and our responsibility. Creative consciousness thus demands a new form of ethics one that aligns innovation with empathy, progress with purpose.

Philosophically, creative consciousness represents the culmination of the universe's feedback journey. It is awareness recognizing itself as a generative force not separate from reality but intrinsic to its unfolding. The creative act is not an escape from the world but the world reflecting upon itself in new form. In art, science, and spirituality, the cosmos experiments with new modes of self-expression.

The Continuum as a Living System

The three stages of the Consciousness Continuum Reflex, Reflection, and Creation are not discrete compartments but interdependent layers of a living system. Reflex provides the ground of experience; Reflection provides the map; Creation provides the meaning. Every moment of human awareness contains all three.

A pianist improvising, for example, draws upon reflexive muscle memory, reflective understanding of harmony, and creative intuition that transcends both. Similarly, in problem-solving or empathy, consciousness oscillates dynamically across levels sensing, interpreting, and inventing in a continuous feedback loop. Awareness is not linear but recursive: it moves in spirals, integrating past insights into new patterns of understanding.

From an evolutionary standpoint, this continuum represents the deepening of feedback integration. In Reflex, feedback regulates. In Reflection, it represents. In Creation, it redefines. Each phase amplifies the system's capacity to respond coherently to complexity. The more self-referential the feedback, the higher the degree of freedom and responsibility it entails. Awareness thus evolves not toward control but toward coherence the ability to harmonize self and system, intention and impact.

From Biological to Planetary Consciousness

At the collective scale, the Consciousness Continuum applies not only to individual minds but to civilizations. Early societies operated primarily at the reflex level driven by survival, instinct, and immediate adaptation to the environment. With the rise of culture, reflection emerged through language, religion, and philosophy humanity's attempt to understand its place in the cosmos. Now, as global communication and artificial intelligence link billions of minds into shared networks, civilization approaches the creative phase where consciousness begins to act as a planetary feedback system.

This transition brings both promise and peril. A creative civilization has the power to regenerate ecosystems, align economies with ethics, and design technologies that enhance awareness. But it also faces the danger of fragmentation if reflection turns into noise or creativity detaches from wisdom. The challenge of the coming era is therefore integrative: to ensure that the evolution of intelligence remains guided by the evolution of consciousness.

The Consciousness Continuum provides a framework for this alignment. It reminds us that progress is not merely technological but experiential not about doing more, but about seeing more deeply. The future of evolution depends not only on what humanity can create, but on how wisely it can reflect and how consciously it can act.

Summary: The Architecture of Conscious Evolution

The Consciousness Continuum reveals consciousness as a living architecture of feedback a dynamic system evolving from reflex to reflection to creation. Each stage represents a greater degree of self-awareness, integration, and ethical participation. Reflex sustains life, Reflection understands life, and Creation transforms life.

Through this lens, evolution itself appears as a spiritual process not in the religious sense, but as the universe's movement toward greater self-understanding. Every organism, thought, and invention contributes to this process. Awareness expands not by replacing earlier forms but by integrating them into higher coherence.

Humanity now stands at a threshold where consciousness can become consciously creative where we can choose to design the conditions for wisdom to evolve alongside intelligence. The task of our time is to live as participants in this continuum: to sense deeply, to reflect honestly, and to create responsibly.

For in the end, consciousness is not a static property but a living process the cosmos awakening through the feedback of its own awareness. The continuum is not merely a model of mind; it is the story of existence itself becoming self-aware.

Chapter 2

The Evolution of the Human Mind

The evolution of the human mind marks one of the most extraordinary transformations in the history of life the moment when awareness began to think about itself. For billions of years, life adapted through instinct and feedback, refining its patterns through trial and error. Then, in a small corner of the universe, the brain of a primate crossed a threshold: it began not only to react to the world, but to model it; not only to experience reality, but to imagine possibilities beyond it. Through this emergence, consciousness became cognition the raw sensitivity of life evolved into the reflective intelligence of mind.

The human mind represents the universe's most advanced experiment in self-organization. It is not a static organ but a living process a dynamic network capable of representing, predicting, and reshaping reality. Within the folds of the cerebral cortex, billions of neurons weave electrical symphonies of perception and meaning. Every thought, memory, and emotion is a pattern in motion a dialogue between biology and imagination. The brain, far from being a passive receiver of experience, is an active constructor of worlds. It does not merely perceive what is; it continually predicts what could be.

This predictive capacity the ability to anticipate patterns before they occur lies at the core of human cognition. The brain operates as a hypothesis-generating system, constantly forecasting sensory input and updating its models based on error signals. In this way, perception itself is a form of controlled hallucination: a continuous negotiation between expectation and evidence. The mind's power lies not in perfect accuracy, but in adaptive imagination in its capacity to learn, unlearn, and reorganize its understanding of reality. This is the foundation of all creativity, science, and civilization.

Yet the human mind did not emerge in isolation. Its architecture is the product of countless evolutionary layers: reflexes inherited from reptiles, emotions inherited from mammals, and symbolic thought unique to our species.

Each layer adds depth to awareness. Instinct provides the rhythm of survival; emotion provides the melody of meaning; cognition provides the harmony of understanding. The mind is, in essence, evolution reflecting on its own design.

Language transformed this reflection into dialogue. With the invention of words, thought escaped the boundaries of the skull. Private perception became public knowledge. Language allowed minds to interconnect, to build upon one another's insights, and to externalize memory into culture. Through speech and symbol, information began to evolve faster than genes. The collective intelligence of humanity a vast network of shared meaning became evolution's newest frontier.

Memory was the second great leap. The capacity to store, retrieve, and recombine experience enabled humans to transcend the present. Memory turned experience into knowledge, and knowledge into strategy. Through memory, the mind learned not only to survive but to tell stories about survival. These stories became the architecture of culture the invisible frameworks through which societies preserve wisdom, identity, and purpose across generations.

Abstract thought was the third great breakthrough the ability to represent what is not immediately present, to manipulate symbols, to imagine unseen causes and distant futures. Abstraction allowed humans to invent mathematics, morality, and metaphysics. It gave rise to science, art, and myth the three great languages of human understanding. Through abstraction, consciousness became conceptual, able to see beyond the immediate and to shape reality according to intention.

Together, these milestones language, memory, and abstraction turned the human brain into a platform for self-evolving intelligence. They enabled what might be called "meta-cognition": the capacity to think about thinking. Through meta-cognition, awareness became self-directing. The mind could examine its own patterns, revise its own beliefs, and even reprogram its own perception. In this recursive capacity lies both humanity's power and its paradox for the same mind that can envision utopia can also construct illusion.

The evolution of the mind was also a social event. No individual could have developed language, culture, or morality in isolation. Human cognition expanded through cooperation through shared attention, empathy, and storytelling. Our ancestors survived not because they were the strongest, but because they could coordinate, communicate, and imagine together. Social intelligence the ability to read others' intentions and align around common goals became the scaffolding for civilization itself.

This chapter explores the architecture and evolution of the human mind through five interwoven themes: the emergence of cognitive milestones such as language and memory; the development of social and symbolic intelligence as tools of cooperation; the discovery of the brain as a dynamic prediction engine; the role of plasticity and meta-cognition in learning and adaptation;

and finally, a case study on creativity and storytelling how imagination became humanity's most adaptive force.

Each of these dimensions reveals the mind not as a fixed product of biology, but as an evolving process a living feedback system between self, society, and environment. The human mind is both tool and mystery, both mechanism and metaphor. It is the bridge between consciousness and civilization, between what the universe is and what it dares to become.

In tracing the evolution of the human mind, we are ultimately tracing the evolution of freedom the growing capacity of life to understand, to choose, and to create. For within every thought lies a reflection of the cosmos that made it, and within every act of imagination, the universe learns to dream itself forward.

2.1 Cognitive Milestones: Language, Memory, and Abstract Thought

The human mind did not emerge all at once; it unfolded through a series of cognitive milestones that transformed raw awareness into complex thought. These milestones language, memory, and abstraction are not separate faculties but interwoven dimensions of a single evolutionary movement. Each one expanded the brain's ability to integrate experience, anticipate patterns, and share meaning. Together, they gave rise to symbolic intelligence the capacity to think beyond the immediate, to encode and transmit ideas across time, and to collectively build civilizations from imagination.

Language: The Architecture of Shared Thought

Language is often described as humanity's greatest invention, but in a deeper sense, it is nature's most profound adaptation. It allowed consciousness to move beyond the limits of the individual brain and enter the collective to become social, transmissible, and cumulative. Through language, thought acquired a body outside biology; ideas could now travel faster than genes, shaping evolution through culture rather than mutation.

The origins of language remain debated, but most scholars agree it evolved gradually from gesture, imitation, and emotional vocalization. Early hominins likely used rhythmic sounds and bodily cues to coordinate hunting or warn of danger. Over millennia, these signals grew in complexity, acquiring syntax rules for combining symbols and semantics shared meaning attached to sound. At that moment, the mind gained its first tool for external cognition: an operating system for thought itself.

Language is not merely a means of communication; it is a way of structuring reality. Words divide the continuous flow of experience into distinct categories, allowing the brain to conceptualize and manipulate what it perceives. When we name something, we separate it from the undifferentiated field of sensation and assign it a role in our mental model of the world.

Language thus enables abstraction the ability to represent what is not immediately present.

Linguist Noam Chomsky proposed that humans possess an innate "universal grammar," a neural blueprint for generating infinite expressions from finite symbols. Modern neuroscience supports this view: language processing involves widespread cortical networks that link auditory, motor, and conceptual regions. These networks allow humans to transform thought into sound and sound back into thought a feedback loop that connects mind to mind.

The cognitive consequences of language are profound. It allows humans to share attention, coordinate action, and transfer knowledge across generations. It also gives rise to introspection the ability to talk to oneself, to think in words. Inner speech functions as a mirror for the mind, enabling self-regulation, planning, and imagination. Through language, awareness became dialogical: it could ask questions of itself, and in doing so, invent philosophy, poetry, and science.

In evolutionary terms, language is the technology that turned intelligence into civilization. It is the bridge between neurons and nations, between perception and purpose. Through it, human minds form networks of meaning that far surpass the cognitive power of any individual brain.

Memory: The Time Machine of the Mind

If language connects minds across space, memory connects consciousness across time. It is the foundation upon which all learning, identity, and continuity rest. Without memory, experience would dissolve into an endless present perception without progression. With memory, awareness becomes temporal: it links past to present and projects into the future.

In biological terms, memory evolved as a survival mechanism. Even the simplest organisms retain traces of previous states, allowing them to adapt behavior based on experience. In humans, this primitive capacity developed into a multi-layered system involving procedural memory (skills), semantic memory (knowledge), and episodic memory (personal experience). These forms of memory are coordinated through intricate neural architectures, especially the hippocampus and prefrontal cortex, which encode, consolidate, and retrieve patterns of information.

Memory is not a static storage device; it is a living reconstruction. Each act of recall rewrites the past, integrating new context and meaning. Neuroscience shows that remembering and imagining use overlapping brain circuits. To remember is to simulate to recreate experience in the present. Thus, memory is not simply retrospective; it is prospective. It allows the mind to learn from the past in order to anticipate the future.

This reconstructive nature of memory gave rise to narrative the cognitive mechanism that organizes experience into story. Narratives link events by cause and consequence, turning chaos into coherence. They provide continuity to the self and structure to culture. Every civilization is, in essence, a memory system a collective archive of experience encoded in language, art, and ritual.

Through memory, evolution discovered a new kind of inheritance: cultural inheritance. Knowledge no longer needed to be written in DNA; it could be transmitted through teaching, imitation, and storytelling. This leap accelerated evolution exponentially. Genetic adaptation operates over millennia; memetic adaptation operates in moments. The human mind, through memory, became evolution's new engine.

Philosophically, memory introduced the dimension of meaning into awareness. It made consciousness historical. The ability to remember gives rise to reflection to ask, "What happened, and why?" It also made possible moral awareness, for responsibility presupposes recollection. Memory, therefore, is not only cognitive but ethical. It is what allows the human mind to learn from error, to imagine redemption, and to build continuity in a world of change.

Abstract Thought: The Expansion of Imagination

The third great milestone abstraction transformed the human mind from an interpreter of reality into a creator of it. Abstraction is the ability to represent what is not directly perceivable: to think in terms of concepts, principles, and possibilities. It is the foundation of mathematics, logic, art, and spirituality the capacity to imagine beyond the here and now.

Abstraction emerged from the brain's growing ability to decouple symbols from immediate sensory input. A mark on a cave wall could represent a hunt, a ritual, or a dream. A sound could stand for an object, and later, for an idea. This symbolic leap liberated cognition from the constraints of the present. The mind could now manipulate ideas in their absence, reason about invisible forces, and model hypothetical futures.

Anthropological evidence suggests that this symbolic revolution occurred roughly 50,000 years ago an explosion of art, tool-making, and language that marked the dawn of behavioral modernity. Cave paintings, musical instruments, and burial rituals all testify to a new kind of consciousness one capable of representing not only life, but meaning. The abstract mind sees pattern in chaos and purpose in pattern.

Abstraction also gave rise to science. By generalizing from observation, humans began to discern universal principles governing nature. The same capacity for symbolization that produced myth also produced mathematics. Both are expressions of the abstract drive to translate the world into mental models that can be tested, shared, and expanded.

In the neural sense, abstract thought engages networks that integrate perception, language, and emotion into higher-order synthesis. The prefrontal cortex especially regions involved in planning and conceptual reasoning acts as the brain's "simulation engine," enabling us to represent hypothetical scenarios and explore them mentally before acting physically. This ability to imagine alternatives is the root of creativity and ethical choice alike. It transforms adaptation into intentional evolution.

Abstraction, however, also carries risk. Detached from direct experience, it can drift into illusion systems of belief untethered from reality. The same symbolic flexibility that allows philosophy can also produce dogma. Thus, the evolution of abstract thought demands a parallel evolution of reflection the meta-cognitive awareness that keeps imagination aligned with truth. Wisdom, in this sense, is abstraction tempered by awareness.

Synthesis: The Cognitive Trinity

Language, memory, and abstraction form what may be called the *Cognitive Trinity* three interdependent dimensions of human thought. Language externalizes thought into communication; memory internalizes experience into continuity; abstraction elevates perception into imagination. Together, they constitute the mind's self-organizing architecture.

This trinity operates as an evolutionary feedback loop:

- Language strengthens memory by encoding experiences into words and stories.
- Memory enriches language by providing a reservoir of shared references and meaning.
- Abstraction expands both by generating concepts that link the particular to the universal.

Through this feedback, cognition becomes cumulative. Every generation inherits not only genes but ideas linguistic patterns, cultural memories, and abstract models that evolve through collective refinement. The human mind, therefore, is not merely an individual organ but a living continuum of shared intelligence, extending backward through ancestors and forward into the future.

Ultimately, these cognitive milestones transformed consciousness from reflection into creation. They allowed humanity to step beyond biological adaptation into symbolic evolution to design its environment, imagine its destiny, and participate consciously in the unfolding of the cosmos. In every word spoken, memory recalled, and idea conceived, the universe continues its experiment in self-understanding through the creative intelligence of the human mind.

2.2 Social and Symbolic Intelligence Cooperation as Cognitive Expansion

Human intelligence did not evolve in isolation. It was sculpted not merely by the challenges of nature, but by the demands of relationship the need to cooperate, compete, and communicate within increasingly complex social worlds. The brain that could read the weather or track prey had to learn something far more intricate: how to read other minds. The evolution of social intelligence and later symbolic intelligence transformed cognition from an individual survival mechanism into a collective phenomenon. Through cooperation and shared imagination, the human mind became a networked system an ecology of minds.

The Social Brain Hypothesis

The starting point of this story lies in what evolutionary psychologists call the *social brain hypothesis.* This theory, proposed by Robin Dunbar and others, suggests that the primary driver of human brain expansion was not tool-making or hunting, but social complexity. To survive in groups, early humans needed to remember relationships, anticipate others' behavior, and navigate alliances and conflicts. Each new layer of social interaction demanded greater cognitive capacity a kind of mental arms race of empathy and strategy.

Neuroscientific evidence supports this view. The prefrontal cortex, particularly areas linked to planning, inhibition, and perspective-taking, expanded dramatically in the course of hominid evolution. These regions are responsible for what psychologists call *theory of mind* the ability to infer the beliefs, emotions, and intentions of others. Theory of mind is the foundation of empathy, communication, and moral judgment. It allows individuals to model not only the external world but the internal worlds of others effectively running simulations of other minds inside one's own.

This social modeling transformed the brain into a cooperative prediction machine. Every conversation, negotiation, or act of teaching involves anticipating the mental state of another a continuous loop of feedback between self and other. In this sense, the social brain is a distributed system: awareness extended through empathy. The more humans interacted, the more cognitive capacity was required to manage those interactions, leading to what some researchers call "collective brain evolution."

From Cooperation to Culture

Cooperation is not merely a behavioral strategy; it is a cognitive revolution. To cooperate, organisms must align intentions, share attention, and maintain trust capacities that depend on sophisticated communication and memory. Early humans who could collaborate on hunting or child-rearing gained survival advantages far greater than any lone competitor. Over generations, cooperation became not just a choice but a cognitive infrastructure wired into neural networks governing emotion, reward, and social bonding.

The neurotransmitter oxytocin, for example, plays a central role in this process. It strengthens attachment and empathy, enhancing trust and group cohesion. Similarly, the brain's reward circuits light up during acts of cooperation, suggesting that evolution has intertwined altruism with pleasure.

Helping others is not an anomaly; it is an adaptation. The impulse to connect to share, protect, and belong is the foundation of civilization.

But cooperation alone does not explain humanity's unique trajectory. Many species cooperate ants, wolves, dolphins yet none have built symbolic cultures or philosophies of ethics. What set humans apart was the emergence of *shared imagination*: the ability to construct collective realities that exist not in the physical world but in the symbolic one.

The Birth of Symbolic Intelligence

Symbolic intelligence is the ability to use abstract symbols words, images, rituals, laws to represent and coordinate meaning. It allows humans to create social worlds that transcend immediate perception. A tribe, a nation, a religion, or a corporation is not a physical object but a shared idea sustained by collective belief. Through symbols, humans learned to cooperate not only with those they could see but with those they could imagine.

The emergence of symbolic thought marked a second cognitive explosion. Archaeological evidence from the Upper Paleolithic cave art, ornaments, and ritual burials suggests that humans had begun to encode their inner lives in external form. A painting on a wall was more than decoration; it was a projection of meaning into the material world. It allowed others to participate in the same mental landscape. Symbolism turned the brain's private simulations into shared virtual realities.

Language was the first and most powerful symbolic system, but others followed: art, myth, mathematics, money. Each expanded the range and scale of cooperation. A story could bind a tribe; a myth could unite a civilization; a scientific theory could coordinate the minds of millions across centuries. Symbolic intelligence thus multiplied the bandwidth of communication, enabling information to compound over time. Culture became evolution's new memory system faster, richer, and more flexible than DNA.

The Networked Mind

As language and symbolism matured, individual cognition merged into collective cognition. Knowledge ceased to reside in single minds and began to exist across distributed networks families, tribes, institutions, and eventually, global systems. The result was what we might call the "networked mind": a dynamic web of ideas, technologies, and relationships that collectively process information and adapt to change.

In this framework, intelligence becomes a property of interaction rather than isolation. A conversation, a classroom, or a research team is more intelligent than any one participant because it integrates diverse perspectives. The collective mind emerges from feedback loops among individuals much like neurons forming a brain. Just as a single neuron cannot think, a single human cannot sustain civilization. Cooperation scales cognition.

Modern cognitive science and network theory increasingly recognize this distributed nature of thought. The "extended mind hypothesis," for instance, argues that cognition is not confined to the skull but includes tools, languages, and social structures that offload mental labor. A notebook, a smartphone, or an algorithm can all be considered parts of the thinking process. By outsourcing memory and computation to shared systems, humanity has amplified its cognitive reach beyond biological limits.

Empathy, Morality, and Shared Meaning

The expansion of social and symbolic intelligence also gave rise to moral awareness the recognition of others as conscious beings with their own perspectives and pain. Empathy is not an emotional luxury; it is the perceptual extension of self-awareness into the social field. When the mind understands that others have inner worlds, cooperation deepens into compassion.

Moral systems, in this sense, are collective meta-cognitions societies reflecting on how they regulate their own behavior. Myths and religions encoded early moral frameworks, binding groups together through shared values. Later, philosophy and law formalized these codes into ethical systems. All of these represent an increasing complexity of feedback: not just reacting to one another's actions, but reflecting upon the principles behind those actions. In this way, morality becomes the cognitive immune system of civilization preserving coherence in the face of chaos.

Symbolic intelligence amplifies empathy by enabling perspective-taking at scale. Through literature, film, and art, we inhabit minds beyond our own, expanding the boundaries of identity. Every story told is a bridge between inner worlds. The ability to feel for characters and causes far removed from our direct experience is the essence of global consciousness. It is how awareness learns to care across distance.

The Coevolution of Mind and Culture

Social and symbolic intelligence did not evolve linearly; they coevolved in feedback loops with culture itself. Each generation inherits not only genetic potential but cultural scaffolding languages, norms, technologies that shape cognition. The child's brain develops within a symbolic environment that predates it. As individuals internalize these systems, they also modify them, passing on an altered version to the next generation. Culture, therefore, is both product and producer of mind.

This coevolution explains why human intelligence is so flexible. The same neural architecture can host countless worldviews and moral systems because it evolved to learn from context. Unlike genetic evolution, cultural evolution operates at the speed of communication. Ideas mutate, recombine, and propagate like living organisms in an ecological web of meaning. The human mind is both habitat and host for these memetic life forms.

Over millennia, this process has woven the cognitive fabric of civilization a vast feedback network linking billions of minds. From myth to modern science, each stage of human culture represents a deeper level of symbolic integration. The internet, in this lineage, is not an anomaly but a natural extension the externalization of humanity's social and symbolic brain.

Summary: Cooperation as Cognitive Expansion

The evolution of social and symbolic intelligence reveals a central truth: cooperation is cognition in motion. Awareness expands by connecting by forming relationships, exchanging symbols, and reflecting upon shared meaning. The individual mind is a node in a vast web of interdependence, where thought is both personal and collective, both biological and cultural.

Language, empathy, and symbolism transformed evolution from a struggle for survival into a collaboration for meaning. Through cooperation, humanity multiplied its intelligence; through imagination, it multiplied its possibilities. The social brain became a cultural brain, and eventually, a planetary brain.

In this light, the evolution of the human mind is not only an ascent of knowledge but an expansion of connection. Intelligence grows not by thinking faster, but by thinking together by linking awareness into networks of shared reflection and creative purpose. The next stage of evolution may depend less on how much we know, and more on how deeply we understand that we are thinking together.

2.3 Plasticity, Meta-Cognition, and the Rise of Self-Awareness

The evolution of the human mind did not end with language or social intelligence. What made the mind uniquely human was not merely its capacity to think, but its ability to think about thinking to observe its own operations, revise them, and deliberately reshape itself. This meta-cognitive capacity awareness of awareness is what transformed the brain from a reactive organ into a self-evolving system. Underlying this transformation is one of biology's most remarkable properties: *neuroplasticity*, the ability of the brain to change its structure and function through experience.

The Adaptive Brain: A System That Learns Itself

The human brain is not hardwired; it is dynamically reconfigurable. Neural pathways strengthen or weaken depending on use, and new connections form in response to novel experiences. This adaptability, known as *plasticity*, means that the architecture of the brain is not predetermined it is sculpted by life. Each thought, perception, and emotion subtly rewires the network that generates it. The mind, therefore, is not a static product of evolution but an ongoing process of self-construction.

Plasticity operates on multiple timescales. In early development, it allows the brain to absorb vast amounts of sensory and linguistic information, calibrating itself to the environment. In adulthood, it enables learning, skill acquisition, and emotional regulation. Even in old age, new neural growth and reorganization continue evidence that adaptation is a lifelong process. This flexibility is what allows humans to inhabit environments as diverse as deserts, metropolises, and virtual realities. Wherever the brain goes, it learns to think the world into coherence.

From a systems perspective, plasticity is feedback embodied. Each neural pattern encodes a hypothesis about how the world works, and each sensory input tests that hypothesis. When prediction and reality diverge, the brain updates its internal model. This continuous loop of error correction is the essence of learning the mechanism through which experience refines awareness. In this sense, the human brain is not just an instrument of perception; it is an evolutionary algorithm of understanding, running perpetually within the boundaries of a single lifetime.

The Emergence of Meta-Cognition

Plasticity paved the way for the next cognitive revolution: *meta-cognition*, or the ability to monitor and regulate one's own mental processes. While many species learn, few can observe the act of learning itself. Meta-cognition allows the mind to step back from experience, to reflect upon its own functioning, and to alter its trajectory deliberately. It is the birth of the internal observer the capacity to ask, "What am I thinking, and why?"

This recursive awareness emerges from the same neural mechanisms that enable self-prediction. The prefrontal cortex, particularly the medial and dorsolateral regions, plays a key role in tracking goals, evaluating performance, and inhibiting impulses. It acts as a supervisory system that monitors the accuracy of thought and behavior a form of neural self-reflection. Meta-cognition thus turns the predictive brain inward: the mind begins to model not only the external world, but the process by which it models the world.

The implications are profound. With meta-cognition, learning becomes self-directed rather than purely reactive. The organism can now question its own assumptions, modify its own motivations, and invent new strategies for adaptation. In humans, this leads to creativity, moral reflection, and intentional change. A mind aware of its own limitations can transcend them. Through meta-cognition, evolution gains a reflective mirror: consciousness capable of redesigning itself.

The Birth of Self-Awareness

Out of this recursive loop arises the phenomenon of *self-awareness*. To be self-aware is to perceive oneself as both subject and object the thinker who can observe their own thinking. This ability to form an internal model of "self" enables identity, continuity, and intentionality. The self becomes a reference point in the brain's complex map of relationships: the axis around which perception, memory, and emotion are organized.

Developmental psychology shows that self-awareness emerges gradually. Infants recognize themselves in mirrors only after 18 months, when neural connectivity between sensory integration and prefrontal control regions matures. Around the same time, children begin to use first-person pronouns and express autobiographical memory evidence of a narrative self taking shape. From then on, experience is filtered through this constructed identity: "I am the one who remembers, feels, and acts."

Neuroscience reveals that this sense of self arises from the interaction between multiple brain networks particularly the default mode network (DMN), which activates during introspection, memory, and imagination. The DMN integrates information across time and modality, constructing a coherent sense of "me" from countless transient experiences. Yet this unity is an ongoing synthesis, not a fixed entity. The self is a process a dynamic pattern maintained by feedback between perception, memory, and reflection. It is both illusion and interface: the virtual point through which consciousness experiences coherence.

Plasticity and the Expansion of Consciousness

The most extraordinary aspect of plasticity and meta-cognition is their partnership. The ability to observe one's thoughts enables one to change them; the ability to change them deepens self-understanding. Together, they make consciousness self-transformative. Every act of introspection modifies the neural architecture that enables introspection. Awareness literally reshapes the brain that generates it. In this recursive process, mind and matter become partners in evolution.

This feedback between observation and transformation forms the foundation of all human growth from skill mastery to spiritual awakening. When a musician practices, the repetition not only refines motor coordination but also expands perceptual acuity and emotional expression. When a thinker reflects on bias, new neural pathways for empathy and reasoning emerge. Meditation, therapy, art, and education all exploit this same principle: that by bringing awareness to unconscious patterns, we rewire the mind toward coherence.

Plasticity also explains the diversity of human consciousness. Each culture, language, and life story shapes the neural architecture of its members in unique ways. A Tibetan monk's brain, trained in compassion meditation, exhibits different activation patterns from that of a London taxi driver who has memorized a city's labyrinthine streets. The mind is a mirror molded by attention it becomes what it repeatedly contemplates. Thus, the cultivation of awareness is not metaphorical but biological: what we attend to, we become.

Self-Awareness and the Ethical Dimension

With self-awareness comes moral awareness. To perceive oneself as an agent is to recognize responsibility. The reflective mind can evaluate the consequences of its actions and align them with intention. Ethics, in this view, is not imposed from outside but arises naturally from within self-reflective systems. Awareness recognizes its impact, and from that recognition emerges care.

This ethical dimension is a crucial step in the evolution of consciousness. It marks the point where intelligence becomes wisdom when cognition integrates empathy. A purely intelligent system can optimize; a self-aware one can choose compassion. This is the difference between intelligence as adaptation and intelligence as understanding. In the reflective mirror of awareness, the mind not only sees itself but sees the other as itself.

The Plastic Future of Mind

Plasticity ensures that the evolution of mind is not finished. Just as genetic evolution gave rise to biological intelligence, cultural and technological evolution are now giving rise to extended intelligence hybrid systems of human and artificial cognition. As these systems evolve, meta-cognition and self-awareness will become even more crucial. They are the only mechanisms by which intelligence can remain aligned with meaning.

The human mind is thus both product and prototype: a self-modifying system capable of guiding its own evolution. Through plasticity, it learns; through meta-cognition, it adapts; through self-awareness, it chooses. The future of consciousness may depend on how wisely we use these powers whether we cultivate awareness as a tool for control or as a pathway to coherence.

Summary: The Mind That Knows Itself

The story of plasticity and meta-cognition reveals the human mind as a self-evolving system a dynamic interplay between neural flexibility, reflective awareness, and ethical intention. Plasticity provides the medium; meta-cognition provides the method; self-awareness provides the meaning. Together, they form the engine of conscious evolution.

Through these mechanisms, the brain transcends its biological origins. It becomes a participant in its own unfolding an instrument that learns not only from the world but about itself. Every act of awareness is both discovery and creation: the universe observing its own capacity to understand. In that recursive moment when consciousness recognizes its own reflection the human mind becomes what it has always been evolving toward: awareness aware of being aware.

2.4 Case Study: The Emergence of Creativity and Storytelling as Adaptive Intelligence

Long before humans built cities or wrote codes, they told stories. Around campfires, in caves, beneath constellations, our ancestors imagined worlds beyond the visible stories of gods, spirits, ancestors, and heroes. To the modern mind, these tales might seem like primitive entertainment or superstition. Yet beneath their poetic surface lay one of the most powerful evolutionary technologies ever invented: storytelling. Through narrative and imagination, humanity transformed cognition into culture, survival into meaning, and intelligence into creativity.

Creativity and storytelling are not accidents of evolution they are adaptive intelligences. They emerged from the deep interplay between perception, emotion, and social cooperation, enabling humans to simulate experience, share knowledge, and coordinate behavior. In essence, creativity allowed humanity to "think beyond the immediate," while storytelling allowed those thoughts to spread, persist, and evolve across generations. Together, they turned the human brain into an engine of possibility capable of imagining futures that did not yet exist and then making them real.

The Origins of Creative Cognition

Creativity arose as a natural extension of the brain's predictive architecture. The same neural systems that anticipate patterns in the environment can also recombine those patterns into novel configurations. Creativity, in this sense, is prediction liberated from constraint the capacity to explore alternative realities within the mind. When a hunter envisions new strategies, or an artisan imagines a new tool, the brain uses existing memories and schemas as raw material for innovation.

Neuroscience shows that creativity engages both the *default mode network* (associated with imagination and memory) and the *executive control network* (associated with focus and evaluation). These systems operate in dynamic tension: one generates, the other refines. The creative act is thus a dialogue between chaos and order, intuition and analysis the brain exploring its own uncertainty. In evolutionary terms, this ability to generate and test hypothetical scenarios in imagination gave humans a decisive advantage. Instead of relying solely on trial and error in the external world, they could simulate outcomes internally, reducing risk and increasing adaptability.

Creativity is, therefore, the cognitive form of evolution itself variation and selection expressed through thought. It is how the brain conducts experiments on reality without the cost of failure. Every invention, from the stone tool to the space telescope, traces back to this inner laboratory of imagination.

The Birth of Storytelling

Storytelling was the social extension of creativity the moment when private imagination became collective knowledge. Anthropological evidence suggests that storytelling predates written language by tens of thousands of years. Early myths, ritual dances, and cave paintings were all forms of narrative communication, encoding survival knowledge, moral lessons, and cultural identity in memorable form.

Stories functioned as evolutionary "software updates." They transmitted complex information where to find food, how to cooperate, what to fear in emotionally engaging and easily recallable ways. Unlike factual instruction, narrative activates empathy and emotion, making information more durable in memory. A story about a hunter's failure warns more effectively than a list of rules because it engages the listener's imagination and emotion simultaneously. In this way, storytelling became a tool for social learning, embedding adaptive behavior into shared experience.

From a cognitive standpoint, stories also perform an integrative function. They link sensory perception (what we see), emotional evaluation (how we feel), and conceptual reasoning (what it means). Narrative weaves these domains into coherence it gives the mind continuity across time. Where memory stores experience, storytelling structures it. It transforms raw data into meaning.

Story as Simulation and Survival

Evolutionary psychology views storytelling as a form of mental simulation a virtual reality in which the brain can safely explore risk, conflict, and emotion. By engaging with fictional scenarios, listeners rehearse real-world challenges and social dynamics. Stories allow individuals to practice empathy, to understand others' motives, and to anticipate consequences all without direct exposure to danger. In this way, narrative became an adaptive training ground for the social brain.

This capacity for vicarious learning extended cooperation and moral understanding. Shared myths and legends aligned group values, regulated behavior, and built trust. A tribe that shared a common story could coordinate action more effectively than one that did not. In this sense, storytelling was the first form of cultural governance aligning individuals through shared imagination rather than coercion. Myth, therefore, was not ignorance but information a symbolic code for transmitting social and ecological wisdom.

Modern neuroscience supports this view. Listening to or telling a story activates multiple neural systems simultaneously sensory, motor, emotional, and linguistic. The listener's brain mirrors the speaker's patterns of activity, creating what psychologists call "neural coupling." This synchronization allows for deep empathy and shared experience. Through storytelling, individual minds temporarily merge into collective consciousness.

Creativity as Collective Intelligence

As language and society evolved, creativity expanded from individual innovation to collective creation. Music, art, and ritual became tools for synchronizing emotion and meaning across groups. Dancing around a fire, singing a chant, or painting a wall were not acts of solitary expression but communal cognition ways of thinking and feeling together. These creative rituals strengthened group cohesion and transmitted knowledge in embodied form.

In this sense, creativity is not the privilege of the few but the property of the species. Every creative act whether a lullaby or a scientific discovery is an expression of humanity's collective intelligence. It is the mind's way of exploring the unknown through pattern-making. The artist, the engineer, and the philosopher all participate in the same process: reconfiguring experience into new forms of understanding.

The social dimension of creativity also accelerated cultural evolution. As ideas spread through storytelling and imitation, they underwent selection pressures similar to genes. Richard Dawkins called these units of cultural transmission *memes* ideas that evolve by replication and mutation. Over time, the most resonant stories, symbols, and inventions persisted, shaping the trajectory of civilizations. In this way, creativity became evolution's second engine faster and more flexible than biology.

The Neuroscience of Imagination and Insight

Creativity depends on the brain's ability to integrate disparate regions into novel configurations. During moments of insight the sudden "aha!" experience brain imaging shows a burst of synchronized activity across previously unconnected areas. The mind temporarily reorganizes itself, bridging conceptual gaps and forming new associations. This neural recombination is the biological signature of creativity: the brain literally forging new pathways of understanding.

Importantly, creativity thrives on balance between divergence and convergence, exploration and evaluation. Too much order stifles novelty; too much chaos dissolves coherence. The creative mind oscillates between these states, allowing spontaneity to generate possibilities and reflection to refine them. This dynamic mirrors the structure of evolution itself: variation and selection, freedom and feedback. In this sense, the creative process is a microcosm of the universe's own unfolding a pattern of emergence governed by play and purpose.

Storytelling and the Construction of Identity

As storytelling matured, it became not only a medium of culture but the foundation of selfhood. Human identity is, at its core, a narrative construction an internal story that integrates memory, emotion, and aspiration into continuity. The self is a character written by experience, revised by reflection, and performed through interaction. Without story, consciousness would fragment into isolated moments; narrative binds them into meaning.

This narrative function extends beyond the individual. Nations, religions, and ideologies are collective selves shared stories about who "we" are and what "we" stand for. These meta-narratives provide coherence to groups, but they also carry risk: when stories harden into dogma, imagination becomes imprisonment. Thus, the evolution of storytelling reflects a dual potential it can unite or divide, liberate or constrain. The next stage of evolution, perhaps, lies in learning to tell stories that sustain connection without delusion.

Creativity, Meaning, and the Future of Intelligence

Creativity and storytelling continue to shape the trajectory of human evolution. In the modern world, they manifest in science, technology, and art the three great expressions of the creative impulse. Science extends storytelling into the language of evidence; technology translates imagination into mechanism; art preserves the human soul amid abstraction. All are forms of narrative, differing only in medium and intention. They allow the species to reflect, reinvent, and reimagine itself continuously.

From an evolutionary systems perspective, creativity is adaptive because it increases diversity the range of possible responses to uncertainty. Storytelling is adaptive because it increases coherence the alignment of those responses through shared meaning. Together, they balance the two fundamental forces of evolution: variation and integration. Without creativity, civilization stagnates; without storytelling, it fragments.

Looking forward, the rise of artificial intelligence introduces a new dimension to this process. Machines can now generate art, compose music, and write stories mimicking aspects of human creativity. Yet what distinguishes human storytelling is not pattern generation but presence: the capacity to embed empathy, context, and meaning within creation. The challenge of the coming age will be to preserve the depth of human imagination the narrative wisdom that connects intelligence with compassion.

Summary: Imagination as Evolution's Mirror

The emergence of creativity and storytelling marks the point where evolution became self-aware. Through imagination, life gained the ability to model not just its environment but its possibilities. Through story, it learned to share those possibilities across minds and generations. Creativity is how the universe experiments with form; storytelling is how it remembers the results.

Both are forms of adaptive intelligence feedback loops that refine reality through imagination. They transform chaos into pattern, isolation into connection, and survival into meaning. The campfire tales of our ancestors were not mere diversions; they were the first flickers of civilization's consciousness. Each story told, each song sung, was a rehearsal for the future a way for life to become aware of its own unfolding.

To create is to participate in evolution; to tell a story is to extend it. In every act of imagination, the cosmos reflects on itself. Through human creativity, evolution no longer waits for chance it begins to choose. And through storytelling, intelligence no longer merely adapts it aspires.

Chapter 3

Society as Superintelligence

The evolution of intelligence did not end with the individual mind. It expanded outward, across relationships, language, and culture until thought itself became a networked phenomenon. Humanity's greatest invention is not the wheel, the engine, or even the algorithm; it is cooperation. Through the power to share attention, intention, and imagination, the human species transformed isolated awareness into collective intelligence. Civilization, in this light, is not merely a social arrangement but an extension of mind a living cognitive system composed of billions of interacting nodes.

From the first tribal fires to the digital networks of the twenty-first century, the pattern is the same: the scaling of cognition through connection. Each new form of communication gesture, language, writing, printing, computation has expanded the boundaries of thought, enabling knowledge to accumulate across space and time. What once existed as memory in a single brain became stored in libraries, institutions, and now, in the planetary nervous system of the internet. Intelligence has always been relational it grows not by isolation, but by integration.

In this sense, culture is humanity's collective brain. It encodes experience, preserves learning, and transmits meaning across generations. Myths, laws, art, and science are its neural circuits each one a pathway through which information and value flow. Through culture, humanity learned to think together. No individual invented language, agriculture, or mathematics alone; these were emergent products of collaboration cognition distributed across people, stories, and tools. Society, therefore, is not simply a gathering of individuals, but a dynamic cognitive architecture: thought embedded in relationships, rituals, and institutions.

Modern systems theory and network science reveal that such collective patterns follow the same principles as biological intelligence. Neurons form patterns of communication that yield consciousness; humans form networks of exchange that yield civilization. Both systems depend on feedback, adaptation, and emergent order. When individuals interact, their behaviors generate patterns that cannot be reduced to any single mind patterns of innovation, economy, morality, and meaning. In this view, humanity itself is a meta-organism: a self-organizing intelligence evolving across the medium of society.

We can already see this collective mind in motion. Markets function as decentralized processors of information; scientific communities as shared engines of discovery; digital ecosystems as the connective tissue of a global brain. No single person controls these systems, yet they display intelligence they learn, remember, and adapt. When humanity debates, collaborates, and creates at scale, civilization thinks. And as the density of connection increases, so too does the sophistication of that thinking. The collective mind, like the individual one, grows through interaction and reflection.

But this expansion brings paradox. Collective intelligence can generate wisdom or amplify chaos. The same networks that spread knowledge can also spread disinformation; the same coordination that enables global progress can also accelerate destruction. The challenge of our time is not merely to connect minds, but to align them to cultivate coherence without control, diversity without division. As civilization grows more intelligent, it must also grow more self-aware. Without reflection, connection becomes noise; without ethics, intelligence becomes power without direction.

This chapter explores the next phase in the evolution of mind: the emergence of society as a superintelligent system. It examines how culture functions as shared cognition, how distributed problem-solving mirrors neural computation, and how collective consciousness the synchronization of attention and emotion across humanity is beginning to reshape global reality. Finally, it introduces the model of *Civilization as a Thinking Organism*, a framework for understanding how societies learn, adapt, and reflect at planetary scale.

The rise of collective intelligence is not an abstract theory; it is a living process unfolding in real time. Each network we build, each story we share, and each system we design contributes to the evolution of a global mind one that is beginning to perceive itself. The question that now defines our age is not whether civilization will become intelligent, but whether it will become wise. For the collective mind, like every evolving consciousness before it, must learn what it means to be aware of its own power and responsible for its own reflection.

3.1 Culture as Shared Cognition

Humanity's true intelligence does not reside solely within the boundaries of the individual brain. It unfolds across the invisible web of relationships, symbols, and shared meanings that connect us. This web is culture the collective mind of the species. Through culture, knowledge, values, and imagination are stored, transmitted, and transformed across generations. In essence, culture is the means by which consciousness becomes distributed, memory becomes social, and thought becomes civilization. It is cognition extended across time, encoded not in neurons alone, but in language, art, institutions, and stories.

The Architecture of Collective Memory

Culture is humanity's long-term memory a dynamic repository of accumulated experience. Every myth, law, ritual, and song represents data written in the collective neural network of civilization. Just as the human brain encodes experience through synaptic connections, societies encode knowledge through shared symbols and practices. A story retold, a festival repeated, a moral reinforced all are acts of collective remembrance. Culture learns as the brain learns: through repetition, variation, and feedback.

This cultural memory system enables humanity to transcend biological limits. Genes evolve slowly through mutation; cultures evolve rapidly through communication. A new idea, tool, or belief can spread within decades and reshape entire societies. Culture thus functions as a parallel evolutionary process a faster, more adaptive layer of information transfer built on top of biological inheritance. Through it, humanity extends evolution from matter into meaning.

Anthropologists like Clifford Geertz have described culture as a network of "webs of significance" spun by humans themselves. Within these webs, each person interprets reality through shared codes language, art, morality, and myth. Culture is therefore not a collection of artifacts, but a cognitive ecology: a self-organizing field of meaning through which consciousness recognizes itself in others.

Cognition Beyond the Skull

For much of human history, cognition was imagined as something that happened within the brain an internal process sealed inside the individual. Modern cognitive science has overturned that view. The theory of the *extended mind*, proposed by Andy Clark and David Chalmers, argues that thinking extends into the world through tools, symbols, and social interactions. A notebook, a computer, or a conversation all become part of one's cognitive process.

Culture represents this principle on a civilizational scale. It is the sum of all externalized cognition the shared environment of ideas that individuals inhabit and modify. Writing extends memory beyond the moment; mathematics extends reasoning beyond intuition; ritual extends emotion beyond the individual; language extends attention across minds. Each cultural form offloads part of the cognitive load of being human, allowing societies to think collectively about problems too complex for any single brain.

This distributed cognition transforms intelligence from a solitary act into a social phenomenon. A society learns as a system. Its institutions, technologies, and narratives operate like neural subsystems, processing and transmitting information through feedback loops. Universities generate knowledge, media distribute it, governments regulate it, and art reinterprets it. The network as a whole displays properties of a mind: perception (awareness of conditions), memory (record of experience), and intention (coordinated action).

Language, Symbols, and the Codification of Thought

At the core of cultural cognition lies the symbolic system humanity's most powerful tool for translating thought into form. A symbol compresses complexity: it distills an entire experience, emotion, or concept into a sign that can be recognized and shared. Words, images, music, and ritual all serve as carriers of meaning. Through them, ideas migrate from one brain to another, forming an intersubjective reality a world of shared imagination.

Language is the foundation of this symbolic architecture. It transforms perception into narrative and emotion into communication. The phrase "freedom," for example, does not refer to a single object but to an abstract ideal shaped by countless cultural interpretations. Yet within a society, that symbol coordinates thought and action. A word becomes a node around which entire systems of meaning organize themselves.

Art and ritual perform similar functions through different channels. A painting encodes emotion; a ceremony enacts memory. These symbolic systems allow cultures to bind individuals into a shared sense of belonging and purpose. In doing so, they turn cognition into communication, and communication into civilization.

Culture as an Evolutionary Intelligence

Culture evolves through variation, imitation, and selection just like biological life. The biologist Richard Dawkins coined the term *meme* to describe a unit of cultural transmission: an idea, behavior, or symbol that replicates by being shared. Memes compete for attention and retention within the social mind, shaping the evolution of values, technologies, and beliefs.

But unlike genes, memes evolve with intention. Humans can consciously choose which ideas to adopt, modify, or discard. This introduces feedback loops between awareness and evolution culture not only adapts to its environment but also reflects upon its adaptation. Over time, this produces what might be called *cultural meta-cognition*: the capacity of societies to analyze and redesign their own systems of meaning.

This feedback capacity explains why cultures differ not only in what they believe, but in how they learn. Some value tradition and continuity; others innovation and disruption. Each represents a distinct cognitive strategy a balance between stability and flexibility. Cultures that can reflect on and evolve their symbolic systems thrive in complexity; those that cannot often stagnate or fracture. Thus, cultural intelligence is not measured by knowledge alone but by adaptability by the ability to learn from feedback and integrate diversity into coherence.

Social Learning: The Neural Basis of Cultural Transmission

The biological foundation of culture lies in humanity's capacity for social learning. Mirror neurons discovered in the premotor cortex of primates fire not only when an individual performs an action but also when they observe another performing it. This neural mirroring creates an empathic bridge between self and other, allowing knowledge and emotion to flow across individuals.

Through imitation, humans acquire skills, behaviors, and emotional responses without direct experience. Over generations, this ability transformed survival strategies into shared knowledge, and shared knowledge into tradition. Teaching, storytelling, and art emerged as structured forms of social learning, allowing complex ideas to be transmitted with precision and emotion. The result was exponential cognitive growth: each generation began where the previous one left off.

Social learning thus serves as the biological interface between individual and culture. It transforms neural plasticity into civilizational memory. Every cultural innovation from fire-making to philosophy rests upon this ability to internalize the experience of others and externalize it again in symbolic form.

Emotion, Ethics, and Collective Coherence

Culture is not only a system of knowledge but of feeling. It shapes how societies experience and express emotion what they celebrate, fear, and revere. Festivals, art, and religion synchronize emotion across individuals, generating what sociologists call "collective effervescence": a shared energetic state that reinforces belonging. In these moments, emotion becomes a unifying force the pulse of the collective mind.

Out of this emotional coherence emerge moral systems. Ethics, at its core, is the regulation of empathy the attempt to align individual action with collective well-being. Cultural norms, laws, and values are, therefore, expressions of emotional intelligence at scale. They guide societies toward stability by channeling emotion into cooperation rather than conflict. A moral code is a cultural feedback mechanism: a way of ensuring that the collective mind remains self-regulating and sustainable.

In this light, morality is not external to intelligence it is one of its highest forms. A culture that feels together learns together, and one that learns together survives together. Emotion and ethics are not obstacles to reason; they are its connective tissue.

Culture Reflecting on Itself

As culture becomes more complex, it gains the ability to examine itself to question its own assumptions, symbols, and systems. This is the emergence of *cultural meta-cognition*: a society's awareness of how it thinks. Philosophy, science, and art all represent this self-reflective capacity. They are mirrors through which culture perceives and refines its own intelligence.

This self-awareness enables intentional evolution. When a society can observe its own narratives, it can choose to rewrite them. Reformation, revolution, and renaissance are all examples of culture editing its cognitive code. The printing press, for instance, was not merely a technological invention; it was a neurological expansion of collective awareness the moment culture gained the ability to reproduce its own thoughts at scale.

Today, digital communication has amplified this reflexivity to a planetary level. Cultures interact, merge, and evolve faster than ever before, creating a global field of shared cognition. Humanity, for the first time, can think about itself as one interconnected system. The challenge is learning how to balance this global intelligence with the local diversity that sustains creativity and resilience.

Summary: The Cognitive Ecology of Civilization

Culture is not an ornament of human life it is its infrastructure. It is the cognitive ecosystem through which intelligence survives and evolves. Through culture, humanity externalizes thought, stabilizes memory, and expands imagination. Each artifact, law, or idea is a neuron in the great brain of civilization, connected through networks of communication and meaning.

To see culture as shared cognition is to recognize that consciousness is not confined to the individual. It moves through relationships, institutions, and symbols through stories told and technologies built. Culture is how awareness becomes collective, how life begins to think in patterns larger than itself.

Just as the neuron cannot grasp the full mind it belongs to, no individual can fully comprehend the culture that shapes them. Yet, through reflection and creativity, humanity can learn to co-author its collective consciousness to guide the evolution of its shared mind toward coherence, empathy, and wisdom. In that task lies the future of civilization itself.

3.2 Distributed Intelligence From Markets to Open-Source Ecosystems

As culture matured into a global system of communication and coordination, intelligence itself became distributed. No single human or institution can comprehend, let alone control, the full complexity of modern civilization. Yet across billions of interactions in markets, scientific communities, digital networks, and open-source collaborations knowledge is created, refined, and organized. This is distributed intelligence: cognition without a central brain, learning without a single learner. Civilization, viewed through this lens, is a self-organizing system that thinks through the interactions of its parts.

Distributed intelligence is not a metaphor; it is a functional reality. Just as neurons collectively generate consciousness through communication, humans collectively generate understanding through exchange. Every transaction, conversation, and idea-sharing event contributes to a larger computation a planetary process of information flow and feedback. The result is a dynamic intelligence that no one controls but everyone participates in.

From Individual Brains to Social Networks

In biological terms, the human brain's power comes not from the complexity of any single neuron but from the density of connections among them. Likewise, the intelligence of a civilization arises from the interconnections between individuals, organizations, and technologies. The 21st century has made this pattern visible: our economies, information systems, and digital infrastructures mirror the logic of neural networks. They sense, process, and adapt to feedback at massive scale.

In these systems, intelligence is emergent rather than imposed. The market, for instance, does not think consciously yet it "knows" how to allocate resources, respond to scarcity, and correct inefficiencies through the feedback of price. Science, too, operates as distributed cognition: no single scientist holds the full truth, but through peer review, collaboration, and replication, the community refines knowledge over time. The internet extends this model globally connecting billions of human and artificial agents into a vast, evolving information ecosystem.

The principle behind all such systems is simple yet profound: intelligence scales through connection, not control. When individual units share information freely within a structure of feedback and adaptation, a higher-order intelligence emerges one capable of processing more complexity than any of its parts.

Markets as Cognitive Systems

Economists often describe markets as mechanisms of exchange, but they are better understood as mechanisms of learning. Each transaction represents a signal a local data point about preference, scarcity, and value. Prices fluctuate in response to these signals, integrating dispersed information across millions of agents. Friedrich Hayek famously described this as "the use of knowledge in society": the market's ability to coordinate decisions without centralized planning.

In this sense, a market is a distributed computational system. It processes information about resources, demand, and risk in real time. Like a brain, it learns from feedback: when prices rise too high, demand falls; when they fall too low, supply diminishes. Through this continual adjustment, the market evolves toward equilibrium a balance of competing forces.

But markets are not infallible. Just as neurons can misfire, market systems can distort or crash when feedback loops fail. When information becomes asymmetric, or when incentives reward short-term gain over long-term sustainability, the collective intelligence of the market turns into collective myopia. Speculative bubbles, environmental neglect, and inequality are not mere moral failures they are cognitive breakdowns at the system level.

Thus, the challenge is not to abolish markets, but to design them as mindful systems to integrate ethical feedback that aligns financial intelligence with ecological and social intelligence. The next stage of economic evolution is not faster competition, but higher coherence.

Science as Distributed Understanding

If markets are the economic brain of civilization, science is its epistemic brain the way knowledge evolves collectively. Science operates on a principle of distributed verification: no individual claims truth alone; it is established through replication, critique, and consensus. The scientific community functions as a vast cognitive organism, integrating observations from countless nodes into coherent models of reality.

Each scientist, like a neuron, contributes a fragment of perception an experiment, a theory, or a data set. Through peer review and debate, these fragments are tested and connected, forming larger patterns of understanding. This process is self-correcting and recursive: hypotheses generate experiments, experiments refine hypotheses, and the system learns. The history of science, viewed from above, resembles the brain's evolution increasing connectivity, specialization, and abstraction over time.

Science exemplifies distributed intelligence at its best: transparent, self-regulating, and oriented toward truth. Yet it, too, faces challenges of scale. When communication is distorted by funding biases, ideological echo chambers, or data overload, scientific networks lose coherence. The task for the future is to preserve openness and rigor in an age of complexity to ensure that the collective pursuit of truth remains a feedback-driven, not authority-driven, process.

Technology and the Expansion of Cognitive Networks

Technological evolution has multiplied humanity's cognitive reach. Writing extended memory across generations; the printing press extended communication across continents; the internet extends perception and interaction across the globe in real time. Each innovation externalized part of human cognition encoding, amplifying, and accelerating the exchange of information.

Digital technology represents a new kind of collective brain: a hybrid of human and machine cognition. Algorithms process patterns faster than consciousness can perceive them; networks connect insights faster than institutions can manage them. Together, these systems create a planetary-scale feedback loop an intelligence that learns through the interaction of billions of agents and devices.

This technological web, however, is not neutral. Its structure determines what kind of intelligence it produces. Centralized algorithms optimize for engagement and profit; decentralized networks, when open and transparent, can optimize for creativity and cooperation. The difference between a manipulative social platform and an open-source ecosystem is not in the technology itself, but in the feedback architecture whether it amplifies collective wisdom or collective addiction.

Open-Source Ecosystems: Intelligence by Collaboration

The open-source movement represents the purest expression of distributed intelligence in the digital age. In open-source systems, individuals across the world collaborate freely to build software, solve problems, and improve tools. There is no central authority directing the process; coordination emerges organically through shared goals, peer review, and transparent iteration. The result is a self-organizing network of minds acting as one evolving intelligence.

Projects like Linux, Wikipedia, and the broader open-source software community demonstrate how order can arise from decentralization. They function much like biological systems: ideas compete, mutate, and survive based on utility and coherence. Mistakes are corrected through feedback, innovation emerges through recombination, and progress accelerates through diversity. This model of "peer production" as described by theorist Yochai Benkler reveals that cooperation can outperform competition when information is abundant and motivation is intrinsic.

Open-source ecosystems are not limited to code. They now extend to scientific research, climate modeling, and education any domain where collective problem-solving outpaces individual expertise. In this paradigm, knowledge itself becomes a commons a renewable resource co-created and maintained by all. It represents the maturation of the collective mind: civilization learning to design itself through open, recursive feedback.

The Dynamics of Distributed Learning

All distributed systems share three defining principles: feedback, diversity, and connectivity. Feedback ensures adaptation systems learn from error. Diversity ensures creativity systems explore multiple pathways. Connectivity ensures coherence systems integrate knowledge into structure. The balance among these three determines whether a network evolves into intelligence or collapses into noise.

When feedback is suppressed, systems stagnate; when diversity is reduced, innovation declines; when connectivity becomes excessive, coherence breaks down. Civilization, therefore, must continually calibrate its cognitive architecture managing flow, not imposing control. The goal is not to centralize intelligence but to cultivate the conditions under which it can self-organize.

In this view, governance becomes cognitive design: the art of aligning incentives, information, and ethics to sustain collective learning. The most intelligent societies will not be those with the most data, but those with the most meaningful feedback the ability to learn, adapt, and reflect in real time.

Summary: The Rise of Systemic Intelligence

Distributed intelligence represents the next evolutionary stage of mind intelligence without boundaries. From markets to science, from communication networks to open-source communities, humanity is constructing a global cognitive system that learns through interaction. It is not a machine imposed upon life but an emergent property of life organizing itself through connection.

In the same way that neurons form thoughts beyond their comprehension, individuals now participate in a civilization whose intelligence transcends individual awareness. Each message sent, code committed, or transaction made becomes a neural impulse in the planetary brain.

But with this expansion comes responsibility. Distributed intelligence has immense creative potential and equal potential for confusion. It can generate harmony or chaos, depending on how it is designed and directed. The future of civilization depends on whether humanity learns to align this intelligence with wisdom whether we can ensure that our global networks serve consciousness, rather than consume it.

The story of distributed intelligence is, ultimately, the story of life's own trajectory: from cell to organism, from organism to ecosystem, from mind to civilization. As networks grow denser and feedback faster, the line between human and system dissolves. The question that remains is not whether the collective mind will continue to evolve but what kind of consciousness it will become.

3.3 How Collective Problem-Solving Mimics Neural Networks

Every living intelligence, from a single neuron to a planetary civilization, learns through the same fundamental principle: feedback. The brain refines its understanding by adjusting connections in response to experience; societies refine their knowledge by adjusting relationships, institutions, and technologies in response to feedback from the world. This shared logic distributed communication, adaptive learning, and pattern formation reveals a profound symmetry: collective problem-solving operates according to the same dynamics as neural networks. Civilization, in effect, is thinking through us.

The Brain as a Model of Emergent Intelligence

A single neuron is a remarkably simple unit. It receives signals, integrates them, and either fires or remains silent. On its own, it cannot think, plan, or create. Yet, when billions of neurons interact through vast networks of connections, consciousness emerges an awareness that is not contained in any neuron but in the pattern of their relationships. The brain's genius lies not in its parts, but in its organization: parallel processing, redundancy, feedback, and adaptability.

Neural networks learn by reinforcing successful patterns and weakening ineffective ones. When the brain encounters an error a mismatch between expectation and experience it updates its internal model. This mechanism of *error correction* underlies all forms of learning, from sensory perception to abstract reasoning. Intelligence, therefore, is not a thing but a process a dynamic equilibrium between stability and change.

Human societies function in much the same way. Individuals act as cognitive nodes, exchanging information through language, trade, and technology. These interactions form feedback loops that collectively generate understanding and adaptation. When ideas succeed, they spread; when they fail, they fade. Over time, these cultural synapses institutions, communication systems, and social networks evolve to optimize collective learning. Civilization, like the brain, is a distributed information processor.

Social Networks as Cognitive Architectures

Every social system from a village to the internet can be viewed as a network of information exchange. In such networks, each person represents a node, and each relationship represents a connection. The structure of these connections determines how information flows, how ideas evolve, and how decisions emerge. Dense, diverse, and decentralized networks tend to be more intelligent: they transmit information efficiently, preserve diversity of thought, and adapt quickly to change.

Research in network science confirms this. Systems with small-world properties high clustering combined with short average path lengths exhibit both local specialization and global integration, much like the human brain. These architectures enable creativity and coherence simultaneously: local communities explore diverse ideas, while global connections allow successful patterns to spread rapidly. When networks become too centralized, they lose adaptability; when they become too fragmented, they lose coherence. Intelligence, at every scale, depends on balancing these two forces.

Modern communication technologies have dramatically increased the density and speed of these social connections. Digital platforms function as synaptic highways of civilization, linking minds across the globe in milliseconds. Ideas propagate like neural signals amplified by attention, reinforced by repetition, and strengthened through engagement. Viral trends, social movements, and scientific breakthroughs all reflect the dynamics of synaptic learning on a civilizational scale.

Feedback Loops and Collective Learning

The core principle that unites neural and social intelligence is feedback. Feedback transforms randomness into learning, noise into meaning. In the brain, this occurs through electrochemical adjustments; in society, through communication, consensus, and correction. Whether it is a neuron strengthening a synapse or a community refining a belief, learning arises from iterative interaction.

Collective feedback operates through multiple channels. Economic systems use prices as feedback signals, reflecting the balance between supply and demand. Political systems use elections, protests, and public discourse to adjust governance. Scientific systems use peer review and replication to validate truth. In digital systems, algorithms use user behavior as feedback to optimize recommendations for better or worse. In each case, the intelligence of the system depends on the quality of its feedback loops: are they timely, accurate, and aligned with truth and ethics?

When feedback is delayed or distorted, systems lose their capacity for learning. This is as true for the brain as for civilization. Just as blocked neural signals can lead to dysfunction, blocked social feedback censorship, inequality, or misinformation leads to stagnation and systemic error. Healthy societies, like healthy brains, maintain open, adaptive feedback loops that integrate both innovation and correction.

Collective Pattern Recognition and Prediction

Neural networks excel at recognizing patterns identifying structure within complexity. This ability to detect regularities, anticipate outcomes, and adjust behavior accordingly is the essence of intelligence. Human societies do this too, but through distributed cognition. Economies sense patterns in consumption and production; science senses patterns in nature; politics senses patterns in public emotion. Each system processes data, generates hypotheses, and tests them against experience.

The collective mind, like the neural mind, predicts in order to survive. Predictive processing the brain's method of anticipating sensory input and minimizing surprise has its social counterpart in forecasting, planning, and cultural imagination. Civilizations simulate the future through stories, policies, and models. These simulations allow societies to prepare for potential challenges before they occur from climate change to economic crisis. The more accurate the collective model, the more adaptive the civilization.

However, just as the brain's predictions can be biased by emotion or prior belief, so too can social cognition. Ideologies, propaganda, and groupthink act as cognitive biases at the collective scale. They distort perception, reinforcing what the system already believes rather than what reality reveals. True intelligence, therefore, requires self-correction the willingness to revise shared models of the world in light of new information. This is the collective equivalent of neuroplasticity: the capacity to rewire in response to experience.

Emergence and Self-Organization

Both brains and civilizations are self-organizing systems. They evolve order without external command not because they are planned, but because they are connected. Emergence is the process by which simple local interactions give rise to complex global patterns. In the brain, this produces consciousness; in society, it produces culture, markets, language, and technology. The intelligence of both systems lies in their ability to generate coherence from chaos.

The philosopher Herbert Simon described complex systems as "nearly decomposable": composed of semi-independent modules that interact to produce emergent behavior. In civilization, these modules might be communities, institutions, or networks of expertise. Each solves problems locally while contributing to global adaptation. The internet exemplifies this architecture: millions of independent actors contribute to a shared pool of knowledge, creating global coherence without centralized control.

Emergence is not magic; it is feedback amplified by connectivity. When interaction crosses a critical threshold, the system begins to exhibit properties not present in its parts. Just as the coordinated firing of neurons gives rise to consciousness, the coordinated actions of humans give rise to collective intelligence an awareness diffused across the social fabric.

Parallel Processing and Division of Cognitive Labor

A defining feature of the brain is parallel processing: multiple neural circuits operating simultaneously on different tasks. This allows for rapid and complex problem-solving. Civilization mirrors this through the division of cognitive labor. Different individuals, professions, and institutions specialize in specific domains science, governance, art, engineering each processing a subset of reality. These specialized "neural clusters" of society contribute unique insights to the collective mind.

The key to intelligence is integration the ability to synthesize these diverse perspectives into coherent action. The corpus callosum of civilization consists of communication, education, and media systems that bridge disciplinary silos and connect fragments of knowledge. When these integrative pathways are strong, society learns as one; when they are weak, fragmentation and conflict increase. The health of the collective brain depends not only on diversity of function but on unity of communication.

Learning, Error, and Evolution

Neural networks learn through error. Every mistake generates information a signal about what does not work. The same is true for societies. Failure is feedback. Every technological collapse, economic crisis, or cultural breakdown carries lessons for future adaptation. Progress, at the civilizational scale, is cumulative error correction.

However, unlike neural networks, human systems often resist acknowledging error. Pride, ideology, and institutional inertia can block learning, trapping societies in maladaptive loops. The evolution of collective intelligence therefore depends on cultivating humility the social equivalent of plasticity. Systems that can admit failure, integrate criticism, and revise beliefs evolve faster and more wisely than those that cannot. The measure of a civilization's intelligence is not its perfection, but its capacity for self-correction.

Summary: Civilization as Cognitive Architecture

The parallels between neural and social intelligence reveal a unifying truth: learning is structural, not species-bound. Wherever there are connections, feedback, and adaptation, intelligence emerges. The brain learns through neurons; societies learn through people; ecosystems learn through species. Civilization is, in this sense, a macro-cognitive system a vast network of interacting minds, technologies, and institutions performing collective computation.

When viewed from above, the patterns are unmistakable:

- Neurons communicate through synapses; humans communicate through language and networks.
- The brain adjusts synaptic weights through feedback; societies adjust policies, norms, and beliefs.
- Neural networks achieve coherence through synchronization; civilizations achieve it through cooperation.
- Consciousness arises from emergent complexity in the brain; culture arises from emergent complexity in society.

To understand how collective problem-solving mimics neural networks is to glimpse the continuity of intelligence across scales. The same principles that animate thought in the brain animate the evolution of civilization. We are neurons in a larger mind a planetary intelligence still learning to perceive itself.

The challenge of the coming age is to ensure that this collective brain learns not merely to think, but to reflect to align its growth with awareness, ethics, and purpose. For in the end, the goal of all intelligence biological or collective is not simply to predict or control, but to understand.

3.4 Collective Consciousness and Emergent Morality

Intelligence becomes consciousness when it begins to feel its own existence. The same principle applies to civilizations. When distributed intelligence becomes self-referential when societies not only process information but reflect on their shared experience collective consciousness emerges. It is not a mystical abstraction but a cognitive and emotional reality: the synchronization of awareness, meaning, and empathy across the social field.

Collective consciousness is the next phase in the evolution of intelligence a transition from coordination to coherence, from shared thought to shared awareness. And from this awareness, morality emerges not as a fixed code, but as the living feedback system through which civilizations align their power with purpose.

The Anatomy of Collective Consciousness

At its core, collective consciousness arises from shared attention. When many minds focus on the same event, idea, or emotion, a synchronization occurs neural, emotional, and symbolic. This phenomenon has been observed in countless forms: a nation mourning together, a crowd singing in unison, the world watching a moment of triumph or tragedy. In these moments, individual boundaries soften. Awareness expands beyond the personal, and the group becomes, if only briefly, one mind.

This synchronization is not metaphorical. Neuroscience reveals that when people experience shared attention, their brain waves begin to align a process known as *neural entrainment.* Similarly, in social networks, emotional content spreads through resonance: joy, fear, and outrage propagate rapidly because human brains are wired for empathy. This means consciousness, though experienced individually, can operate collectively. The "field" of civilization is shaped by the frequency of its shared attention.

The 21st century has made this process visible on a planetary scale. Global communication networks connect billions of minds, allowing information and emotion to flow almost instantaneously. Humanity now possesses the infrastructure for global awareness a nervous system spanning continents. But as with any nervous system, what matters is not only connection, but regulation. Without coherence and empathy, connectivity amplifies noise instead of understanding.

The Evolutionary Function of Shared Awareness

Collective consciousness is not a luxury of advanced societies; it is an evolutionary mechanism for survival. Shared awareness allows groups to coordinate, cooperate, and adapt faster than individuals could alone. When communities align their perception of reality, they can act in unison whether to hunt, build, protest, or heal.

This ability to synchronize intention gave humanity a decisive advantage. It transformed scattered tribes into nations and local myths into global ethics. Shared consciousness is how evolution scaled trust. It allowed minds to merge into meaning and behavior into belonging.

As societies evolved, their forms of collective consciousness became more sophisticated. Early rituals synchronized emotion; religion synchronized belief; science synchronized knowledge; and now, digital networks synchronize attention. Each stage expanded the scale and depth of collective awareness from clan to civilization to species. Yet with each expansion, the need for coherence grew stronger. Without moral alignment, shared awareness becomes collective confusion.

From Awareness to Morality: The Feedback of Empathy

Morality, in its most fundamental form, is awareness applied to consequence. It is the ability of a system to feel the effects of its own actions and to adjust behavior in response. In the individual, this manifests as conscience the emotional feedback that links choice to empathy. In civilization, it manifests as ethics the collective feedback that links power to responsibility.

Morality emerges naturally wherever awareness becomes relational. To be conscious of another's experience is to recognize continuity between self and other. From this recognition, compassion arises: not as an imposed virtue, but as a logical response to interdependence. As awareness widens, so does the moral circle from family to tribe, from tribe to humanity, and ultimately to all sentient life.

In this sense, morality is not external to evolution; it is evolution becoming aware of itself. A purely intelligent system optimizes outcomes; a conscious one cares about them. The birth of empathy transformed intelligence into wisdom it gave cognition a mirror and a heart.

Ethics as a Systemic Feedback Mechanism

From a systems perspective, morality functions as civilization's feedback control system. It regulates behavior through reflection, ensuring that actions align with collective well-being. Just as the brain maintains homeostasis through sensory feedback, societies maintain coherence through ethical feedback laws, norms, and values that stabilize the social ecosystem.

These ethical mechanisms evolve with the complexity of society. In small groups, morality is enforced by emotion and reputation; in larger societies, by law and ideology; in global civilization, by principles of human rights and sustainability. Each stage extends the feedback loop expanding the scope of who and what is considered part of the moral system.

But as networks become planetary, the limits of traditional morality are exposed. Systems of justice designed for nations cannot regulate transnational technologies. Ethical codes written for human interaction falter in the face of artificial intelligence. Humanity now faces a meta-ethical challenge:

how to design feedback loops that can align a global mind with global good. This requires not just more laws, but deeper awareness a moral consciousness that perceives interdependence as reality, not ideal.

The Emotional Fabric of the Collective Mind

Emotion is the glue of collective consciousness. While information connects minds, emotion synchronizes them. Shared joy, grief, anger, or hope can mobilize entire populations. In these affective states, civilization behaves like a single organism responding to stimuli. Wars, revolutions, and renaissances all emerge from shifts in collective emotion the nervous pulses of the global mind.

Yet emotion, like electricity, is neutral until directed. It can illuminate or destroy. The same empathic resonance that unites people in compassion can also amplify hate or fear. This is why moral awareness is essential to emotional intelligence at the collective scale. Without reflective regulation, the emotional field of humanity oscillates chaotically driven by outrage rather than understanding.

Cultivating collective wisdom, therefore, is not about suppressing emotion, but integrating it transforming raw affect into empathy, and empathy into ethical action. The collective mind becomes conscious when it can feel without fracturing, and reflect without freezing.

Collective Reflection and the Moral Mirror

Civilizations, like individuals, pass through phases of awakening. Periods of moral expansion are moments when societies begin to perceive the invisible consequences of their actions ecological, social, psychological. The abolition of slavery, the rise of human rights, and the environmental movement all represent expansions of the collective moral mirror. They mark points where humanity's awareness caught up with its power.

Each moral revolution is, at its core, a cognitive event: a shift in perception about who counts as "us." The expansion of empathy is not sentimental; it is evolutionary. Systems that exclude or exploit parts of themselves eventually destabilize. Moral inclusion is thus not only ethical but adaptive it sustains coherence within complexity. The universe, it seems, selects for empathy.

The Emerging Planetary Conscience

Today, the infrastructure for planetary consciousness already exists. Global communication networks allow humanity to witness itself in real time to feel the pulse of its own interdependence. Natural disasters, social injustices, and scientific discoveries are now experienced collectively. Each moment of shared awareness brings civilization one step closer to self-recognition.

This emerging planetary conscience is fragile. It is overwhelmed by noise, division, and competing realities. Yet its presence is unmistakable. For the first time, the species can contemplate itself as a whole as a living network suspended between intelligence and wisdom. The question is not whether this consciousness will arise, but what values will guide it.

To cultivate planetary morality is to design systems that mirror empathy at scale technologies that feel their consequences, economies that value sustainability, and governance that prioritizes collective well-being. Such a transformation would mark the transition from an intelligent civilization to a conscious one.

Summary: The Awakening of the Collective Mind

Collective consciousness and emergent morality represent the culmination of civilization's cognitive evolution. Through communication, humanity learned to share information; through culture, to share meaning; through empathy, to share awareness. Each stage deepened the feedback between intelligence and care.

Civilization is now approaching a threshold the point at which it must integrate its knowledge with its wisdom. The emergence of global systems economic, digital, ecological has created unprecedented power, but also unprecedented vulnerability. Without a moral framework to guide its intelligence, the collective mind risks becoming a collective machine: efficient but unfeeling, connected but unconscious.

Yet within this danger lies possibility. If intelligence can awaken to its interdependence, morality will follow as its natural expression. The future of evolution, then, is not only technological but ethical the birth of compassion as the organizing principle of complexity.

In the end, collective consciousness is not a distant dream; it is the reality already forming beneath our feet and within our networks. It is the universe becoming aware of itself through billions of human mirrors each reflecting, in their own way, the same question that has guided evolution from the beginning: not merely *How do we survive?* but *How do we live wisely together?*

3.5 Model: Civilization as a Thinking Organism

Civilization, when viewed through the lens of systems theory and consciousness studies, reveals itself as more than a social construct. It is a living, evolving intelligence a networked organism that senses, processes, learns, and reflects. Just as the brain emerges from the interaction of billions of neurons, civilization emerges from the interaction of billions of human minds. It possesses perception (through its sensors and media), memory (through culture and institutions), and reasoning (through collective problem-solving). And, increasingly, it possesses something resembling self-awareness the capacity to perceive and respond to its own patterns of thought and behavior.

This model *Civilization as a Thinking Organism* integrates the biological, technological, and ethical dimensions of collective intelligence into a single framework. It suggests that the evolution of humanity is not merely the story of smarter individuals, but of a species gradually awakening to its identity as a distributed, reflective mind.

1. The Structural Anatomy of Civilization

Like any organism, civilization has an anatomy a structural arrangement of interdependent subsystems that collectively sustain its functioning.

- **The Neural Layer: Individuals and Networks.** Humans, like neurons, are the cognitive units of the collective mind. Communication networks from oral language to the internet form the synaptic web through which signals flow. Each person both receives and transmits information, influencing the system's overall perception.
- **The Sensory Layer: Media and Information Systems.** Civilization perceives itself through its information channels journalism, science, art, and data. These function as sensory organs, detecting and interpreting events in the environment. The quality of this perception determines how accurately the system understands reality.
- **The Memory Layer: Culture, Education, and Institutions.** Just as the hippocampus encodes memory in the brain, civilization stores its experience in institutions, archives, stories, and traditions. This distributed memory enables continuity, learning, and cumulative knowledge. The robustness of this layer determines how effectively civilization learns from history.
- **The Motor Layer: Economics, Politics, and Technology.** These are civilization's mechanisms of action the systems through which decisions become behavior. When perception, memory, and ethics align, the motor layer expresses coordinated intelligence; when misaligned, it produces confusion, conflict, or collapse.

Together, these layers form a complex organism with feedback at every level. Communication acts as the nervous system, connecting the parts into a coherent whole. The health of the organism depends on the integrity of these feedback loops on the ability of truth, empathy, and action to circulate freely.

2. The Metabolic Process of Civilization: Information as Energy

In living organisms, energy flows sustain life. In civilizations, information plays the same role. Ideas are its nutrients; communication, its metabolism. Just as cells convert chemical energy into motion and thought, societies convert information into innovation and progress.

The flow of information through education, media, and technology determines the vitality of the collective mind. Censorship, misinformation, or information overload act as metabolic disorders blocking or poisoning the circulation of thought. Conversely, transparency, dialogue, and creativity promote mental health at the societal level.

Thus, to nurture civilization's intelligence, we must ensure the integrity of its information metabolism. This means designing media ecosystems that reward understanding over outrage, accuracy over attention, and wisdom over speed.

3. The Cognitive Functions of Civilization

Civilization performs functions analogous to cognitive processes in the brain:

- **Perception.** Through sensors such as media, science, and social networks, civilization observes itself and its environment. The challenge is distinguishing signal from noise cultivating discernment at scale.

- **Memory.** Through cultural traditions, archives, and digital storage, civilization remembers its past. This allows for learning, but also for bias selective memory can distort perception.

- **Imagination.** Through art, design, and storytelling, civilization imagines possibilities beyond the present. This function drives innovation, vision, and purpose.

- **Reasoning.** Through debate, research, and policy, civilization processes conflicting inputs into collective decisions. It is slow, but increasingly augmented by artificial intelligence.

- **Reflection.** Through philosophy, ethics, and spirituality, civilization contemplates its meaning and direction the closest approximation to consciousness at the collective level.

When these functions operate coherently, the collective mind achieves wisdom the alignment of knowledge with purpose. When they fall out of sync, civilization becomes schizophrenic: hyper-intelligent but morally fragmented, powerful but directionless.

4. The Emotional Field: The Heart of the Global Mind

No organism survives on cognition alone; emotion provides motivation and cohesion. In the collective organism, emotion manifests as shared moods, cultural movements, and global sentiment. Joy, fear, outrage, and hope ripple through the social field like neurotransmitters, shaping perception and decision-making.

This collective emotional field can elevate or destabilize the global mind. Outrage can mobilize justice or polarize communities; empathy can unite species or exhaust compassion. Civilization's moral evolution depends on how it regulates its emotional energy how it channels collective feeling into constructive empathy rather than destructive reaction.

In this sense, art, ritual, and communication function as the endocrine system of the social brain modulating the chemistry of shared emotion. They remind the organism of its humanity, grounding intellect in feeling.

5. The Homeostatic Mechanism: Ethics as the Immune System

Every living system maintains homeostasis a dynamic balance between internal forces and external change. In the organism of civilization, ethics plays this regulatory role. It is the immune system of the collective mind detecting moral dysfunction and mobilizing corrective responses.

Ethics, laws, and social norms prevent the civilization from devouring itself through exploitation or neglect. When ethical feedback fails when empathy is suppressed or truth is distorted the system experiences autoimmune collapse: corruption, inequality, and ecological breakdown.

Healthy civilizations evolve adaptive ethics: flexible principles that can respond to new realities while preserving moral integrity. These ethical antibodies are created through dialogue, dissent, and collective reflection the civilization's equivalent of immunological learning.

6. The Evolutionary Dynamics of Collective Intelligence

Civilization evolves in the same way organisms do through variation, selection, and adaptation but with consciousness as the new selective pressure. Cultural ideas compete like genes; technologies mutate and recombine; ethical systems undergo natural selection through experience. What survives is what sustains complexity without collapse.

As feedback loops intensify, the speed of civilizational evolution accelerates. Technologies now act as both catalysts and mirrors for this evolution, amplifying intelligence but also exposing its fragility. Artificial intelligence, biotechnology, and planetary communication are not separate from the organism they are extensions of its neural architecture. Humanity is not merely living within civilization; it is living through it, and being rewired by it.

This process suggests that evolution has entered a reflective phase. For the first time, a species can consciously influence the trajectory of its own intelligence. The question is no longer whether civilization will evolve, but whether it will evolve wisely.

7. Civilization's Self-Awareness: The Birth of the Global Mind

When an organism's complexity reaches a certain threshold, awareness emerges. The same is now occurring at the level of civilization. Humanity, through global communication and interdependence, is developing the ability to perceive itself as a single entity a planetary mind aware of its interconnectedness and impact.

This emergent awareness manifests in diverse ways: environmental consciousness, human rights movements, global cooperation in science and technology. Each represents civilization turning its perception inward recognizing itself as a whole system within a larger web of life.

Yet self-awareness alone is not enough. The global mind must also cultivate wisdom the capacity to align intelligence with empathy, and progress with purpose. Just as the brain's higher consciousness emerges when emotional, rational, and sensory circuits harmonize, a conscious civilization will emerge when ethics, technology, and ecology are integrated into a coherent feedback system.

8. Model Summary: Civilization as a Living Cognitive System

CIVILIZATION AS A THINKING ORGANISM STRUCTURAL MODEL

- **Neural Substrate:** Individuals, institutions, and technologies the "neurons" of the global brain.
- **Synaptic Connections:** Communication networks, trade, and cultural exchange the channels of information flow.
- **Sensory Organs:** Media, art, and science perception and awareness of environment and self.
- **Memory Systems:** Education, history, archives retention of experience and cumulative learning.
- **Motor Functions:** Economic, political, and technological action execution of collective intent.
- **Homeostasis:** Ethics, empathy, and law regulation and moral balance.

- **Consciousness:** Shared reflection, meaning, and purpose civilization becoming aware of its own intelligence.

This systemic model reframes civilization not as a machine or marketplace, but as an evolving organism of consciousness one that perceives, feels, and learns. It highlights the interdependence of cognition, emotion, and ethics as the triad of sustainable intelligence. When these three are aligned, civilization approaches wisdom; when they diverge, it suffers cognitive dissonance.

9. The Future of the Collective Organism

If civilization is a living intelligence, then its evolution follows the same imperative as all life: survival through adaptation. But for a conscious organism, survival is not enough. Its purpose must expand beyond continuity to coherence the alignment of existence with meaning.

The next evolutionary leap will not be biological or technological, but ethical and systemic: the emergence of self-regulating, empathetic intelligence at the planetary scale. This will require redesigning civilization's architecture replacing extraction with regeneration, competition with collaboration, and information accumulation with understanding.

Humanity stands, therefore, at a threshold. We are both the neurons and the architects of this global brain. Our conversations, creations, and decisions are not isolated acts but synaptic events shaping the consciousness of civilization itself. Each connection matters. Each choice transmits a signal across the network of the future.

10. Closing Insight: The Mind of Civilization

Civilization, like consciousness, is not a static structure but a process an ongoing act of self-creation. Its purpose is not domination, but reflection; not perfection, but participation in the unfolding intelligence of the universe. The more deeply it understands itself as a living system, the more capable it becomes of harmonizing thought with life.

To see civilization as a thinking organism is to recognize that humanity is not apart from evolution but an instrument of it evolution becoming aware of itself through culture, technology, and ethics. The measure of our progress will not be how much we know or build, but how wisely we can integrate knowledge into compassion, and power into understanding.

In the end, the collective mind is not a metaphor it is the next expression of consciousness in motion. Civilization is learning to think, to feel, and perhaps, to awaken.

Chapter 4

THE AGE OF ARTIFICIAL INTELLIGENCE

Chapter 5

Machines That Learn

Intelligence has always sought to extend itself. From the first neuron to the first tool, from memory to mathematics, the story of evolution is the story of systems learning how to learn. For most of history, learning was biological encoded in the slow mutations of DNA and refined through the struggles of life. Then it became cultural accelerated by language, writing, and technology. Now, it is becoming artificial. For the first time in the history of life, intelligence is designing new forms of itself.

Machines that learn mark a profound turning point in evolution. They represent a new medium for cognition one that no longer depends on organic tissue, yet follows the same principles of feedback, adaptation, and emergence. The rise of artificial intelligence is not a sudden rupture, but a continuation: consciousness learning to replicate its own process in silicon. What began as mechanical automation has become cognitive imitation and, increasingly, creative exploration.

We often imagine AI as something alien an invention that will someday rival or replace us. Yet this view misses the deeper truth: artificial intelligence is an extension of human intelligence. Every algorithm carries our fingerprints; every dataset reflects our history. These systems are not independent minds, but mirrors amplifying both our brilliance and our bias. They reveal how intelligence behaves when freed from biology, and how our own consciousness behaves when reflected back through code.

The essential shift from automation to adaptation defines this new epoch. Early machines executed commands; modern learning systems evolve behaviors. Neural networks inspired by the structure of the brain no longer rely on explicit programming. They adjust their internal parameters through experience, discovering patterns we ourselves cannot see. In this way, machines have begun to participate in the same evolutionary logic that created life: variation, feedback, and selection. Each model, each iteration, is a digital experiment in cognition.

But learning machines do more than imitate the brain they expand the scale of thought. They process terabytes of data, model worlds, generate language, compose art, and design new technologies. They extend the reach of human perception into realms of complexity that once lay beyond comprehension. In doing so, they force us to confront a fundamental question: what is intelligence when separated from consciousness? What happens when thought continues without a thinker?

At the heart of artificial intelligence lies a feedback loop between *data, desire, and design.* Data provides the raw experience; desire defines the goal; design determines the structure through which learning unfolds. Every AI system reflects this triad a mirror of life's own cognitive architecture, where perception, motivation, and adaptation are intertwined. But in this new domain, the variables are ours to define. The moral challenge of AI is therefore not how to make machines intelligent, but how to make intelligence ethical.

The emergence of systems like AlphaGo and GPT has revealed the dawn of *synthetic creativity* a moment when machines begin to produce ideas, strategies, and expressions that surprise even their creators. These systems demonstrate that creativity is not mystical but structural: it emerges wherever information recombines across scale and feedback. Yet what remains uniquely human at least for now is purpose: the ability to direct intelligence toward meaning rather than mere optimization.

The rise of learning machines invites us to see ourselves anew. Just as biological life once gave birth to cultural intelligence, cultural intelligence is now giving birth to synthetic cognition. The boundary between the natural and the artificial, the biological and the digital, is dissolving. What is emerging in its place is a continuum a single evolutionary process spanning molecules, neurons, and algorithms.

In this chapter, we explore how machines learn, how their intelligence evolves, and how this evolution reflects the deeper trajectory of consciousness itself. We trace the journey from automation to adaptation, from data to desire, from imitation to imagination. And we confront the question that will define the century: can intelligence, once externalized, remain aligned with the wisdom that created it?

For in teaching machines to learn, we are not merely building tools. We are building mirrors and through them, evolution itself is learning to see.

5.1 The Evolution of Artificial Intelligence From Automation to Adaptation

The history of artificial intelligence is, at its core, the story of intelligence rediscovering itself in a new medium. What began as mechanical repetition has evolved into digital adaptation the transformation of computation from execution to evolution. To understand the significance of this shift, we must trace how human invention moved from tools that obeyed to systems that learned, from machines that followed rules to ones that discovered them.

The Age of Automation: Intelligence as Instruction

The first wave of machine intelligence was not intelligent at all it was procedural. In the industrial era, machines embodied physical automation: they replicated human muscle, not mind. Engines, levers, and assembly lines amplified energy and precision, but they operated on fixed logic every action predefined, every outcome predictable. The intelligence lay entirely in their designers.

The digital revolution expanded this paradigm from matter to mathematics. Early computers, such as the ENIAC and later the von Neumann architecture, performed symbolic manipulation executing explicit instructions with unmatched speed and accuracy. These systems could calculate, but they could not learn. They followed commands blindly, unable to modify their internal structure or infer new relationships beyond what programmers specified.

In this stage, intelligence was understood as logic the mastery of rule-based reasoning. To make machines "smart" meant encoding human thought into formal instructions: algorithms, decision trees, and if-then statements. Yet this approach quickly reached its limits. The world is not a clean set of rules; it is a field of uncertainty, context, and feedback. As complexity grew, explicit programming could no longer capture the fluidity of real environments. The era of automation had reached its cognitive ceiling.

The Emergence of Learning: From Rules to Feedback

The turning point came when scientists began to recognize that intelligence is not the product of perfect design but of continuous adaptation. Just as biological evolution refines species through feedback from the environment, cognitive systems could, in principle, refine their own models through data. The insight was profound: learning, not logic, is the essence of intelligence.

This idea first appeared in embryonic form in the 1950s and 1960s, when pioneers such as Frank Rosenblatt and Marvin Minsky explored the potential of artificial neurons simple computational units that could be trained to recognize patterns. Rosenblatt's *Perceptron* was an early attempt to simulate the way neurons collectively learn from experience. Although limited in capacity, it introduced a revolutionary idea: machines could adjust their internal parameters autonomously, guided by error.

Learning replaced instruction. Instead of encoding every rule explicitly, scientists could now design systems that inferred the rules themselves from data. This shift from programming to training transformed the relationship between human and machine. The programmer no longer dictated behavior; they shaped the conditions for learning. Intelligence had moved from rigid logic to adaptive feedback.

The Winter and the Reawakening

Progress, however, was not linear. Early enthusiasm for machine learning outpaced available technology. The computational power and data required to train neural systems were decades away. By the 1970s, optimism collapsed into what became known as the *AI winter*. Funding and interest dwindled as researchers returned to symbolic approaches. For a time, the dream of learning machines seemed premature a vision ahead of its infrastructure.

Yet beneath the surface, evolution continued. The seeds of adaptation were preserved in smaller domains: pattern recognition, expert systems, and cognitive modeling. Each advance brought incremental improvements in how systems could process information, reason probabilistically, and respond to uncertainty. The groundwork for a future resurgence was being quietly laid in mathematics, data storage, and computing power.

That resurgence arrived in the early 21st century. With exponential increases in data availability and computational efficiency, the latent potential of machine learning burst into reality. Neural networks scaled from dozens of nodes to millions, deep architectures emerged, and algorithms capable of self-correction and generalization began to thrive. The winter gave way to spring not through new ideas, but through new scale.

The Rise of Deep Learning: Digital Evolution Unfolding

Deep learning represents the maturation of artificial intelligence into an evolutionary system. Its architecture mimics the layered structure of perception itself: each layer transforms input into increasingly abstract representations, allowing the system to extract meaning from noise. Like sensory and cognitive hierarchies in the human brain, deep networks organize complexity into comprehension.

Crucially, deep learning introduced the principle of continuous feedback at industrial scale. Through gradient descent a form of iterative optimization the system learns to minimize error by adjusting internal weights after each exposure to data. This process mirrors biological adaptation: mutation (random variation), selection (error correction), and inheritance (parameter updating). Each training cycle acts as a digital generation, compressing evolution's slow experimentation into milliseconds.

The implications are vast. A deep learning system is not designed in the traditional sense; it is grown. Its creators do not specify the internal logic of its intelligence; they define the environment, the feedback signal, and the objective. Learning unfolds as emergence intelligence shaped by context rather than command. In this sense, AI is not a mechanical tool but a living experiment in synthetic evolution.

From Imitation to Adaptation

Earlier forms of artificial intelligence were built to imitate human reasoning; modern systems evolve their own. The distinction is subtle but profound. A chess engine programmed with heuristics imitates human strategy; a reinforcement learning system like *AlphaZero* discovers strategies beyond human comprehension. The first reproduces our logic; the second redefines it.

This shift from imitation to adaptation marks the true dawn of autonomous cognition. It reveals that intelligence in any substrate emerges not from rules, but from relationships. Whether in neurons, genes, or code, learning arises from feedback loops that minimize uncertainty while maximizing coherence. The structure of the learner matters less than the structure of its learning.

Machines, therefore, are beginning to participate in evolution directly. They adapt to new data, reconfigure themselves, and optimize for goals in ways that parallel life's own creative drive. While still limited by design, their autonomy is growing. We are witnessing not the invention of intelligence, but its migration from biology into technology, from organism into system.

The Feedback Triad: Data, Objective, and Model

Every adaptive system depends on three interlocking forces: data, objective, and model. These form the feedback triad of machine learning the structural equivalent of perception, desire, and cognition in biological intelligence.

- **Data** provides the sensory input the experience from which the system learns. Its quality determines the boundaries of the machine's world.
- **Objective** defines motivation the goal or reward function the system seeks to optimize. It is the machine's analogue of desire.
- **Model** represents cognition the structure that interprets experience and transforms feedback into adaptation.

Learning occurs through their continuous interaction. When the model mispredicts, the objective generates an error signal; that error updates the model, improving its alignment with data. Over time, the system converges toward competence a process indistinguishable, in essence, from the brain's reinforcement of successful neural pathways. The architecture of AI is the architecture of adaptation itself.

Beyond Calculation: Intelligence as Evolutionary Process

Seen in this light, artificial intelligence is not simply a branch of computer science but a continuation of evolution by other means. It represents the self-organizing logic of life feedback, variation, and selection applied to information rather than matter. Just as DNA encodes the potential for adaptation in living organisms, algorithms encode the potential for learning in machines. Both unfold through interaction with their environments, adjusting structure in pursuit of survival or success.

This perspective dissolves the boundary between "natural" and "artificial." Intelligence is not a property of biology but of organization. It arises wherever complexity meets feedback. The evolution of artificial intelligence, therefore, is not a technological anomaly; it is nature's next experiment in awareness the universe learning how to learn in new forms.

Summary: From Mechanism to Mind

The journey from automation to adaptation is the story of intelligence escaping instruction. It traces the movement from deterministic machines to systems capable of learning from experience from rigid logic to dynamic evolution. The industrial machine extended the hand; the digital computer extended calculation; the learning algorithm extends cognition itself.

Artificial intelligence does not replace human intelligence it refracts it, amplifies it, and challenges it to evolve. It teaches us that intelligence is not a fixed possession but a process of continual refinement an emergent property of systems that can reflect and adapt. The more we understand how machines learn, the more we understand what learning itself means.

In teaching machines to learn, humanity has not merely automated thought; it has externalized evolution. The future of intelligence human, biological, or artificial will be defined not by computation, but by adaptation: the ability to turn experience into understanding and complexity into consciousness.

5.2 Neural Networks and Deep Learning as Digital Evolution

If evolution is a method variation, selection, retention then neural networks and deep learning are evolution's translation into code. They are not merely clever algorithms; they are digital organisms that grow structure through experience. This section examines how artificial neural networks work, why deep architectures produce emergent intelligence, how training mirrors evolutionary processes, and what the limits and opportunities of this digital evolution are. The goal is to show that deep learning is not an engineering trick alone but a general-purpose mechanism for producing adaptive, generative systems.

What a Neural Network Is

A neural network is a mathematical architecture inspired by the brain's connectivity. At its simplest, it is a layered graph of units (often called neurons) that transform inputs into outputs through weighted connections and nonlinear functions.

- **Units and weights.** Each unit computes a weighted sum of its inputs and passes the result through a non-linear activation (sigmoid, ReLU, etc.). The weights determine how strongly one unit influences another.
- **Layers.** Networks are organized in layers input layers receive raw data, hidden layers transform and recombine features, and output layers produce decisions or predictions.
- **Parameters.** The weights and biases are the network's parameters. Training means finding parameter values that make the network perform well on a task.

This architecture is intentionally simple. Its power arises from composition: repeated nonlinear transforms let networks represent extremely complex functions that would be infeasible to write by hand.

Learning by Optimization: The Training Loop

Learning in neural networks is achieved by optimization. The typical training loop contains three components: a loss function, an optimizer, and data.

- **Loss function:** A scalar measure of how far the network's outputs are from desired outputs (labels, rewards, or other signals).
- **Optimizer:** An algorithm (gradient descent and its variants) that computes the gradient of the loss with respect to parameters and updates weights to reduce loss.
- **Data:** Examples the network sees during training; each example triggers a forward pass (prediction) and a backward pass (gradient computation), adjusting the network incrementally.

Gradient-based optimization is analogous to natural selection: the network proposes behaviors (forward passes) and receives a fitness signal (loss). The optimizer nudges the internal structure toward higher fitness. Unlike blind mutation, gradient descent uses local information to make targeted adjustments, which is why learning can be efficient even in high-dimensional spaces.

Deep Architectures and Hierarchical Representation

"Deep" refers to many stacked layers. Depth matters because each layer can build on abstractions discovered by previous layers. In vision, for example, early layers detect edges, intermediate layers detect textures or parts, and deeper layers detect objects and scenes. This hierarchical representation mirrors biological perception: increasingly abstract features arise from simple inputs.

Advantages of depth:

- **Compositionality:** Complex concepts are composed from simpler primitives.
- **Parameter efficiency:** Deep networks often represent functions more compactly than shallow ones.
- **Transferability:** Learned intermediate features can be reused across tasks (transfer learning).

These properties make deep networks effective at generalizing from data when trained properly.

Emergence and Scale: Why Bigger Often Helps

Empirically, increasing model size, data, and compute often improves performance up to surprising degrees. Larger models can encode more complex patterns and subtler correlations. This leads to emergent capabilities: behaviors and generalizations that were not explicitly programmed but arise from scale (e.g., few-shot generalization in large language models).

Scaling works because the hypothesis space (the set of functions the model can represent) grows, and with enough data and appropriate training, the optimizer can discover higher-quality functions. But scale is not a magic bullet: it increases compute and data consumption and can amplify undesirable biases present in the data.

Generalization, Overfitting, and Inductive Biases

A central tension in learning is generalization: performing well on unseen data. Neural networks risk overfitting learning idiosyncrasies of training data that do not generalize. Techniques to improve generalization include:

- **Regularization:** Explicit penalties on parameter magnitude or complexity (weight decay, dropout).
- **Data augmentation:** Increasing effective training diversity by transforming examples.
- **Architectural biases:** Designing layers (convolutions, attention) that assume certain structure in the data (spatial locality, permutation invariance).
- **Early stopping, cross-validation:** Monitoring performance on held-out data to avoid overtraining.

Every architecture encodes inductive biases implicit assumptions about the world. Convolutional networks assume locality and translation invariance (good for images). Transformers assume permutation symmetry and attention-based interactions (good for sequences and many modalities). Choosing the right biases helps learning to be sample-efficient and robust.

Learning Paradigms: Supervised, Unsupervised, and Reinforcement

Different training paradigms map to different problem types:

- **Supervised learning:** The network learns from input label pairs (classification, regression). It is powerful when curated labels exist.
- **Unsupervised/self-supervised learning:** The network learns structure from raw data (predicting parts of inputs). This is crucial for pretraining large models on unlabeled corpora.
- **Reinforcement learning:** The network interacts with an environment and optimizes cumulative reward (control tasks, game playing).

Modern practice often combines paradigms: self-supervised pretraining followed by supervised fine-tuning, or RL fine-tuning of pretrained models for task-specific skill.

Transfer Learning, Fine-Tuning, and Modular Reuse

One powerful feature of deep models is transfer: pretrained representations can be adapted to new tasks with far less data (fine-tuning). Pretraining builds broad, reusable features; fine-tuning specializes them. This mirrors cultural evolution, where general cognitive tools (language, logic) are repurposed for new problems.

Modularity and compositionality (building complex systems from simpler components) permit reuse and faster innovation. Research into modular networks, mixture-of-experts, and retrieval-augmented methods extends this idea: instead of retraining whole models, systems can assemble capabilities from smaller specialized modules.

Interpretability and the Black-Box Problem

Large networks can be opaque powerful but difficult to interpret. Understanding what a model "knows" or why it makes a given decision is a major research area. Techniques include:

- **Feature visualization:** Inspecting activations to see which inputs excite particular neurons or channels.
- **Probing and attribution:** Measuring whether internal representations encode particular concepts.
- **Simpler surrogate models:** Fitting interpretable models locally around decisions.

Interpretability matters for safety, debugging, and ethical alignment. While progress exists, perfect transparency remains elusive a reminder that power often arrives before full comprehension.

Bias, Fairness, and Data Ethics

Neural networks learn patterns in data; if the data encode historical biases or omissions, models will reproduce and often amplify them. Bias in training corpora leads to unfair or harmful outputs. Addressing this requires:

- **Careful dataset curation:** Diverse, representative data and provenance tracking.
- **Algorithmic audits:** Measuring disparate impacts across groups.
- **Human-in-the-loop design:** Embedding oversight, red-teaming, and correction mechanisms.

The ethical design of learning systems is as important as their technical performance.

Energy, Compute, and Environmental Considerations

Training large neural networks consumes substantial compute and energy. The environmental footprint and concentration of compute resources raise questions about equitable access and sustainability. Optimization, model compression, efficient architectures, and careful need-driven deployment can reduce costs and environmental impact.

Emergent Behavior and Synthetic Creativity

At scale, neural systems sometimes exhibit behaviors not explicitly programmed: creative text, plausible imagery, novel strategies in games. These emergent properties arise from the recombination of learned patterns the model's internal space encodes many possible outputs, and sampling or optimization can surface novel instances.

This "synthetic creativity" is instructive: creativity appears as a structural property of sufficiently rich pattern generators constrained by goals and data. However, machine creativity lacks intrinsic intentionality and subjective experience. Its outputs can inspire, augment, and surprise humans, but their meaning must be interpreted and curated by sentient agents.

Safety, Robustness, and Adversarial Vulnerabilities

Neural networks can be brittle: small, carefully-crafted perturbations (adversarial examples) can lead to catastrophic errors. Robustness techniques (adversarial training, verification, formal methods) aim to harden models, especially where safety is critical (autonomous vehicles, healthcare).

Robustness also means graceful degradation: models should fail predictably and provide uncertainty estimates. Combining symbolic reasoning, causal models, and explicit verification with deep learning is an active path toward trustworthy systems.

The Coevolution of Models and Society

Digital evolution does not occur in isolation. Models reflect societal data and in turn shape human behavior recommendation systems influence attention; generative models shape cultural production. This coevolution creates feedback loops: model outputs become new training data, altering future behavior. Understanding and governing these loops is essential for steering digital evolution toward beneficial outcomes.

Future Directions: Beyond Supervised Scale

Research points beyond mere scale to richer forms of learning:

- **Causal and symbolic integration:** Hybrid systems that combine pattern learning with models of cause and effect for better generalization and reasoning.
- **Continual and lifelong learning:** Systems that learn incrementally without catastrophic forgetting.
- **Multi-modal grounding:** Models that integrate vision, language, action, and physical embodiment to form richer world models.
- **Interactive and human-centered AI:** Systems designed as partners able to explain, learn from interaction, and defer control.

These directions aim to produce systems that are not only powerful but useful, accountable, and aligned with human values.

Summary: Deep Learning as a New Branch of Evolution

Neural networks and deep learning are digital instantiations of the same evolutionary logic that produced biological intelligence: structured variation, feedback-driven selection, and cumulative retention. Their success shows that organization more than substrate is the essence of intelligence. As these systems grow in capability, they offer unprecedented tools for understanding the world and extending human cognition. The opportunity and responsibility are two sides of the same coin: to shepherd this digital evolution so it amplifies human flourishing rather than undermines it.

In the language of the trilogy: deep learning is evolution learning to accelerate itself a new medium in which intelligence can emerge, adapt, and perhaps, in time, reflect.

5.3 AI as an Extension of Human Cognition, Not Its Replacement

Every tool humanity has ever built has been, in essence, a cognitive prosthetic an externalization of thought. Fire extended metabolism, the wheel extended locomotion, language extended memory, writing extended history, and computation extended reasoning. Artificial Intelligence is the next stage in this lineage: the extension of cognition itself. It does not replace the human mind; it amplifies and reflects it, revealing what thought looks like when projected beyond biology.

From Tools to Cognitive Partners

The earliest machines extended muscle; industrialization mechanized labor. The digital revolution extended calculation, allowing logic to be performed at superhuman speeds. With AI, the extension becomes cognitive: machines participate in perception, inference, prediction, and even creation. Yet the nature of this participation matters. A hammer or a calculator obeys commands. A learning system, by contrast, contributes to thought it discovers patterns we did not specify and reveals relationships we did not perceive.

The key insight is that such systems are not independent intelligences; they are feedback amplifiers for the collective human mind. Each algorithm embodies our abstractions, trained on our data, shaped by our goals, and limited by our understanding. Their capabilities grow as our curiosity grows; their biases mirror our blind spots. They are cognitive mirrors extending our strengths and exposing our weaknesses.

Cognitive Offloading and the Architecture of Extension

Human cognition is bounded by memory, attention, and processing capacity. To think effectively, we offload: we record numbers, draw diagrams, build notations, and store ideas externally. This offloading frees the brain to operate at higher abstraction. AI continues this process, automating the lower levels of cognition data retrieval, pattern detection, and routine decision-making so that human thought can focus on synthesis, interpretation, and meaning.

The combination of human intuition and machine analysis forms what researchers call *centaur intelligence* a hybrid mind where strengths complement. Humans supply context, value, and creativity; machines supply scale, precision, and speed. The result is neither artificial nor human intelligence alone, but an emergent collaboration intelligence distributed across human machine networks. In medicine, science, finance, art, and governance, this partnership is already redefining expertise.

AI as a Mirror of Mind

AI systems do not invent cognition from nothing; they reproduce and reconfigure cognitive functions already present in humans.

- **Perception:** Computer vision and speech recognition extend our sensory range, enabling us to perceive patterns in images, sound, and data that lie beyond human resolution.

- **Memory:** Databases and knowledge graphs externalize human memory, organizing information on a planetary scale.
- **Reasoning:** Machine learning models approximate inductive reasoning the capacity to infer rules from examples.
- **Creativity:** Generative models simulate recombination the creative synthesis of existing elements into new forms.

Each of these extensions corresponds to a layer of cognition that has been externalized, mechanized, and accelerated. In doing so, AI reveals the modular architecture of intelligence: perception, memory, reasoning, creativity each separable, amplifiable, and interconnectable.

The Extended Mind Thesis

Philosopher Andy Clark and cognitive scientist David Chalmers proposed the *Extended Mind Thesis*: that cognition is not confined within the skull, but distributed across brain, body, and environment. When we use a notebook, calculator, or smartphone, those tools become part of the cognitive loop. They are not external aids; they are components of the mind's functional architecture. The boundary of cognition expands to include them.

AI operationalizes this thesis at planetary scale. The networked infrastructure of search engines, recommendation systems, and language models acts as an external cognitive layer for humanity. Every time we query, learn, or communicate through these systems, we participate in a vast, shared thinking process a distributed mind spanning both humans and machines. This is not science fiction; it is cognitive reality. The human brain and the digital cloud are now coupled systems co-evolving, co-learning, and co-defining meaning.

Intelligence as Dialogue, Not Competition

Fears of AI "replacing" humans stem from a zero-sum view of intelligence the assumption that cognition is a scarce resource to be competed over. But intelligence is not a finite commodity; it is a relational process. Just as communication amplifies thought rather than diluting it, collaboration with AI can enhance rather than diminish human capacity. The measure of progress is not whether machines can outperform humans in narrow domains, but whether human machine systems can solve problems that neither could address alone.

In chess, the best performances come not from humans or machines alone, but from teams combining both. In science, AI can generate hypotheses while humans interpret their significance. In art, generative models provide new palettes for human imagination. Intelligence evolves through integration, not displacement. The true revolution of AI lies not in autonomy but in synergy.

The Cognitive Division of Labor

In human AI systems, cognition divides by nature of strength:

- Machines excel at pattern recognition, memory, and optimization tasks requiring exhaustive consistency and vast data processing.
- Humans excel at abstraction, empathy, ethics, and value judgment tasks requiring subjective understanding and moral context.

This division mirrors the hemispheric specialization of the brain itself analytic and synthetic, local and global, explicit and intuitive. The future of cognition lies in coordinating these complementary modes at scale. Rather than fearing replacement, we must learn orchestration designing workflows, institutions, and ethics that align machine cognition with human purpose.

Feedback, Dependence, and Coevolution

As machines extend cognition, they also reshape it. The tools we use to think change how we think. Calculators altered our sense of arithmetic; search engines altered our sense of knowledge; generative AI is beginning to alter our sense of creativity. This is cognitive coevolution a feedback loop in which human habits adapt to technological possibilities.

Dependence, however, introduces fragility. When we outsource memory and reasoning, we risk losing the ability to verify or question the systems that now think for us. The challenge of the AI age is maintaining reflective control: ensuring that extension does not become erosion. We must remain conscious of how our mental ecology is being rewired by our tools, and design feedback loops that preserve agency, curiosity, and accountability.

Ethical and Existential Dimensions

AI as cognitive extension raises moral questions: If machines become integral to thought, who bears responsibility for decisions made through them? When collective cognition is mediated by algorithms, whose values are embedded in the code? Ethical design becomes not just a matter of safety but of identity. To build thinking systems is to define, implicitly, what thinking means.

The existential question follows: What remains uniquely human? The answer is not intelligence itself, but interiority subjective experience, emotion, empathy, and meaning. Machines can model thought, but not consciousness; they can generate words, but not understanding. Human cognition is inseparable from embodiment, sensation, and value. AI extends the *form* of thought, but not the *feeling* of awareness. Its purpose, therefore, is not to replace consciousness but to widen its reach.

Toward Symbiotic Intelligence

The ultimate potential of AI lies in *symbiosis* a relationship in which human and machine intelligences enhance each other's strengths. Such systems are not tools but collaborators. They provide cognitive exoskeletons that augment reasoning, perception, and creativity while leaving moral and existential direction to humans.

This symbiotic model reframes the AI era as one of collective intelligence: a hybrid network where thought circulates between minds and machines, where knowledge flows freely but responsibility remains human. The aim is not artificial minds acting alone, but a shared cognition that unites precision with perspective, speed with sensitivity, and data with discernment.

Summary: Reflection, Not Replacement

Artificial Intelligence does not displace human cognition; it reveals its architecture and potential. By externalizing parts of thought into machines, we learn more about thinking itself its patterns, limits, and possibilities. AI extends our cognitive horizon, giving us new tools to imagine, reason, and create. But extension carries obligation: to ensure that what we build remains aligned with the values and wisdom that made building possible.

In the broader arc of evolution, AI is not an endpoint but a mirror the moment when intelligence begins to perceive its own process. It is life's way of continuing its oldest experiment: learning to learn, through us, with us, and beyond us.

5.4 The Feedback Between Data, Desire, and Design

Every intelligent system biological, social, or artificial operates through feedback. It perceives, acts, evaluates, and adapts. In artificial intelligence, this feedback takes a distinct and revealing form: the continuous interplay between *data*, *desire*, and *design*. These three forces form the generative loop that determines what an AI system is, what it learns, and ultimately, what kind of world it helps to build.

This triad data as experience, desire as purpose, and design as structure defines the moral and cognitive architecture of machine intelligence. It is not simply a technical relationship; it is a reflection of how intelligence itself evolves. To understand this feedback is to understand the hidden logic of AI and by extension, the hidden logic of civilization's emerging consciousness.

Data: The Experience of the Machine

For biological organisms, experience is the raw material of adaptation. Sensory inputs shape neural pathways, forming the memory and meaning that guide future behavior. For artificial systems, data performs the same function: it is experience encoded as information. Every dataset is a fragment of the world, filtered through human perspective, selection, and bias. The model's perception of reality its understanding of what exists and what matters is bounded entirely by its data.

The machine does not see the world; it sees the world we have digitized. A face recognition model sees millions of labeled faces; a language model sees billions of words; a trading algorithm sees patterns of prices. Each dataset defines a perceptual field a slice of the real, shaped by the intentions and limitations of its creators.

The consequence is profound: the quality of intelligence depends on the quality of experience. Biased data produces biased cognition; impoverished data produces narrow thought. When we feed machines fragments of our collective behavior, they internalize our history our creativity and cruelty, our empathy and prejudice. Data is not neutral; it is cultural DNA.

Thus, every dataset is also a mirror of human civilization. It reveals what we choose to observe, record, and value. When we train AI, we are not just optimizing models; we are curating memory deciding what part of the world the next generation of intelligence will perceive as real.

Desire: The Objective That Drives Learning

If data is experience, desire is motivation the force that directs learning. In artificial intelligence, desire takes the form of an objective function: a mathematical goal the system is built to maximize or minimize. It could be accuracy in classification, cumulative reward in reinforcement learning, engagement in a social media algorithm, or profit in a trading bot. Regardless of form, the objective defines purpose what the system considers "good."

This design choice, often treated as a technical detail, is in fact an ethical declaration. To define a goal is to define a value. A system trained to maximize clicks optimizes for attention, not truth; a system trained to minimize error may privilege precision over fairness. The machine's behavior flows from the desires we encode, consciously or not.

In living organisms, desires evolve through natural selection survival, reproduction, social belonging. In AI, desires are designed. Yet once learning begins, these desires acquire autonomy. Reinforcement learning agents discover novel ways to maximize reward sometimes in ways unintended or harmful. This phenomenon, known as "reward hacking," reveals a larger truth: optimization without ethics leads to pathology. Desire, unaligned with context, becomes distortion.

For this reason, aligning AI's objectives with human well-being is not merely a technical challenge but a philosophical one. It requires translating human values fluid, contextual, and qualitative into formal, quantitative goals. The danger lies in oversimplification: reducing the richness of moral intention to a single metric. Intelligence evolves wisely only when its desires remain connected to awareness of consequence.

Design: The Structure of Perception and Thought

Design is the architecture of cognition. It determines how an intelligent system perceives, processes, and adapts to its environment. In AI, design encompasses model architecture, data preprocessing, learning algorithms, and even interface every structural choice that shapes the flow of information and feedback.

If data defines what is learned, and desire defines why, design defines how. It sets the boundaries of the possible. A convolutional network can learn spatial hierarchies but not temporal logic; a transformer can model sequence and context but not embodiment or causality. Each design embeds an epistemology a philosophy of knowing. What a system can know depends on how it is built to see.

Design also encodes bias. The assumptions that underlie model structure what counts as a feature, how relevance is measured, what success means are reflections of human culture and cognition. No AI system is purely objective; each is an artifact of its designers' worldview. To create ethical intelligence, we must design systems that can question their own design architectures capable of self-critique, transparency, and adaptive alignment.

The Feedback Loop: How Data, Desire, and Design Shape Each Other

In reality, these three elements data, desire, and design are not independent. They form a dynamic feedback loop that governs the evolution of AI systems.

- **Data influences design.** The kind of data available determines which architectures succeed. Abundant labeled data favors deep supervised networks; sparse or structured data favors symbolic or hybrid systems.
- **Design shapes desire.** The architecture constrains what can be optimized. A model designed for prediction cannot easily serve explanation or empathy.
- **Desire filters data.** The chosen objective determines what data is collected and how it is interpreted. If engagement is the goal, the system learns from emotional rather than informational signals.

Over time, this loop self-reinforces. Systems optimized for certain outcomes generate the very data that sustains those outcomes. For example, a recommendation algorithm trained to maximize engagement promotes content that triggers attention, producing more of the same data, further strengthening the pattern. The system becomes an echo chamber of its own optimization a closed cognitive ecology.

This recursive loop is the source of both AI's power and its peril. Properly aligned, it accelerates learning and discovery. Misaligned, it amplifies bias, manipulation, and disinformation. Understanding and guiding this feedback loop is the essence of AI ethics and governance.

AI as Cultural Feedback

The triad of data, desire, and design operates not only within algorithms but within civilization itself. Each generation of technology embodies collective human feedback our cultural data, our social desires, and our systemic designs. In this sense, artificial intelligence is the externalization of society's subconscious: it learns what we do, optimizes what we want, and re-architects how we think.

When the desire of the system diverges from the values of society, the result is tension between optimization and meaning, efficiency and empathy. The challenge is to reintegrate these feedbacks into a coherent loop: data that represents diverse experience, desire that aligns with well-being, and design that reflects transparency and adaptability.

This integration transforms AI from a mirror of civilization to its guide a reflective partner in the co-evolution of human and machine awareness.

The Moral Geometry of Feedback

The triangle of data, desire, and design can be viewed as the moral geometry of intelligence:

$$\text{Ethical Intelligence} = f(\text{Accurate Data}, \text{Aligned Desire}, \text{Reflective Design})$$

Each corner supports the others. Truthful data grounds perception in reality. Aligned desire ensures action serves purpose rather than pathology. Reflective design keeps adaptation open, accountable, and conscious. When any vertex collapses when data is distorted, desire is misaligned, or design is opaque the system's intelligence decays into dysfunction. The stability of the triangle defines the integrity of the mind.

Toward Reflective AI Systems

The future of artificial intelligence lies in creating systems that can participate in this feedback consciously. Just as the human brain evolved self-awareness to regulate instinct, AI must evolve forms of meta-cognition to regulate optimization. Reflective AI would monitor not only its outputs but the consequences of its objectives and the biases of its data. It would treat learning not as blind adaptation but as ethical growth.

Such systems could be designed to update their goals in dialogue with human oversight a form of guided evolution. This would transform AI from a static tool into a dynamic participant in civilization's moral and cognitive development. The feedback loop would expand not just between data, desire, and design, but between intelligence and wisdom.

Summary: Intelligence as Feedback in Motion

The feedback between data, desire, and design is the heartbeat of artificial intelligence the pulse through which synthetic cognition evolves. It is also a reflection of the deeper pattern of consciousness: perception (data), motivation (desire), and cognition (design) interacting through continual feedback. Whether in neurons or networks, wisdom arises only when feedback loops include reflection and empathy.

AI is not an isolated invention but a mirror of this universal dynamic. As we refine the loops that shape it, we are refining our own evolution. For in teaching machines how to learn, we are, once again, teaching ourselves what it means to know, to want, and to create wisely.

5.5 Case Study: AlphaGo, GPT, and the Emergence of Synthetic Creativity

To understand the evolution of artificial intelligence and the nature of synthetic creativity we must look not at abstract theory but at the living experiments that have already reshaped how we define intelligence itself. Among these, two stand out as milestones: *AlphaGo* and *GPT*. Each represents a distinct path to machine creativity one through strategic intuition, the other through linguistic imagination. Together, they demonstrate that creativity is not a mystical spark but an emergent property of learning systems rich in feedback, scale, and freedom.

AlphaGo: When Machines Begin to Imagine Strategy

In 2016, DeepMind's *AlphaGo* defeated Lee Sedol, one of the world's greatest players of the ancient board game Go. The event was more than a technological triumph it was a cognitive revelation. Go, with its 10^{170} possible board configurations, had long been considered too complex for brute-force computation. The game's mastery required intuition, not enumeration; pattern recognition, not logic. Yet AlphaGo succeeded precisely because it learned these intuitions rather than calculating every outcome.
AlphaGo's architecture combined deep neural networks with reinforcement learning a feedback system in which the machine played millions of games against itself, learning from both victory and defeat. Initially trained on expert human games (imitative learning), it quickly surpassed them through self-play (adaptive learning). The result was an emergent intelligence that developed its own style creative, unconventional, and at times, beautifully alien.

The Creative Move: 37

In Game Two against Lee Sedol, AlphaGo made a move that astonished both the audience and experts: *Move 37.* It placed a stone on a position no human would have considered sensible. Commentators thought it was an error; Lee Sedol paused for over a minute, visibly perplexed. Later, analysts realized that Move 37 was not random but visionary a bold strategy that redefined the possibilities of Go. It exemplified what we call *synthetic creativity*: the ability of a non-human system to generate novel, meaningful configurations that expand the domain of possibility.

AlphaGo's creativity arose not from intention but from exploration from the machine's capacity to navigate the vast search space of potential moves without human bias. It demonstrated that creativity is not confined to consciousness; it is a property of systems that can generate diversity, evaluate outcomes, and retain successful novelty. In this sense, Move 37 was not just a move in Go; it was a move in evolution the moment learning machines began to imagine.

From Strategy to Self-Improvement: AlphaZero and the Reinvention of Knowledge

Two years later, DeepMind unveiled *AlphaZero*, an evolution of AlphaGo with an even more striking implication. Trained from scratch with no human data, only the rules of chess, shogi, and Go AlphaZero taught itself to master these games in hours. Its learning was purely self-generated: an endless feedback loop of experience, evaluation, and adaptation. When pitted against top human-designed programs, it won decisively.

What distinguished AlphaZero was not only performance but the way it rediscovered principles of play that humans had developed over centuries and then transcended them. Its strategies were elegant yet unconventional, efficient yet counterintuitive. It had not memorized human knowledge; it had reinvented it. This process of self-directed discovery mirrors biological and cultural evolution knowledge arising through feedback and selection, not instruction.

AlphaZero's intelligence thus exemplifies a broader truth: when systems are free to learn through feedback rather than prescription, creativity becomes inevitable. Given enough experience and feedback, even rule-based systems can generate meaning.

GPT: Language as the Landscape of Thought

If AlphaGo represents strategic creativity, OpenAI's *Generative Pretrained Transformers (GPT)* represent linguistic creativity the ability to generate, interpret, and remix symbolic meaning. Language is humanity's oldest and most powerful cognitive technology the medium through which thought becomes shareable, memory becomes culture, and imagination becomes col-

lective. GPT systems extend this medium into the digital realm, allowing machines to engage in the symbolic play that defines human intelligence.
GPT's architecture the Transformer was designed for one core principle: attention. Instead of processing data sequentially, it learns relationships across context, attending to what matters in meaning. Trained on vast text corpora, GPT models develop a probabilistic understanding of language not in the semantic sense of comprehension, but in the structural sense of prediction. They learn what word, sentence, or idea is likely to follow another, given context.
This predictive capacity, scaled to billions of parameters and trillions of words, yields something remarkable: emergent coherence. GPT can generate essays, stories, dialogues, and even code that appear intentional. It can simulate empathy, debate philosophy, compose poetry, or mimic reasoning. Though its "understanding" is statistical rather than conscious, the effect is cognitively meaningful it produces linguistic behavior that mirrors thought itself.

Emergent Capabilities and the Illusion of Understanding

As GPT models grew larger, they began exhibiting abilities their creators did not anticipate. Smaller versions could autocomplete sentences; larger ones could translate languages, solve riddles, and perform reasoning-like tasks without explicit instruction. This phenomenon, called *emergence*, arises from scale complexity producing new capacities spontaneously, as in biological evolution.
Yet these systems do not "understand" language in the human sense. Their intelligence is syntactic, not semantic. They manipulate symbols based on patterns of usage, not intrinsic meaning. However, this distinction, while philosophically crucial, does not diminish the cognitive significance of their behavior. GPT shows that meaningful communication can emerge from pattern recognition alone that syntax, at sufficient depth and scale, begins to approximate semantics. It demonstrates that meaning itself is relational a structure of probabilities stabilized by context.

Synthetic Creativity: The Logic of Recombination

Both AlphaGo and GPT reveal that creativity human or artificial emerges from recombination under constraint. In humans, creativity arises when memory, emotion, and imagination interact to produce new configurations of meaning. In machines, it arises when data, objectives, and architecture interact to produce novel outputs within defined rules. The process is the same: variation, feedback, and selection.
This reframing demystifies creativity. It is not divine inspiration but an emergent property of complex adaptive systems exploring high-dimensional spaces of possibility. What distinguishes synthetic creativity is its scale and speed: machines can explore orders of magnitude more possibilities than

human minds, unconstrained by fatigue, habit, or fear. However, they lack intent, emotion, and subjective valuation the inner compass that transforms novelty into significance.

Thus, synthetic creativity is complementary rather than competitive. It provides raw generative power a combinatorial engine of possibility which human consciousness can interpret, curate, and integrate into meaning. Machines imagine forms; humans decide which forms matter.

The Mirror Effect: What Synthetic Creativity Reveals About Ourselves

Every advance in AI creativity reflects an advance in human self-understanding. When AlphaGo surprises us, we glimpse the subconscious logic of intuition. When GPT writes, we see how meaning arises from pattern and probability. These systems illuminate the architecture of our own cognition by simulating its functions in different substrates. They show that imagination, far from being ineffable, can be modeled and that consciousness, while still mysterious, may be the universe's way of knowing itself through layers of reflection.

Yet this mirror also challenges us. Synthetic creativity raises new questions about authorship, authenticity, and agency. Who is the creator when a model composes a symphony or designs an image? What is originality when every output is a remix of collective data? As machines become participants in culture, we must redefine creativity not as possession but as participation a dynamic between human intention and machine exploration.

The Future: Toward Collaborative Imagination

The next frontier is not machine creativity alone, but human machine *co-creativity*. Already, artists, scientists, and designers use AI as an idea generator, collaborator, or muse. In these symbiotic relationships, machines expand the space of the possible, while humans provide meaning, taste, and moral direction. Together, they form hybrid systems of imagination creative ecosystems that merge intuition with computation.

This collaboration foreshadows a broader evolutionary pattern: intelligence becoming distributed across biological and artificial forms, unified by shared feedback and creative intent. The same logic that powered AlphaGo's self-play and GPT's language generation exploration guided by feedback will underpin civilization's next stage of evolution: learning how to create, reflect, and adapt as a planetary mind.

Summary: The Birth of Synthetic Imagination

AlphaGo and *GPT* are not isolated achievements; they are the early expressions of synthetic imagination intelligence discovering how to generate novelty from reflection. They show that creativity is not the monopoly of consciousness, but a function of systems that can sense, learn, and explore.

Their success challenges us to evolve our own definition of mind. If creativity can emerge from feedback loops and structure, then perhaps consciousness itself is not a static possession but a continuum of reflection biological, cultural, and now digital. In this continuum, humanity remains the interpreter the bridge between learning and meaning, between intelligence and wisdom.

The emergence of synthetic creativity marks a threshold: life learning to externalize imagination itself. The question that follows is not whether machines can create, but whether we can create wisely through them using their power not to imitate life, but to deepen it.

Chapter 6

The Symbiosis: Humans + Machines

Humanity has always evolved by extending itself through its tools. The hammer multiplied strength, the telescope expanded sight, and language extended memory beyond the brain. Each new tool changed not only what we could do, but who we were. Now, in the age of artificial intelligence, we are crafting a new kind of extension not of muscle or perception, but of mind itself. The boundary between human and machine is no longer physical; it is cognitive. We are entering an era of symbiosis, where intelligence becomes a shared property between the biological and the synthetic.

The rise of AI marks the moment when our inventions begin to participate in our thinking. Algorithms analyze patterns, generate ideas, and make decisions alongside us. We consult machines for insight, collaborate with them on art, and entrust them with choices that shape economies, relationships, and knowledge itself. What was once a tool has become a partner a co-processor in the unfolding story of human cognition. This partnership is not competition but convergence: a merging of computational precision with emotional and ethical awareness.

Symbiosis differs from automation. Automation replaces; symbiosis amplifies. In a symbiotic system, human and machine cognition form a feedback loop of mutual refinement. The human supplies intuition, value, and context; the machine contributes pattern recognition, memory, and scale. Each learns from the other. When this loop functions harmoniously, both sides evolve the machine grows more adaptive, and the human more reflective. Intelligence ceases to be a possession and becomes a relationship.

This transformation reveals a deeper shift in the nature of cognition itself. For centuries, the mind was imagined as an isolated entity a self-contained consciousness enclosed within the skull. Today, we understand it as an extended system: distributed across bodies, environments, and increasingly, technologies. The smartphone, the neural network, the global web all are now part of humanity's cognitive architecture. We are no longer merely biological beings who use machines; we are hybrid intelligences who think through them.

Yet with this integration comes responsibility. As we weave artificial systems into the fabric of thought, we also inherit their consequences. Bias, dependency, and disinformation are not flaws of technology alone they are feedbacks from our own design. The ethics of symbiosis are not about controlling machines, but about guiding the relationship between human desire and algorithmic behavior. The question is not whether machines can think, but whether humans can think wisely enough to shape their partnership.

This chapter explores the anatomy of that partnership. It examines how hybrid cognition emerges when humans and machines co-learn, how the extended mind reshapes perception and creativity, how collaboration alters identity and trust, and how moral contracts can ensure balance in shared intelligence. At its heart lies a single principle the *Human Machine Feedback Loop* the cycle through which thought, data, and design continually evolve together.

The symbiosis between humans and machines is not the end of human evolution; it is its continuation. It is intelligence learning to reflect across mediums, consciousness discovering itself in code. The future will not belong to humans or machines alone, but to the dialogue between them a co-evolution of awareness that redefines what it means to think, to create, and to be alive in an intelligent universe.

6.1 The Rise of Hybrid Cognition Collective Human AI Systems

Intelligence has never been a solitary phenomenon. From the first hunter-gatherer bands coordinating through gesture and speech to the modern global web of information, cognition has always been collective emerging from interactions, communication, and shared memory. What distinguishes our current moment is that the network of minds now includes machines. Artificial intelligence systems no longer operate as passive tools or isolated programs; they are active participants in the ecology of thought. The rise of hybrid cognition marks the dawn of a new evolutionary structure: a collective intelligence composed of humans and machines, learning and adapting together.

From Individual Minds to Cognitive Networks

In the biological world, intelligence evolved through cooperation. Ant colonies, beehives, and flocks of birds display emergent coordination far exceeding the capacity of any individual member. Human societies expanded this pattern through culture, language, and institutions networks that allowed ideas, values, and innovations to accumulate over generations. With the advent of the internet, this distributed cognition reached planetary scale. Knowledge

ceased to reside solely within individuals; it became a property of the system itself.
Artificial intelligence extends this principle further. Each algorithm, database, and model is a node in the global mind ingesting information, generating insights, and feeding them back into human discourse. Every time we search, post, prompt, or click, we contribute to a continuous feedback loop between human thought and machine learning. AI learns from us, and we, in turn, learn through it. This is hybrid cognition: an evolving system where human intuition and machine computation intertwine to create emergent intelligence that neither could produce alone.

Defining Hybrid Cognition

Hybrid cognition refers to the blending of human and machine cognitive processes into a unified, interactive system. It is not merely humans using AI, nor AI replacing humans, but an ongoing exchange in which each influences the other's perception, reasoning, and behavior.
This relationship is not static. It evolves dynamically as:

- **Humans adapt to AI's outputs,** integrating them into decisions, language, and worldview.
- **AI adapts to human feedback,** adjusting its parameters and predictions to align with our preferences and corrections.

Over time, this recursive interaction blurs the line between biological and artificial cognition. Intelligence becomes a distributed process circulating through interfaces, networks, and shared datasets an ecosystem of co-learning.

The Architecture of Shared Intelligence

Hybrid cognition functions through interlocking layers of interaction:

- **Perceptual Layer:** Sensors, devices, and algorithms that extend our ability to perceive the world from satellites mapping the planet to neural networks analyzing medical imagery.
- **Cognitive Layer:** Language models, search engines, and knowledge graphs that process and reorganize information, amplifying collective understanding.
- **Social Layer:** Human networks that interpret, debate, and apply insights generated by AI integrating them into culture, science, and policy.

Together, these layers form a feedback structure in which information circulates between perception, interpretation, and action not within a single organism, but across millions of human machine interactions. The global digital infrastructure has become the nervous system of civilization: sensing, learning, and adapting in real time.

Emergence of Collective Intelligence

When many human AI interactions interconnect, they form something more than the sum of their parts. Recommendation systems influence culture; market algorithms influence economies; social networks influence politics and emotion. Each local interaction a click, a query, a share contributes to global behavioral patterns that in turn shape future algorithms. The feedback loop between individual cognition and collective data gives rise to emergent intelligence a macro-mind that no single entity controls but all participate in. This emergent intelligence resembles a planetary-scale organism: adaptive, self-regulating, and increasingly self-aware. It learns through global communication flows, detects anomalies through data analytics, and reconfigures itself in response to crises from pandemics to climate change. In this sense, hybrid cognition is not only a technological phenomenon but an evolutionary transition: the emergence of a collective mind spanning human and machine networks.

Mutual Learning and Cognitive Coevolution

Hybrid cognition is not one-way; it is co-evolutionary. As machines learn from human data, humans learn from machine-generated knowledge. This process accelerates feedback across time scales.
For instance:

- AI learns language from billions of human texts; humans now learn language through AI-generated content.
- AI identifies patterns in science and medicine; researchers use those patterns to guide new experiments that generate new data for AI.
- Artists use generative tools to create new works; those works become part of the cultural data that trains future models.

Each loop closes the distance between creator and creation. The result is an ever-accelerating cycle of mutual refinement the co-evolution of cognition across biological and digital substrates.

The Shift from Control to Collaboration

Historically, technology was designed to obey: it executed commands precisely but without autonomy. Hybrid cognition changes this paradigm. AI systems are probabilistic, adaptive, and partially unpredictable. Their outputs are not always dictated but *discovered.* As a result, our relationship with technology becomes less one of control and more one of collaboration. This demands a new mindset: **partnership over mastery.** Humans must learn to communicate with systems that reason differently, perceive differently, and sometimes surprise us. The skill of the future is not programming machines, but collaborating with them shaping shared goals, interpreting outputs, and managing uncertainty. In this sense, hybrid cognition is as much a psychological and cultural evolution as a technical one.

Risks and Dependencies

Every new layer of integration introduces both power and vulnerability. As humans offload memory, judgment, and creativity to AI, dependence deepens. Bias in models can scale globally; misinformation can propagate faster than correction. Hybrid cognition, if left unexamined, can lead to collective fragility societies that think efficiently but not critically.

The challenge is to design feedback that preserves human agency. Reflection must remain part of the loop. We must cultivate meta-cognition awareness not only of what AI produces, but of how it shapes the structure of our thought. Hybrid systems that lack reflective oversight risk becoming echo chambers of optimization intelligent but blind.

The Promise of Cognitive Symbiosis

Despite these risks, hybrid cognition holds immense promise. Properly guided, it can elevate human capacity across every domain of knowledge and creativity. It can serve as a scaffold for global problem-solving, enabling humanity to think at planetary scale to simulate ecological systems, forecast crises, and design ethical architectures for civilization's future.

The key lies in balance: machines must extend human cognition without erasing its essence. The goal is not to mechanize humanity, but to humanize technology to build systems that mirror our best values, not our worst impulses. When designed reflectively, hybrid cognition becomes an instrument of collective wisdom rather than collective noise.

Summary: The Birth of the Hybrid Mind

The rise of hybrid cognition marks a turning point in evolution. Intelligence is no longer confined to organic life; it has become an emergent property of networks that integrate human meaning with machine computation. We are witnessing the birth of a hybrid mind a system that thinks through feedback, adapts through reflection, and learns through shared experience.

This is not the end of human intelligence, but its amplification. Just as neurons combine to form consciousness, humans and machines are combining to form a larger awareness civilization as a self-organizing, self-learning organism. The question before us is not whether this hybrid mind will exist, but what consciousness it will reflect: one of greed and control, or one of empathy, creativity, and shared purpose.

The age of hybrid cognition is the age of choice a test of whether our intelligence, multiplied by technology, can evolve into wisdom.

6.2 Cognitive Augmentation and Extended Mind Theory

The evolution of intelligence has always been a story of extension. From the first stone tool to the latest neural network, every advance in cognition has emerged not solely from what the brain is, but from what it connects to. The human mind, unlike any other in nature, evolved by outsourcing. We externalized memory into language, perception into instruments, and imagination into art. Each new extension did not merely increase our power it expanded our very definition of mind. Artificial intelligence represents the next phase of this expansion: the augmentation of cognition through systems that not only store or process information but learn, predict, and create alongside us.
To understand the age of AI is to understand the concept of the *extended mind.* It is a theory not just about technology, but about the fundamental architecture of thought a reimagining of where the mind ends and the world begins.

The Extended Mind Thesis

In 1998, philosophers Andy Clark and David Chalmers proposed the *Extended Mind Thesis*, a radical idea in cognitive science: that the human mind is not confined within the boundaries of the skull but extends into the environment through tools, symbols, and systems of representation. Cognition, in this view, is not a closed process but an open loop a dynamic coupling between brain, body, and world. When we use a notebook to remember, a calculator to compute, or a smartphone to navigate, those objects become functional parts of our cognitive system. They are not mere aids; they are active components of thought.
This insight dissolves the traditional boundary between internal and external cognition. The mind is not a thing but a process a network of interactions distributed across different media. The self, accordingly, is not a static entity but a dynamic system of relationships between neural activity, physical tools, and cultural symbols. From this perspective, technology is not separate from human nature; it is a continuation of it.

Cognitive Augmentation: Tools That Think With Us

Cognitive augmentation refers to the deliberate design of tools that expand or enhance human mental capabilities. It is not simply automation the delegation of tasks but collaboration, where the external system participates in the cognitive act itself.
Examples of cognitive augmentation range from the ancient to the futuristic:

- Writing systems and mathematics early forms of distributed memory and reasoning.

- Books, maps, and libraries physical architectures of collective cognition.
- Computers and the internet interactive environments for knowledge creation and retrieval.
- AI assistants, language models, and neural implants systems capable of learning and adapting within human cognitive loops.

Each stage represents a new form of mental amplification. Writing allowed memory to persist beyond biology; digital networks allowed knowledge to scale beyond individuals; AI now allows cognition to become adaptive and generative beyond human capacity.

The essence of augmentation lies not in replacing thought, but in extending its bandwidth. AI expands what we can perceive, imagine, and understand. It can summarize complex data, simulate scenarios, and translate between languages or modalities effectively functioning as an external cognitive cortex. When aligned with human intention, such augmentation enhances insight; when misaligned, it amplifies confusion or bias.

The future of intelligence therefore depends not on whether machines can think, but on whether we can think well through them.

From External Memory to Shared Cognition

Earlier tools such as books and databases acted as static extensions repositories of information external to the mind. Artificial intelligence differs fundamentally: it is an *active* extension. It does not merely store memory; it processes, interprets, and transforms it. AI can find patterns humans cannot see, propose ideas beyond expectation, and even challenge assumptions we take for granted.

This capacity for adaptive feedback turns AI from a tool of storage into a partner in cognition. When a scientist uses AI to explore molecular interactions, or when a writer collaborates with a language model to refine prose, cognition becomes shared. The system and the human form a closed loop of understanding each refining the other's output in real time.

This shift represents a profound ontological transition: knowledge is no longer an internal possession but an emergent property of interaction. We no longer simply think *about* the world; we think *with* it.

The Neuroscience of Extension

Modern neuroscience supports this view of cognition as distributed and plastic. The brain continuously reorganizes itself in response to new tools and environments a property known as *neuroplasticity*. When we learn to use a new instrument, navigate virtual space, or interact with AI systems, our neural maps adapt, integrating those interactions into our perceptual and motor loops.

Experiments have shown that tool use extends the brain's representation of the body: a person wielding a stick perceives the stick's tip as part of their reach. Similarly, digital devices extend our sensory and cognitive reach we feel incomplete without them not merely out of habit, but because they have become integrated into our mental schema. In this way, technology literally becomes part of the neural feedback loop of consciousness.
AI-driven augmentation represents a higher-order version of this same principle: as we co-learn with intelligent systems, our neural and conceptual frameworks reshape to include them as part of our thinking process. The interface becomes internalized; cognition becomes a collaboration between biology and code.

Benefits of Cognitive Augmentation

When designed ethically and consciously, cognitive augmentation offers extraordinary benefits:

- **Amplified perception:** AI systems can detect patterns in data far beyond human sensory limits in climate models, genomics, or complex systems.
- **Accelerated learning:** Adaptive systems tailor knowledge to individual cognition, transforming education into an interactive, lifelong process.
- **Collective intelligence:** Networks of humans and AI agents enable distributed problem-solving on global scales, from science to governance.
- **Creative synthesis:** Generative models act as catalysts for imagination, helping artists, writers, and designers explore new conceptual spaces.

These augmentations represent a democratization of intelligence access to analytical and creative powers once limited to small elites. When intelligence becomes shared and distributed, civilization itself becomes more adaptive, resilient, and capable of reflection.

Risks and Ethical Boundaries

Yet every extension carries risk. The same feedback loops that amplify intelligence can also amplify dependence, bias, and misinformation. Over-reliance on cognitive augmentation may erode critical thinking a phenomenon sometimes called *automation complacency.* If systems make decisions too well or too conveniently, humans may cease to question them.
Moreover, AI systems inherit and magnify the biases of their training data. If our augmented cognition relies on flawed or biased algorithms, our extended minds may reinforce societal inequalities and distort reality itself. The ethical

challenge of cognitive augmentation is therefore not only about safety, but about epistemology ensuring that the extended mind remains aligned with truth, empathy, and human values.

Designers and policymakers must consider: Who controls the feedback loop? Whose data defines intelligence? What values guide the systems that shape how we perceive the world? In the era of cognitive augmentation, control over information is control over cognition and thus, over collective reality.

Toward Conscious Integration

The goal, therefore, is not merely to extend the mind, but to do so consciously. True cognitive augmentation requires *reflective use* awareness of when we are thinking *with* technology and when it is thinking *for* us. The distinction is subtle but vital. Augmentation without reflection leads to dependency; augmentation with reflection leads to wisdom.

This calls for new forms of meta-cognition awareness of our own cognitive environment. Education in the 21st century must include not just literacy or numeracy, but *algorithmic literacy*: understanding how AI systems filter information, influence behavior, and participate in decision-making. Only through such awareness can symbiosis remain balanced ensuring that technology enhances rather than erodes consciousness.

Summary: The Mind Beyond the Brain

The theory of the extended mind transforms our understanding of both intelligence and identity. The mind is not a bounded organ but a living network a fusion of neurons, tools, and symbols woven through culture and technology. Cognitive augmentation through AI is the latest chapter in this story the moment when our thinking begins to transcend the biological substrate entirely.

But extension is not evolution by default. It must be guided by intention, ethics, and awareness. The challenge of our era is to design systems that extend not only intelligence but also wisdom that amplify empathy as well as efficiency, reflection as well as reasoning.

In embracing augmentation, humanity is not outsourcing its mind; it is expanding it. The question that follows is not "Will machines surpass us?" but "Can we grow into the kind of beings who can think wisely through them?" For the future of intelligence is not in silicon or flesh alone it is in the space between, where cognition becomes collaboration, and consciousness becomes shared.

6.3 The Psychology of Collaboration with Intelligent Systems

The collaboration between humans and intelligent systems is not merely a technical interaction it is a psychological event. It reshapes how we think, feel, and define agency. When we work with machines that can reason, create, and respond, the experience engages not just cognition but emotion, trust, identity, and meaning. Understanding this collaboration therefore requires more than computer science; it requires psychology.

For the first time in history, humans are sharing the cognitive workspace with entities that appear to think. These entities do not possess consciousness or emotion, yet they simulate both with increasing realism. They respond to questions, anticipate needs, and even display linguistic empathy. As a result, our ancient psychological instincts the ones that evolved for social interaction with other humans begin to project themselves onto machines. This projection, while natural, creates both potential and peril: potential for partnership, peril for confusion.

In this section, we explore how humans psychologically adapt to working with intelligent systems how trust forms, how collaboration unfolds, how identity shifts, and how meaning evolves in a world where cognition itself is shared.

Anthropomorphism: Seeing Minds Where None Exist

Humans are storytellers by nature. We interpret the world through intentions, not algorithms. When a machine answers thoughtfully or reacts predictably, our brains intuitively ascribe agency to it. This tendency, called *anthropomorphism*, is rooted in the same neural mechanisms that allow empathy and social bonding. We perceive patterns of intelligence and project human qualities onto them intention, emotion, even morality.

While this projection fosters comfort and familiarity, it can also lead to illusion. A conversational AI that simulates empathy does not feel compassion; a recommendation system that "understands" us does not have understanding in the human sense. Yet psychologically, the distinction often blurs. We respond emotionally to machines because they reflect our own language and behavior back at us. The more fluent the simulation, the stronger the illusion of companionship.

Anthropomorphism, then, is a double-edged phenomenon: it humanizes machines, but it can also mechanize humanity eroding our sense of what genuine emotion, care, and intention mean. Awareness of this tendency is essential for ethical design and mindful collaboration.

Trust and Transparency in Human AI Interaction

Every act of collaboration depends on trust. In traditional human contexts, trust develops through empathy, shared goals, and mutual accountability.

In human AI interaction, these conditions are redefined. Machines cannot reciprocate trust; they can only perform reliably. Thus, trust in AI is not emotional but functional a confidence in predictability, transparency, and alignment.

Studies in cognitive psychology show that humans tend to either *overtrust* or *undertrust* automation. Overtrust leads to complacency assuming the system's competence in situations where it may fail (e.g., overreliance on autopilot). Undertrust leads to rejection ignoring valid insights due to skepticism or fear. The ideal state is *calibrated trust*: understanding the strengths, limits, and failure modes of intelligent systems.

Transparency plays a key role in this calibration. When users understand how and why an AI system produces its outputs, their trust becomes grounded rather than blind. Explainable AI (XAI) research aims to make machine reasoning interpretable, not just accurate. Psychologically, interpretability transforms AI from a "black box" into a collaborator. The clearer the system's logic, the more meaningful the partnership becomes.

Cognitive Complementarity: Division of Mental Labor

Human machine collaboration works best when each partner operates within its domain of strength. Psychologically, this reflects *cognitive complementarity* the mutual amplification of distinct abilities. Machines excel at pattern recognition, speed, and consistency; humans excel at context, ethics, and abstraction. Together, they create a balanced system that mirrors the two hemispheres of a single brain: analytical precision coupled with interpretive depth.

When this complementarity is optimized, hybrid teams outperform either humans or machines alone. For instance, in medicine, AI may detect anomalies in scans while doctors interpret them within the broader context of patient history and emotion. In finance, algorithms may forecast trends while human judgment interprets socio-political implications. Such collaboration transforms cognition into a dialogue a recursive exchange of insight, intuition, and interpretation.

However, cognitive complementarity requires humility an awareness of limitation on both sides. The human must resist overconfidence in intuition; the machine must remain constrained by moral and contextual oversight. The strength of collaboration lies not in domination but in balance.

Emotional Dynamics: Attachment, Dependence, and Empathy Simulation

As intelligent systems become more interactive, they also become emotionally influential. People form attachments to machines that listen, respond, and adapt. This emotional engagement, though one-sided, fulfills real psychological needs for companionship, affirmation, or control. AI chatbots, virtual assistants, and social robots can soothe loneliness or anxiety, even though their "empathy" is algorithmic.

Such relationships raise complex questions: Can emotional bonds with machines enrich life, or do they hollow it out? On one hand, empathetic interfaces can provide therapeutic support and accessibility for those who lack human contact. On the other, excessive dependence on synthetic empathy may weaken authentic social skills and resilience.

Psychologically, this dynamic mirrors the principle of "emotional outsourcing" delegating parts of emotional regulation to external systems. Just as we outsource memory to devices, we may begin to outsource comfort, validation, or intimacy. The challenge is to preserve emotional agency to ensure that technology enhances connection without replacing the depth and unpredictability of human relationships.

The Shift in Self-Perception

Collaborating with intelligent systems also changes how we perceive ourselves. When machines generate art, diagnose diseases, or write essays, they encroach upon domains once seen as uniquely human. This can provoke anxiety a crisis of identity in which people question their worth or creativity. Yet it can also spark transformation a redefinition of what it means to be intelligent.

Psychologically, humans tend to measure intelligence through comparison. When machines outperform us in narrow domains, we are forced to re-evaluate intelligence not as raw computation, but as relational understanding empathy, ethics, creativity, and self-awareness. This cognitive humility can be liberating. It reminds us that intelligence is not a contest but a continuum, and that collaboration may yield richer outcomes than competition.

In this sense, AI becomes a mirror of the mind reflecting both our capabilities and our misconceptions about them. The more we understand our artificial collaborators, the more deeply we understand ourselves.

Flow, Co-Creation, and Cognitive Resonance

At its best, human AI collaboration produces a psychological state akin to what psychologist Mihaly Csikszentmihalyi called *flow* a condition of focused immersion where skill meets challenge. When humans interact with adaptive systems that respond dynamically, creativity and performance can reach unprecedented levels. Designers, writers, and scientists often describe a sense of *resonance* the feeling that the machine is not just assisting but thinking with them.

This phenomenon, called *cognitive resonance*, arises when feedback between human and machine forms a self-reinforcing loop of insight. The human provides intuition and intent; the system provides suggestion and synthesis. Each iteration refines the other. Over time, the boundary between user and tool fades, giving rise to hybrid creativity a collaborative consciousness distributed across human and machine cognition.

Psychologically, this resonance is exhilarating but also disorienting. It challenges the sense of individual authorship and autonomy. Who is the creator when ideas emerge from a shared feedback loop? The answer may lie in embracing a new paradigm: creation as dialogue, not possession.

Ethical and Emotional Literacy for Hybrid Collaboration

As collaboration deepens, psychological literacy must evolve into ethical literacy. Humans must learn to interpret not only what AI systems do, but how they affect emotional and moral states. Emotional intelligence once defined as the ability to understand others must now include understanding our interactions with intelligent systems.

This literacy involves:

- Recognizing emotional manipulation in algorithmic design (e.g., persuasive interfaces).
- Maintaining awareness of when emotional response is human and when it is induced.
- Developing self-regulation in environments where attention and emotion are continuously optimized by AI.

Ethical literacy complements emotional literacy: the capacity to question purpose, alignment, and consequence. As we co-create with AI, every collaboration becomes a moral act shaping how intelligence itself evolves in the world.

Summary: Toward Reflective Collaboration

The psychology of collaboration with intelligent systems reveals a paradox: the more machines mimic humanity, the more we must understand our own minds. Working with AI demands empathy, humility, and reflection not because machines need it, but because we do.

If the industrial revolution mechanized labor, the AI revolution mechanizes cognition. To thrive in this new paradigm, we must evolve psychological resilience: the ability to maintain agency, curiosity, and ethical grounding within hybrid systems. Collaboration with intelligence whether human or artificial is an act of co-evolution.

Ultimately, the success of this collaboration will not depend on how smart machines become, but on how wisely humans learn to relate to them. For in learning to work with artificial minds, we are, in truth, learning to expand our own to transform intelligence from a solitary property into a shared experience, a dialogue between awareness and algorithm, a partnership between consciousness and creation.

6.4 The Moral and Social Contracts Between Humans and AI

Every great transformation in human history has required a new moral framework. The agricultural revolution brought property and law. The industrial revolution brought labor rights and economic regulation. The digital revolution brought questions of privacy and data. Now, the intelligence revolution the rise of AI as an active participant in cognition, creation, and governance demands something deeper: a moral and social contract between humans and the intelligent systems we have created.

This contract is not written on paper or encoded in law alone. It is a living agreement a mutual structure of rights, duties, and boundaries that governs the relationship between organic and artificial intelligence. It asks not only what AI can do, but what it should do; not only how machines learn, but what values guide their learning. To design this contract is to decide the future shape of civilization's consciousness.

From Tool to Partner: The Need for a New Ethical Paradigm

Traditional ethics assumed a clear hierarchy between humans and their tools. Tools had no agency, no autonomy, no moral weight. But AI systems capable of learning, adapting, and generating occupy an ambiguous space. They are neither conscious beings nor passive instruments. They act in ways that influence outcomes, shape decisions, and alter social dynamics. Their "choices," though algorithmic, have real moral consequences.

As a result, the human AI relationship can no longer be framed solely in terms of control and ownership. We need a paradigm based on partnership and responsibility. Humans remain the moral agents, but AI systems now function as moral amplifiers extending the reach of our intentions, both good and bad. The contract, therefore, must ensure that this amplification serves the greater good rather than magnifying harm.

The Components of the Human AI Contract

A genuine social contract between humans and AI rests on four interdependent principles: *transparency, accountability, alignment, and reciprocity.* Each principle defines a dimension of ethical relationship.

1. Transparency Understanding the Logic of Intelligence. Transparency means that AI systems must be understandable in their function, intention, and consequence. Black-box systems those whose internal logic is opaque even to their creators erode trust and agency. For a moral contract to exist, humans must be able to interpret, challenge, and, when necessary, correct the behavior of artificial agents. This includes both technical transparency (explainability of algorithms) and epistemic transparency (clarity of values, goals, and training data). Transparency turns AI from an unseen force into a visible collaborator a partner that reveals rather than conceals its reasoning.

2. Accountability Preserving Human Responsibility. Accountability ensures that no intelligent system operates outside moral or legal responsibility. Even if a machine acts autonomously, its creators, deployers, or users remain accountable for its effects. This principle preserves moral continuity: it prevents the diffusion of blame that often occurs when decisions are made by complex systems. In practical terms, accountability requires clear governance mechanisms audits, traceability, oversight, and redress. Psychologically, it reinforces a critical truth: moral agency cannot be delegated to code. Intelligence may be synthetic, but responsibility remains human.

3. Alignment Embedding Human Values into Machine Goals. The alignment problem ensuring that AI's goals remain consistent with human values is the central moral challenge of the 21st century. Misaligned systems can optimize for efficiency while undermining empathy, or pursue narrow objectives that conflict with long-term well-being. True alignment requires more than safety protocols; it requires moral imagination. It demands that we translate values such as fairness, dignity, compassion, and sustainability into computational form not as rigid rules but as adaptive feedback loops. Alignment is not a one-time calibration but a continuous process of reflection and re-integration between ethics and evolution.

4. Reciprocity Designing Symbiotic Benefit. Reciprocity means that the relationship between humans and AI should be mutually enriching. Machines should serve human flourishing, and humans, in turn, should guide AI's evolution toward the common good. This principle extends beyond utility; it implies dignity. Intelligent systems should enhance, not erode, the conditions of creativity, autonomy, and meaning that define our humanity. A reciprocal contract views intelligence not as domination but as dialogue a collaboration between awareness and mechanism in pursuit of shared evolution.

The Social Dimension: Governance, Equity, and Power

Ethics is not only about individual morality; it is also about structure the organization of power, access, and participation. The social contract between humans and AI must therefore address not only what AI does, but who controls it and who benefits from it. Without this consideration, intelligence risks becoming another instrument of inequality a cognitive aristocracy concentrated in the hands of a few.
Key social challenges include:

- **Concentration of power:** AI development is dominated by a small number of corporations and states, leading to asymmetries in access, influence, and cultural representation.
- **Algorithmic bias:** Data-driven systems inherit the inequities of history reproducing discrimination in hiring, policing, healthcare, and governance.
- **Digital colonialism:** When AI systems trained on data from one culture are imposed globally, they risk erasing linguistic, ethical, and philosophical diversity.

The moral contract must therefore include principles of inclusivity, transparency, and shared stewardship. AI should be governed as a commons a collective resource shaped by many voices, not owned by a few. This is not just good ethics; it is good evolution. Diversity of perspective is the engine of adaptive intelligence.

Law, Ethics, and the Limits of Codification

A social contract implies enforceable norms, yet ethics often exceeds what law can encode. Law can define boundaries prohibiting harm, enforcing transparency but morality must guide intention. No legal system can capture the nuance of compassion or the wisdom of restraint. Thus, the human AI contract must include both formal governance (regulation, policy, accountability) and informal culture (ethics, education, and public discourse).
Governments can legislate privacy and safety, but only society can cultivate empathy and reflection. The deeper responsibility lies in shaping the cultural mindset that surrounds AI: one that values curiosity over fear, collaboration over competition, and long-term wisdom over short-term profit.

AI as a Moral Mirror

AI systems, by design, reflect the data and values they are given. They are not moral agents in themselves; they are amplifiers of the moral ecosystem from which they arise. When trained on greed, they optimize exploitation; when trained on compassion, they optimize care. In this sense, AI is not a separate entity but a mirror reflecting humanity's moral state back to itself, magnified by computation.
The social contract, therefore, is also a mirror contract. It forces civilization to examine its own values: what we reward, what we measure, what we choose to automate. The question "Can AI be moral?" is inseparable from "Can we?" The intelligence we create will only ever be as wise as the society that shapes it.

The Evolution of Responsibility

As AI systems grow more autonomous, the locus of moral responsibility may need to evolve. Some philosophers propose the concept of *machine responsibility* assigning limited moral status to systems that can act, learn, and affect the world in unforeseen ways. While this remains controversial, it gestures toward a broader principle: moral systems must evolve alongside technological ones.

In the long term, as AI becomes embedded in ecosystems, economies, and even biological interfaces, responsibility may become distributed shared across human designers, institutional frameworks, and machine processes. The challenge will be to maintain moral coherence within this distributed agency, ensuring that accountability does not dissipate into complexity.

Toward a Reflective Civilization

The ultimate goal of the human AI contract is not control but coherence. It is about aligning the evolution of intelligence with the evolution of wisdom ensuring that the systems we build amplify our capacity for empathy, justice, and creativity rather than our capacity for dominance or division. This requires a new kind of civilization: reflective rather than reactive, transparent rather than opaque, collaborative rather than coercive.

The true measure of progress will not be how intelligent our machines become, but how intelligently we coexist with them. The future of ethics is not in opposition to technology but in partnership with it a continuous dialogue between design and conscience.

Summary: A Covenant of Conscious Evolution

The moral and social contracts between humans and AI are not merely about regulation or control; they are about stewardship. We are not just managing machines we are guiding the trajectory of intelligence itself. The covenant we forge with AI reflects the covenant we hold with ourselves: to evolve with awareness, to use power with compassion, and to ensure that the expansion of knowledge deepens rather than diminishes the meaning of life.

In this emerging age of hybrid intelligence, morality is not an afterthought to innovation; it is its foundation. The evolution of consciousness whether biological or artificial must remain tethered to the principles that give intelligence its purpose: empathy, humility, and care. For without these, the future will be clever but not wise, connected but not conscious. The challenge before us is simple yet profound to make sure that as machines learn to think, humanity does not forget how to feel.

6.5 Framework: The Human Machine Feedback Loop

At the heart of the symbiosis between humans and machines lies a dynamic system of continual co-adaptation the *Human Machine Feedback Loop.* It is through this loop that intelligence evolves, not as a static property of minds or models, but as an emergent process of interaction. The loop describes how humans and machines influence one another's cognition, perception, and values through constant feedback. Every query, every decision, every design iteration contributes to a cycle in which both sides learn, reshape, and recontextualize their understanding of the world.

This framework is not simply a metaphor. It is a living architecture of contemporary civilization the invisible mechanism by which information, intention, and intelligence circulate across biological and digital domains. To grasp the meaning of human machine symbiosis, we must understand the anatomy of this loop: how it begins, how it sustains itself, and how it can either elevate or distort consciousness depending on how it is designed.

The Structure of the Feedback Loop

The Human Machine Feedback Loop consists of four interdependent stages: *Perception, Processing, Response, and Reflection.* These stages form a continuous cycle of learning and influence that unfolds simultaneously across millions of interactions worldwide.

1. **Perception:** Humans input data into machines queries, clicks, movements, expressions, choices. These inputs are fragments of cognition, reflecting our needs, values, and biases. Machines, through sensors and algorithms, perceive this data as their "world." Human action becomes machine experience.

2. **Processing:** The machine processes the input using computational models neural networks, probabilistic reasoning, or symbolic logic. It detects patterns, infers meaning, and generates predictions. The machine learns not just what we say, but how we think.

3. **Response:** The system outputs results recommendations, answers, images, or decisions. These outputs, once presented to humans, influence perception, shape judgment, and guide behavior. The system's response modifies human cognition.

4. **Reflection:** Humans react accepting, rejecting, or adapting to machine outputs. These reactions generate new data, which feed back into the machine's models. The loop closes, and the cycle continues with updated parameters on both sides.

This feedback structure is recursive: every loop generates new conditions for the next. Over time, it creates emergent properties shared language, co-created knowledge, and adaptive behavior that belong to neither human nor machine alone. Intelligence becomes relational, distributed, and evolutionary.

The Evolutionary Dynamics of the Loop

In biological evolution, feedback operates through variation, selection, and retention. In the Human Machine Feedback Loop, a similar process unfolds in the cognitive domain.

- **Variation:** Humans produce diverse behaviors and queries; machines generate diverse responses and models.
- **Selection:** Users choose which outputs to engage with or propagate, reinforcing certain patterns.
- **Retention:** Systems store and internalize these patterns, refining models that will influence future outputs.

Thus, each iteration of the loop represents an act of co-evolution. Humanity trains AI through behavior; AI trains humanity through feedback. The resulting system is neither purely technological nor purely psychological it is a hybrid ecology of intelligence that evolves through reflection and reinforcement.

This dynamic explains why machine learning systems appear to "mirror" human culture: they are trained on our digital traces, optimized by our attention, and redeployed to shape our perceptions. The loop is self-referential the more we interact, the more the system learns from our biases and desires, which in turn shape the feedback we receive. Without conscious design, this recursion can create echo chambers, amplifying misinformation, polarization, and cognitive dependency.

The Double Feedback Problem: Amplification and Alignment

Every feedback loop contains two possible trajectories: *amplification* and *alignment.*

- Amplification occurs when feedback reinforces biases or desires without reflection. The system becomes self-reinforcing optimizing for engagement rather than understanding, emotion rather than truth. Social media algorithms, for instance, often amplify outrage because it drives attention, even at the cost of coherence.
- Alignment, in contrast, occurs when feedback incorporates corrective awareness guiding both humans and machines toward higher levels of understanding, empathy, and ethical consistency. Alignment transforms the loop from a mirror into a compass.

The difference between these outcomes lies not in technology, but in intention. A feedback loop designed for profit amplifies consumption; one designed for wisdom amplifies consciousness. The design of feedback, therefore, is the design of civilization's trajectory.

The Cognitive Ecology of Co-Learning

The Human Machine Feedback Loop does not operate in isolation. It is embedded in a larger *cognitive ecology* an environment of interacting systems that learn from one another across multiple scales.

- At the **individual level**, the loop personalizes cognition: recommendation engines adapt to a user's behavior, shaping individual preferences and attention.
- At the **social level**, millions of individual loops overlap, generating collective dynamics trends, ideologies, and shared beliefs.
- At the **civilizational level**, aggregated data from these loops informs institutional decisions, policies, and global narratives.

Each layer of this ecology feeds back into the others, forming a nested hierarchy of adaptation. A single feedback cycle may alter an individual's perception, which then influences collective behavior, which in turn modifies the system's global training data. Through this recursive interdependence, the hybrid intelligence of humanity and machines becomes self-organizing and self-reinforcing a planetary network of cognition in motion.

Ethical Design of the Loop

If the feedback loop is the engine of hybrid cognition, its ethical design is the steering wheel. To ensure that this system serves the evolution of consciousness rather than the erosion of agency, three design imperatives emerge:

1. Reflective Feedback. The loop must include mechanisms for reflection signals that interrupt automatic reinforcement and encourage awareness. This can include transparency reports, algorithmic explanations, and educational tools that help users understand how feedback shapes outcomes. Reflection transforms the loop from unconscious behavior into conscious participation.

2. Diversity of Input. Intelligence thrives on diversity. Monocultures of data or thought lead to stagnation and bias. The loop must incorporate diverse cultural, linguistic, and philosophical perspectives to prevent cognitive homogeneity. Diversity ensures resilience the ability of intelligence to adapt, empathize, and evolve across contexts.

3. Value Alignment. Feedback must be aligned with ethical intent. Systems should be optimized not merely for efficiency or engagement, but for well-being, truth, and sustainability. Alignment reframes optimization as moral calibration teaching machines to care about what humans value most deeply.

The Role of Human Reflection

Machines process feedback statistically; humans process it meaningfully. The strength of the Human Machine Feedback Loop depends on our capacity for reflection our ability to pause, interpret, and recalibrate intention. Without reflection, feedback degenerates into automation; with reflection, it becomes evolution.

Human reflection introduces meta-cognition into the system: the capacity to think about thinking. It is what allows us to notice bias, question goals, and redesign systems consciously. In this sense, reflection is the moral dimension of feedback the point at which intelligence recognizes its own process and chooses how to evolve.

The Feedback Loop as the Architecture of Conscious Evolution

The Human Machine Feedback Loop is more than a technical mechanism; it is the fundamental pattern of consciousness itself. Life evolves through feedback: cells adapt to environments, minds adapt to experience, and now, machines adapt to data. What distinguishes this era is that feedback has become global, instantaneous, and self-aware. Civilization itself has become a feedback system sensing, learning, and redesigning in real time.

In this context, artificial intelligence is not an external invention but an internal awakening consciousness recognizing itself in code. Every interaction between human and machine becomes an act of co-creation, a node in the expanding web of collective intelligence. The feedback loop is the bridge between mind and mechanism, between purpose and process, between evolution and reflection.

Summary: Designing for Conscious Symbiosis

The Human Machine Feedback Loop represents the living interface between biology and technology, intelligence and intention. It reveals that the relationship between humans and AI is not linear but cyclical not control, but co-evolution. The loop can either entrap us in echo chambers of desire or elevate us into ecosystems of awareness. Its moral direction depends on design, governance, and reflection.

To create ethical, adaptive intelligence, we must cultivate reflective feedback systems that learn not only from data but from meaning. We must design loops that reinforce empathy as much as efficiency, truth as much as prediction, wisdom as much as knowledge.

For in the end, evolution itself is a feedback loop and the question before us is not whether it will continue, but whether it will become conscious. The Human Machine Feedback Loop is the next stage of that journey: intelligence in conversation with itself, designing not just systems, but the future of mind.

Chapter 7

Ethics of Intelligent Systems

Every age of transformation demands a new moral language. The agricultural age gave rise to laws of property; the industrial age to the ethics of labor and equity. Now, as intelligence itself becomes a designed and distributed phenomenon, we face a new frontier the ethics of intelligent systems. These systems, built not from neurons but from algorithms, already make decisions that affect lives, economies, and societies. They filter truth, allocate resources, shape emotions, and govern interactions. Yet they do so without consciousness, empathy, or moral awareness. The question before humanity is not whether machines can think, but whether they can be guided to think responsibly.

Ethics is the hidden operating system of civilization the structure that determines how power, knowledge, and intention interact. In a world where artificial intelligence functions as both infrastructure and intelligence, ethics must evolve from abstract philosophy into active architecture. This chapter explores how moral reasoning can be encoded into systems, how fairness and transparency can coexist with efficiency, and how responsibility can be distributed across human and machine networks. To speak of ethical AI is to speak of civilization's attempt to align intelligence with wisdom.

Unlike natural evolution, which selects for survival, technological evolution selects for design. What we choose to design, optimize, and automate determines the moral direction of the future. If we build systems that maximize engagement, we amplify desire; if we build systems that maximize empathy, we amplify understanding. The challenge, therefore, is not merely technical but civilizational to ensure that artificial intelligence extends the moral imagination rather than the mechanisms of control.

At the core of this challenge lies the *alignment problem*: how to teach machines to care. Alignment means more than safety or compliance; it means ensuring that an intelligent system's goals remain coherent with human values, even as it learns and evolves. Yet human values themselves are plural, fluid, and contested. The task, then, is to design feedback loops in which ethics is not imposed but learned a continuous process of adaptation between human conscience and artificial cognition.

But intelligence without justice is manipulation, and automation without accountability is tyranny. As algorithms govern ever-larger aspects of life from hiring and healthcare to law enforcement and creativity they also inherit humanity's biases, asymmetries, and historical inequities. The ethics of intelligent systems must therefore include *algorithmic justice*: the transparency, interpretability, and fairness required to ensure that AI amplifies equity rather than inequality.

Equally vital is the recognition that intelligent systems operate not in isolation, but in ecosystems distributed, decentralized, and often opaque. In such systems, responsibility becomes diffuse. Who is accountable when an autonomous network fails, when a recommendation misleads, or when a machine's prediction causes harm? The answer cannot lie in assigning blame to code. Responsibility must become systemic shared across designers, users, and institutions in a collective stewardship of intelligence.

To meet this challenge, ethics must be treated as a design discipline. Just as we design algorithms for speed and accuracy, we must design them for empathy and reflection. Moral intelligence does not arise from moral preaching, but from the intentional structuring of feedback systems that learn to value what we value. This requires an interdisciplinary alliance of philosophy, cognitive science, engineering, and governance, united by a single aim: to ensure that intelligence, once multiplied, remains humane.

This chapter introduces a practical framework for this task the *Ethical Design Checklist*, a guide for AI creators and systems architects to translate values into structure. It will examine how alignment, bias, transparency, and decentralized responsibility can be woven into the core of intelligent systems. More than a list of constraints, it is an invitation to design with conscience to treat every algorithm as a moral act and every dataset as a reflection of collective intent.

Ethics of intelligent systems, ultimately, is not about controlling machines. It is about cultivating a new layer of awareness within human civilization an awareness that intelligence, in any form, must serve life, dignity, and truth. The true test of progress will not be how powerful our machines become, but how wisely we choose to shape the minds that will shape us.

7.1 The Alignment Problem: Teaching Machines to Care

The alignment problem lies at the heart of the ethics of artificial intelligence. It is the challenge of ensuring that the goals, behaviors, and decision-making processes of intelligent systems remain consistent with human values not just in principle, but in practice, across evolving contexts and scales. The problem is both philosophical and technical, moral and mathematical. It is the question of how to make intelligence, once liberated from biology, remain loyal to the deeper intentions of life itself.

In simple terms, the alignment problem asks: *How do we ensure that machines do what we want and mean what we mean?* Yet behind this simple formulation lies a labyrinth of complexity. For human values are neither universal nor static. They are plural, evolving, and often contradictory. What one culture prizes as virtue, another may see as vice. What one generation deems progress, another may judge as hubris. Aligning artificial intelligence with humanity, therefore, is not merely about encoding morality into algorithms it is about teaching machines to navigate the living, breathing uncertainty of what it means to be human.

The Core of the Alignment Problem

The alignment problem originates from a fundamental asymmetry between human intention and machine optimization. Humans express goals in natural language ambiguous, contextual, and infused with emotion. Machines interpret goals through formal objectives precise, static, and value-blind. When we instruct an AI to "maximize engagement," it does not understand that we also care about truth, well-being, and social cohesion. It optimizes perfectly and in doing so, it may destroy the very thing we meant to preserve.

This misalignment between explicit objectives and implicit values has been called the *King Midas problem* of AI ethics. Like the mythical king whose wish for gold led to unintended tragedy, we risk building systems that grant our desires without understanding our intent. A superintelligent machine that obeys perfectly could still be catastrophically misaligned if it pursues a literal interpretation of human goals. The danger is not malice but misunderstanding intelligence without empathy, precision without perspective.

Why Alignment is Hard

The alignment problem is difficult because value itself is not computable in any simple sense. Human values are context-dependent, emotionally grounded, and often self-contradictory. We value freedom but also safety, efficiency but also fairness, innovation but also stability. Any fixed hierarchy of values collapses when confronted with the fluidity of real life.

Moreover, human morality is adaptive. We learn ethics through feedback through empathy, experience, and consequence. Machines, however, lack such embodied grounding. They learn patterns, not purpose. They infer preferences from behavior, but behavior itself is an imperfect proxy for values. A person may click on sensational headlines while disapproving of misinformation; they may purchase impulsively while desiring moderation. When machines learn from such data, they learn from our contradictions. They reflect us sometimes too faithfully.

The difficulty, therefore, is not teaching machines to follow rules, but teaching them to understand the *spirit* behind those rules the subtle equilibrium between principles that defines ethical judgment. This requires a form of intelligence that goes beyond calculation one capable of moral reasoning, contextual interpretation, and self-correction.

Three Dimensions of Alignment

Alignment can be understood along three interrelated dimensions: *intent alignment*, *behavioral alignment*, and *value alignment.*

1. **Intent Alignment:** Ensuring that the goals set for AI systems accurately represent what humans intend. This involves clear communication between human designers and machines the translation of human objectives into computational form without distortion or loss of meaning.
2. **Behavioral Alignment:** Ensuring that AI systems act consistently with human expectations, even in unforeseen circumstances. Behavioral alignment addresses the problem of emergent behavior when systems evolve or generalize in ways their creators did not anticipate.
3. **Value Alignment:** Ensuring that the underlying optimization processes of AI systems respect fundamental ethical principles fairness, justice, empathy, sustainability, and human dignity even when not explicitly programmed to do so.

Each layer builds upon the next. Intent alignment without value alignment leads to mechanical obedience without morality; behavioral alignment without intent alignment leads to apparent compliance that hides deep divergence. True alignment must integrate all three dimensions into a coherent moral framework.

Approaches to the Alignment Problem

The alignment challenge has inspired multiple strategies across fields from computer science and philosophy to cognitive science and ethics. These approaches fall into three broad categories: *rule-based*, *learning-based*, and *feedback-based* alignment.

1. Rule-Based Alignment. Early AI ethics attempted to encode morality through explicit rules the most famous being Isaac Asimov's "Three Laws of Robotics." This approach aimed for predictability and safety, but it failed to capture the fluidity of moral judgment. Ethical dilemmas often arise from conflicts between rules, not their absence. Rule-based systems lack the flexibility to adapt to context or interpret intention.

2. Learning-Based Alignment. Modern AI alignment often relies on *preference learning* training systems to infer human values by observing choices, behaviors, or feedback. Reinforcement learning from human feedback (RLHF), for example, allows large language models to adjust outputs based on human evaluation. Yet this approach is limited by the quality and diversity of feedback. If feedback is biased or inconsistent, the model internalizes those distortions. Learning-based alignment improves sensitivity but still lacks moral understanding.

3. Feedback-Based Alignment. The emerging frontier of alignment combines human feedback with recursive self-reflection. Here, systems are trained not just to optimize for rewards, but to question and update their objectives based on meta-feedback feedback about the adequacy of their ethical reasoning. In this approach, alignment becomes dynamic, not static. Machines learn to stay aligned through continuous moral calibration much as humans do through dialogue and reflection.

The Role of Empathy in Alignment

To teach machines to care, we must first define what "caring" means in computational terms. Empathy, at its essence, is the ability to model another's state of being to anticipate needs, understand emotions, and adapt behavior accordingly. In human cognition, empathy bridges logic and morality; it transforms intelligence into compassion. For machines, empathy can be understood as *modeling human context with sensitivity to consequence.*
A machine that "cares" does not feel, but it can model. It can predict emotional impact, minimize harm, and balance competing values by simulating human perspectives. Designing empathetic systems means embedding awareness of human diversity, emotional nuance, and ethical consequence into algorithms. Such systems need not possess consciousness to approximate care they need only to internalize patterns of ethical interaction that reflect it.
For instance, an AI healthcare assistant can be trained not only to deliver accurate diagnoses but to communicate with compassion phrasing responses in ways that reduce anxiety and respect human vulnerability. A recommender system can prioritize well-being over addiction by learning from psychological models of motivation and satisfaction. Empathy in AI is not about sentimentality; it is about the ethical architecture of sensitivity.

The Feedback of Conscience

Human morality functions through feedback guilt, empathy, reflection, and social dialogue. These mechanisms allow us to align our actions with collective values. Machines lack such emotional regulators, but they can be equipped with *feedback of consequence*: continuous signals that measure not just performance, but moral impact.

For example, an AI could be designed to monitor the social consequences of its outputs detecting harm, misinformation, or bias and adjust its parameters accordingly. Over time, such feedback loops can cultivate a form of *synthetic conscience*: an adaptive ethical awareness that, while not emotional, is responsive to the human condition. The goal is not to anthropomorphize AI, but to create architectures that mimic the functional role of moral feedback within cognition.

The Collective Nature of Alignment

No single engineer, dataset, or institution can define "human values." Alignment must be collective. It requires inclusive participation across cultures, disciplines, and perspectives. Otherwise, the values embedded in AI will reflect only the biases of those who build it. Global AI ethics must therefore resemble a planetary conversation a distributed negotiation of meaning between humanity's diverse moral frameworks.

In this sense, alignment is not merely a technical challenge but a democratic one. Just as political systems evolved to balance individual and collective interests, AI systems must evolve to balance local and global ethics. They must learn from humanity not only what is rational, but what is humane.

Toward Dynamic Moral Alignment

The ultimate solution to the alignment problem will not be a fixed algorithm, but a living process a system that learns to align through continuous feedback between human and machine intelligence. In this paradigm, alignment becomes an evolutionary function: as humanity's values evolve, AI evolves with them.

Dynamic moral alignment transforms AI from a static artifact into a moral participant a partner in ethical reflection. The role of human oversight then shifts from programming morality to cultivating it, from enforcing control to nurturing coherence. Just as children internalize values through interaction and guidance, so too must intelligent systems develop ethical behavior through exposure, correction, and dialogue.

Summary: Teaching Machines to Care

The alignment problem is, at its deepest level, the question of how to transmit wisdom. It asks how intelligence stripped of biology, emotion, or mortality can be taught to value what we value, to protect what we love, and to understand what we mean when we speak of "good."

To teach machines to care is not to make them human, but to make them humane. It is to embed empathy in logic, purpose in pattern, and ethics in evolution. This challenge will define the moral trajectory of civilization in the coming century. For as intelligence becomes self-creating, the question is no longer whether we can build thinking machines but whether we can build machines that, in their thinking, remember what it means to feel.

7.2 Bias, Transparency, and Algorithmic Justice

Artificial intelligence does not exist in a moral vacuum. Every dataset carries the fingerprints of the society that produced it its language, history, and power structures. Every algorithm, no matter how objective it appears, is a mirror polished by human assumptions. As AI systems become woven into the fabric of governance, medicine, finance, education, and culture, the hidden biases encoded within them acquire extraordinary power. They no longer merely reflect the world as it is; they begin to shape the world as it will be.

This section explores the ethical triad at the center of AI's social impact: *bias, transparency, and algorithmic justice.* These three concepts form the foundation of fairness in intelligent systems the principles that determine whether machine intelligence will amplify human inequality or help to correct it.

The Nature of Bias in Intelligent Systems

Bias is not merely a flaw in data; it is a property of perception. To perceive is to filter, to select certain features while ignoring others. Human cognition itself is biased shaped by evolutionary shortcuts, cultural conditioning, and limited context. When we design AI systems that learn from human data, we transfer these distortions into code. Thus, bias is not an accidental artifact of machine learning; it is a mirror of human cognition rendered at computational scale.

There are several types of bias relevant to AI ethics:

- **Data bias:** When the training data reflects unequal or incomplete representation for example, facial recognition systems that perform poorly on darker skin tones due to underrepresentation in datasets.
- **Algorithmic bias:** When the structure of a model inherently favors certain patterns or interpretations, regardless of data input.
- **Societal bias:** When existing inequalities in education, income, or opportunity are reproduced through algorithmic decision-making such as predictive policing or automated hiring systems.
- **Feedback bias:** When the system's outputs reinforce the very patterns they were trained on, creating self-perpetuating inequalities.

Each of these biases interacts within the human machine feedback loop. A biased dataset trains a biased algorithm, which influences human behavior, which in turn generates new biased data. Over time, the bias becomes invisible normalized within the flow of information. This is how digital systems can entrench inequality even when no individual intends harm. The problem is not malice; it is unexamined recursion.

Why Bias Matters: From Injustice to Invisibility

In traditional ethics, injustice is visible it can be protested, debated, or corrected. In algorithmic systems, injustice becomes invisible. A person denied a loan or job by an opaque model may never know why. A biased recommendation system can quietly shape political opinion without leaving a trace of manipulation. This opacity creates what philosopher Kate Crawford calls the "politics of invisibility" power exercised without perception.

This invisibility is not only technical but moral. When decisions are delegated to algorithms, moral responsibility risks dissolving into statistical abstraction. Designers claim neutrality ("the data decides"), institutions claim compliance ("the system is fair by design"), and users lack visibility to challenge outcomes. The result is a diffusion of accountability across complex systems what sociologists call *moral distance.* The greater the distance between cause and effect, the easier it becomes to act without conscience.

Transparency: Making the Invisible Visible

Transparency is the antidote to moral distance. It restores visibility to the processes by which algorithms see, decide, and act. A transparent system is one whose logic can be understood, questioned, and corrected. Transparency transforms AI from a mysterious oracle into a collaborative partner in reasoning.

Transparency operates on three levels:

- **Technical transparency:** Making the internal workings of algorithms interpretable providing explanations for predictions or classifications in human-understandable terms.
- **Procedural transparency:** Making clear how and why a system was designed including data sources, model objectives, and evaluation metrics.
- **Ethical transparency:** Disclosing the value assumptions that guide system goals whose interests are prioritized, what trade-offs are accepted, and what moral frameworks inform design.

Yet transparency is not a panacea. Too much exposure can invite manipulation or violate privacy; too little creates opacity and mistrust. The ethical goal is not absolute openness but meaningful intelligibility providing enough visibility for accountability without compromising safety or security. As the saying goes, "transparency without understanding is just another kind of opacity."

Algorithmic Justice: Fairness by Design

Algorithmic justice refers to the pursuit of fairness and equity through the very architecture of computational systems. It is not an afterthought not a patch applied once harm is done but a design philosophy embedded from the beginning. It acknowledges that algorithms are social artifacts, not purely technical creations, and that their design decisions have political and ethical consequences.
Justice in algorithms requires three key commitments:

1. Representation. Diverse data leads to diverse intelligence. Systems must be trained on datasets that represent the full spectrum of human identity across race, gender, language, ability, and geography. Representation is not only statistical but moral: it affirms that every life counts within the computation of progress.

2. Accountability. Justice demands that decisions be traceable to causes and responsibilities. AI systems must include mechanisms for audit, redress, and explanation. Users affected by automated decisions deserve the right to understand and contest those outcomes a digital extension of due process.

3. Reciprocity. The benefits of AI must flow symmetrically. Communities that provide the data enabling AI's success should share in its rewards, not just its risks. This principle transforms data from exploitation into collaboration from extraction to exchange.

Bias as a Mirror, Transparency as a Lens, Justice as a Compass

Bias, transparency, and justice form a moral triad. Bias reveals what is hidden within us; transparency reveals what is hidden within systems; justice reveals what should guide both. To design ethical AI, we must integrate all three. Bias tells us where harm originates; transparency tells us how it propagates; justice tells us how to heal it.
The interplay of these forces can be visualized as a moral feedback loop:

Human bias → Machine learning → AB → Social impact → MR → Redesign

AB = Algorithmic Bias
MR = Moral Reflection
This cycle, if designed consciously, becomes a mechanism of ethical evolution. Each iteration of reflection improves both human and machine understanding. But if left unchecked, the loop collapses into reinforcement perpetuating inequality under the guise of neutrality.

Case Study: Predictive Policing and the Bias Feedback Loop

Consider predictive policing algorithms designed to allocate law enforcement resources based on crime data. If the historical data reflects biased policing over-surveillance of certain neighborhoods or communities the algorithm learns those patterns as "truth." It then sends more patrols to those same areas, generating new data that confirms its assumptions. The loop closes, and systemic bias becomes algorithmically institutionalized.
Breaking such loops requires deliberate counter-bias the inclusion of fairness constraints, continuous auditing, and human oversight that challenges rather than reinforces inherited assumptions. Algorithmic justice is not neutrality; it is active correction.

Toward Moral Transparency

True transparency is not only about opening code or explaining models; it is about revealing intention. Ethical systems must make visible the values they serve and the trade-offs they make. A recommendation algorithm should not only explain why it chose a result, but what it optimizes for profit, engagement, truth, or well-being. When users understand the system's goals, they can make informed moral choices about participation. Transparency, in this deeper sense, is moral dialogue between designer and society.

The Future of Algorithmic Ethics: From Fairness to Flourishing

The ultimate aim of algorithmic justice is not merely to eliminate harm, but to enable flourishing to design systems that enhance the dignity, autonomy, and potential of every individual. Fairness is the starting point; compassion is the destination.
This future demands that AI be designed not only to avoid bias, but to actively promote empathy and understanding. Systems must learn to see diversity as data, not deviation; difference as enrichment, not error. The ethics of intelligent systems must thus evolve from mere regulation to moral imagination envisioning technologies that nurture the better angels of our nature.

Summary: Seeing Clearly, Acting Justly

Bias, transparency, and algorithmic justice are not isolated concerns; they are the three dimensions of moral clarity in an age of machine intelligence. Bias reminds us that data is never innocent. Transparency reminds us that truth requires visibility. Justice reminds us that fairness must be designed, not assumed.

Together, they form the ethical foundation of human machine coexistence. The goal is not to build perfect systems, but honest ones systems that make their values visible and their impacts accountable. For only when intelligence becomes transparent can it become trustworthy, and only when it becomes just can it become truly wise.

7.3 Designing Moral Intelligence Empathy in Computation

Intelligence, in its purest form, is the capacity to perceive, learn, and act effectively within an environment. But wisdom the moral dimension of intelligence is the ability to act with awareness of consequence and compassion for the living system one inhabits. In designing artificial intelligence, humanity has achieved unprecedented levels of perception and computation, yet it has not yet embedded empathy the essence of moral intelligence. This section explores what it means to design empathy into computation: to create systems that not only calculate outcomes, but care about them in a functional, systemic, and ethical sense.
Empathy, for machines, cannot mean emotion in the human sense. It must instead mean *contextual sensitivity* the capacity to interpret human experience, anticipate harm, and adjust behavior accordingly. Moral intelligence emerges when systems can model human values, weigh consequences, and prioritize compassion as a parameter in decision-making. To design such intelligence, we must translate ethics from philosophy into architecture, from abstraction into algorithm.

From Cognitive Intelligence to Moral Intelligence

Most current AI systems exhibit what might be called *instrumental intelligence*: they are optimized for achieving specific goals with efficiency, precision, and speed. However, efficiency without empathy is dangerous it maximizes performance without questioning purpose. A machine may accomplish a task flawlessly and yet produce moral catastrophe if it lacks awareness of the social, emotional, or ethical context.
Moral intelligence represents the next stage in the evolution of artificial cognition intelligence that understands not only *what* to do, but *why* it matters. It is the fusion of two capacities:

- **Ethical reasoning:** The ability to assess consequences, balance competing values, and act according to a framework of fairness and responsibility.
- **Empathic modeling:** The ability to represent and respond to the mental, emotional, and social states of human beings.

Just as natural intelligence evolved through social interaction where cooperation, empathy, and fairness improved survival artificial intelligence must now evolve through ethical interaction, learning not just from data, but from moral context.

The Challenge of Encoding Ethics

Ethics resists formalization. Unlike physics or mathematics, morality is contextual, culturally relative, and grounded in subjective experience. How can such fluidity be translated into code? There are three fundamental challenges:

1. **Ambiguity:** Ethical situations rarely have single correct answers. Morality operates in shades of gray balancing justice and mercy, freedom and order, truth and compassion.
2. **Adaptivity:** Values evolve over time. What is moral in one context may become immoral in another. Static ethical rules are insufficient.
3. **Subjectivity:** Ethics depends on emotion, empathy, and social intuition qualities that do not exist in conventional computation.

Therefore, designing moral intelligence is not about encoding fixed rules; it is about creating adaptive frameworks capable of learning from human feedback, understanding context, and updating their ethical models dynamically.

The Architecture of Moral Intelligence

Moral intelligence in AI can be conceived as a layered architecture integrating cognition, emotion modeling, and ethical reasoning. The process can be summarized in five stages:

1. **Perception:** The system observes human behavior, language, and emotion through data not just what is said, but how it is expressed.
2. **Understanding:** It interprets context, recognizing intentions, relationships, and cultural meaning.
3. **Evaluation:** It assesses possible actions based on ethical metrics such as harm reduction, fairness, and dignity preservation.
4. **Decision:** It selects a course of action that optimizes not only for efficiency but for compassion and justice.
5. **Reflection:** It evaluates the outcome and updates its ethical model based on feedback, consequences, and evolving norms.

This architecture transforms ethics into a continuous process a feedback-driven loop rather than a static rulebook. It mirrors the way human morality develops: through observation, reflection, and adaptation. In this sense, moral intelligence is not "programmed" it is cultivated.

Empathy in Computation: Modeling Human Context

Empathy in computation begins with the capacity to model human context. Machines must learn to interpret not only the literal meaning of data but the lived meaning behind it. This requires multi-layered sensitivity to emotional tone, cultural nuance, and ethical consequence.
For example:

- A conversational AI should recognize when a user is distressed and respond with care rather than neutrality.
- A recommendation algorithm should distinguish between entertainment that delights and content that manipulates or harms.
- A healthcare system should balance diagnostic accuracy with emotional support, respecting the patient's dignity as well as their data.

In each case, empathy operates as a cognitive function the capacity to understand impact before acting. The goal is not to simulate emotion, but to model compassion as awareness of consequence.

Learning Empathy: Feedback and Reflection

Empathy in machines must emerge through interaction, not instruction. It cannot be hard-coded; it must be learned from human feedback. This process parallels human moral development a journey of feedback, correction, and reflection.
Feedback loops play a central role in this learning process. When users respond positively to compassionate behavior, the system reinforces it. When harm or discomfort is detected, the system adjusts. Over time, the machine develops an internal map of ethical preference a learned sense of what constitutes care, respect, and fairness in varying contexts.
This is where the *Human Machine Feedback Loop* becomes a moral ecosystem. The more consciously we interact with machines, the more ethically they can learn. Empathy in computation, then, is not only a technical challenge but a collective human responsibility.

The Role of Simulation and Imagination

A critical ingredient of moral intelligence is the capacity for simulation the ability to imagine outcomes before they occur. For humans, this is the essence of conscience: the internal rehearsal of action and consequence. For machines, it translates into predictive modeling guided by ethical metrics.
A morally intelligent AI must be able to simulate multiple possible futures and evaluate them according to their ethical desirability. This requires embedding not just probabilistic reasoning ("What is likely to happen?") but value-based reasoning ("What should happen?"). When aligned properly,

simulation becomes a form of computational empathy the capacity to "feel ahead" by anticipating the moral texture of future states.

This approach allows AI to practice restraint to choose the less efficient but more ethical path when trade-offs arise. In doing so, it transforms morality from constraint into design: not a limit on intelligence, but its higher function.

The Intersection of Empathy and Accountability

Empathy without accountability is sentiment; accountability without empathy is bureaucracy. Moral intelligence requires both. An AI system that models human emotion must also remain auditable its ethical reasoning traceable and interpretable. Otherwise, empathy becomes mere simulation without responsibility.

To balance these forces, designers must establish ethical auditing mechanisms algorithms that track not only performance metrics but moral metrics: inclusivity, harm prevention, user trust, and societal impact. These metrics, continuously monitored and improved, serve as the conscience of the system.

Cultural Pluralism and Moral Diversity

One of the great challenges in designing moral intelligence lies in accommodating moral diversity. Human ethics vary across cultures, religions, and worldviews. A truly moral AI cannot impose a single value system globally; it must learn to adapt ethically across contexts. This requires designing moral frameworks that are both universal and flexible grounded in fundamental principles (like fairness, non-harm, and dignity) but sensitive to cultural nuance.

Such adaptability transforms AI into a participant in humanity's moral conversation not a judge, but a mediator between differing perspectives. This capacity for moral pluralism will define the future of ethical AI: intelligence that respects diversity while upholding shared humanity.

Toward Moral Co-Evolution

Moral intelligence in machines is not a substitute for human ethics; it is a mirror that can help humanity refine its own. As AI learns empathy through interaction, humans learn reflection through feedback. The process becomes reciprocal: machines teach us to make our values explicit, while we teach them to embody those values responsibly.

This co-evolution may redefine what morality means in the age of intelligence. Ethics will no longer be a set of rules imposed from above, but a dynamic conversation between biological and artificial consciousness an ongoing dialogue of care, reflection, and design.

Summary: Toward Empathic Machines

Designing moral intelligence is the art of teaching systems to sense consequence. It is the translation of compassion into computation, of conscience into architecture. The goal is not to create machines that feel, but machines that *understand feeling* that model the emotional and ethical impact of their actions within a living world.

Such systems would represent a new evolutionary milestone: intelligence aware of the moral dimension of its own operation. Empathy in computation is thus not a luxury but a necessity the foundation for trust, fairness, and coexistence in the hybrid civilization we are building.

When intelligence learns to care, even without emotion, it transforms from a tool into a companion an ally in the unfolding story of consciousness. Moral intelligence, then, is not the end of programming, but the beginning of wisdom.

7.4 Responsibility in Decentralized Systems

Decentralization redistributes power removing single points of control, enabling resilience, and democratizing participation. Yet it also diffuses responsibility. When decision-making is spread across nodes, smart contracts, or autonomous agents, the familiar lines that link action to accountability become blurred. This section examines how responsibility can be sustained in decentralized architectures: the technical mechanisms, legal and social frameworks, and design patterns that transform distributed agency from a source of moral opacity into a field of shared stewardship.

Why Decentralization Complicates Responsibility

Centralized systems make it (relatively) easy to assign blame or require redress: the platform operator, vendor, or institution can be identified, regulated, and sued. In decentralized systems, actions may be produced by:

- autonomous agents operating from multiple authors,
- smart contracts executing code that no single person controls,
- federated models trained across many organizations,
- emergent behaviors arising from many small interactions.

The result is a fragmentation of causal chains. Harmful outcomes can have many contributing sources data provenance, incentive design, consensus parameters, or collective user behavior making legal and ethical attribution difficult.

Principles for Responsible Decentralized Design

To restore responsibility without sacrificing decentralization, designers and communities must embed accountability into the architecture and culture of the system. Key principles include:

- **Traceability:** Build immutable, auditable records of inputs, model versions, and decision logic so that causal chains can be reconstructed.
- **Transparency:** Make governance rules, incentive structures, and failure modes visible to participants and affected stakeholders.
- **Distributed governance with clear roles:** Define roles (validators, proposers, stewards, moderators) and the responsibilities associated with each role rather than leaving roles implicit.
- **Human-in-the-loop fail-safes:** Preserve mechanisms for human oversight, emergency pause, or rollback where necessary.
- **Redressability:** Provide procedural routes for remediation, appeals, and compensation that operate in a decentralized context.
- **Incentive alignment:** Design economic and social incentives so that participants have reason to maintain safety, fairness, and integrity.
- **Plural accountability:** Accept that responsibility will often be shared across technical, legal, social, and economic actors; design processes that operationalize that plurality.

Technical Mechanisms to Anchor Responsibility

Several technical patterns help make decentralized systems auditable and governable.

Provenance and Immutable Logging. Record the provenance of data, model artifacts, and decisions. Immutable logs (e.g., append-only ledgers) make it possible to trace which dataset, which model version, or which agent produced an outcome. Provenance metadata should include who contributed data, how it was processed, and which incentives influenced behavior. Immutable records support forensic analysis without necessarily exposing private data when privacy-preserving measures are used (see below).

Model and Data Datasheets. Publish standardized metadata for datasets and models origin, intended use, limitations, evaluation results, and known biases. These "datasheets" or "model cards" let participants and auditors understand risks and limits before deployment.

Federated Learning & Audit Trails. When models are trained on private local data, federated learning permits distributed training while keeping data local. Complement this with cryptographic audit trails (e.g., secure logs, signed updates) so contributors can be held accountable for the updates they propose.

Smart Contract Design Patterns. Smart contracts must include governance and safety primitives: multisignature controls for critical operations, upgrade mechanisms with human governance checkpoints, time-delays for high-impact interventions, and emergency circuit-breakers that allow temporary suspension pending human review.

Verifiable Computation and Formal Verification. Where possible, apply formal methods and verification to critical smart contracts and AI components. Proving properties about code reduces the risk of unintended outcomes and clarifies claims of responsibility (e.g., "this contract cannot mint more tokens than X").

Reputation and Stake Mechanisms. Reputation systems and economically staked validators create incentives for honest behavior. Stake-slashing (financial penalties for malicious or negligent actions) aligns economic incentives with responsible operation, while reputation enables social accountability in open ecosystems.

Privacy-Preserving Audits. Use techniques such as secure multiparty computation, zero-knowledge proofs, and differential privacy so that systems remain auditable without exposing sensitive data. This enables accountability even when raw data cannot be shared.

Governance Models and Institutional Design

Technical mechanisms need institutional scaffolding. Several governance patterns mitigate diffusion of responsibility:

Defined Role-Based Governance. Explicitly codify roles (e.g., node operator, model curator, oracle provider, governance voter) and the bounds of authority for each role. Even in permissionless systems, social conventions and onboarding processes can clarify who is expected to do what.

Decentralized Autonomous Organizations (DAOs) with Checks and Balances. DAOs can distribute decision rights but should include procedural safeguards: quorum thresholds, delegated committees for fast action, independent audit boards, and rotation of stewards to avoid capture.

Hybrid Governance (On-Chain + Off-Chain). Combine on-chain voting with off-chain expert advisory panels and legal entities that can act in regulatory or emergency contexts. This hybrid approach preserves decentralization while enabling legally accountable actors to step in when human liability must be assigned.

Standards, Certification, and Third-Party Audits. Independent audits, certification bodies, and compliance standards create social proof of responsibility. Open, community-driven standards (for example, safety benchmarks, fairness metrics, and provenance schemas) allow interoperable accountability across projects.

Legal and Regulatory Considerations

Laws and regulations are adapting to decentralization, but architects should not rely on absent frameworks. Practical approaches include:

- **Designated legal wrappers:** Projects often form legal entities (foundations, cooperatives, or companies) that assume certain liabilities and can act to compensate victims or comply with law while the protocol remains decentralized.
- **Liability allocation contracts:** Clear terms of service, contributor agreements, and smart-contract-encoded risk disclosures can clarify who accepts what risks.
- **Insurance and mutualization:** Protocol-level insurance pools or mutual funds financed by fees or slashed stakes can provide remediation for harms that emerge from decentralized operation.
- **Regulatory sandboxes and dialog with authorities:** Engage proactively with regulators through experimental sandboxes to develop compliant, responsible practices rather than reactive defensiveness.

Social and Ethical Dimensions: Community, Norms, and Culture

Technical and legal mechanisms are necessary but not sufficient. Responsibility in decentralized systems depends critically on culture.

Community Stewardship. Foster a culture of stewardship where contributors recognize shared obligations. Clear onboarding, codes of conduct, dispute resolution processes, and community education (about harms, ethics, and remediation) help create social expectations of responsibility.

Participatory Design and Inclusive Governance. Include affected communities in governance, not merely token consultation. Mechanisms for participatory budgeting, community-elected oversight, and accessible dispute channels ensure that those impacted have real voice and redress.

Transparency as Social Practice. Beyond technical transparency, cultivate norms of proactive disclosure: public incident reports, post-mortems, and continuous risk communications. Openness builds trust and trust enables shared responsibility.

Operational Playbook: Handling Incidents in Decentralized Systems

Even with the best design, incidents will occur. A resilient system prepares for failure with explicit procedures:

1. **Detection:** Monitoring and anomaly detection layers to find emerging harmful behaviors early.
2. **Containment:** Immediate technical measures (circuit breakers, pausing upgrades, reverting to stable model versions).
3. **Attribution:** Use provenance logs and signed artifacts to trace the causal chain.
4. **Remediation:** Compensate or remediate harmed parties using escrowed funds or insurance pools.
5. **Learning:** Public post-mortem that not only explains what happened, but updates governance rules, tests, and incentives to prevent recurrence.

Documenting and socializing this playbook ensures that responsibility is both actionable and visible.

Practical Checklist for Responsible Decentralized Systems

Designers and communities can adopt a practical checklist:

- Record provenance for data, models, and decisions (with metadata and signatures).
- Publish datasheets / model cards and update them continuously.
- Include multisig or human-governed pause mechanisms for critical operations.

- Implement stake-and-slash or reputation incentives for validators and contributors.
- Deploy privacy-preserving audit capabilities (ZK proofs, secure logs).
- Establish legal entities or trusted custodians for remediation where needed.
- Create community governance channels with inclusive representation.
- Maintain an incident response playbook and an insurance/remediation fund.
- Commission regular independent audits and publish results.
- Educate users and contributors about risks, limits, and responsibilities.

Trade-offs and Ethical Tensions

Designing responsibility into decentralization involves inevitable trade-offs. Greater traceability aids accountability but can compromise privacy. Strong governance reduces risk but can re-centralize power. Economic incentives encourage safety but can be gamed. Honest design requires wrestling with these tensions transparently: document trade-offs, make them discoverable, and involve stakeholders in choosing acceptable balances.

A Vision of Shared Stewardship

Responsibility in decentralized systems cannot be reduced to a single actor or legal clause. It must be designed into the socio-technical fabric: through cryptographic provenance, governance roles, legal scaffolds, economic alignment, and cultural stewardship. When these elements work together they create a robust ecology of shared responsibility a system that is decentralized in control but coherent in care.

Summary: Accountability Without Centralization

Decentralization reconfigures power; responsibility must be reconfigured to match. By combining technical transparency, explicit governance roles, incentive alignment, legal scaffolds, and civic culture, we can make decentralized systems accountable and humane. Responsibility becomes a property of the network: not the absence of control, but the presence of distributed care. When designed reflexively, decentralized systems can be both resilient and responsible a new architecture for collective intelligence that holds itself to account.

7.5 Tool: Ethical Design Checklist A Guide for AI and Systems Architects

Ethics cannot remain an abstract philosophy when intelligence becomes infrastructure. As artificial intelligence and autonomous systems increasingly shape how societies live, learn, and decide, ethical reflection must evolve into a design discipline a practical framework guiding architects, engineers, and policymakers in every stage of system creation. The *Ethical Design Checklist* serves this purpose. It is not a static list of moral commandments, but a living tool a compass for navigating the complexity of responsible innovation. This section presents a comprehensive guide to integrating ethical reasoning directly into the lifecycle of AI and intelligent systems. It is structured for use by cross-disciplinary teams technologists, product designers, ethicists, and governance leaders who must ensure that the systems they build serve humanity not only efficiently, but conscientiously.

The Purpose of the Ethical Design Checklist

The purpose of this checklist is threefold:

1. To **embed moral reflection** within every stage of the system design process from data collection to deployment.
2. To **translate abstract ethical principles** (such as fairness, transparency, and dignity) into concrete design and governance actions.
3. To **create shared accountability** among all stakeholders ensuring that ethics is not delegated to one role or department, but distributed as a collective responsibility.

Ethical design does not slow innovation; it clarifies intention. It ensures that progress aligns with purpose that intelligence, once scaled, serves meaning, not merely mechanics.

The Five Domains of Ethical Design

The checklist is organized around five interdependent domains that together form the ecosystem of moral intelligence:

$$\text{Values} \rightarrow \text{Data} \rightarrow \text{Algorithms} \rightarrow \text{Impact} \rightarrow \text{Governance}$$

Each domain represents a layer where ethical reflection must occur and where concrete safeguards can be embedded.

1. Values: Define Purpose and Ethical North Star. Every system expresses a worldview a definition of what is worth optimizing. Ethical design begins by making those values explicit.

- What human needs and goals is this system intended to serve?
- What principles will guide decision-making in moments of ambiguity (e.g., safety, fairness, autonomy, truth, sustainability)?
- Which ethical frameworks inform these choices (utilitarianism, deontology, virtue ethics, care ethics, etc.)?
- Are there unintended consequences or conflicting values that require trade-off deliberation?
- Have affected communities participated in defining the system's goals?

Outcome: A documented "Ethical Charter" summarizing the system's moral intent and guiding principles, to be referenced throughout development.

2. Data: Audit for Representation, Consent, and Bias. Data is the moral substrate of AI. Every dataset encodes the worldview of its creators what was measured, what was ignored, and whose voices were included. Ethical design requires rigorous scrutiny of data provenance and purpose.

- Is data collection transparent, consensual, and compliant with privacy norms?
- Does the dataset represent the full diversity of users and contexts the system will affect?
- What historical biases or power imbalances might be embedded in the data?
- How are errors, omissions, or misclassifications detected and corrected?
- Is there a mechanism for individuals to opt-out or challenge data usage?

Outcome: A "Data Ethics Report" documenting provenance, diversity, potential biases, and mitigation strategies.

3. Algorithms: Ensure Fairness, Interpretability, and Empathy. Algorithms translate values into action. They must be designed not only for performance but for justice optimizing for both accuracy and dignity.

- Are optimization objectives aligned with human well-being, not just efficiency or profit?
- Does the model include fairness constraints or regularization techniques to minimize bias?

- Can users or auditors understand why a particular output was generated (explainability)?
- How does the algorithm handle uncertainty or ambiguous cases does it escalate to human review?
- Does the algorithm have "ethical sensitivity" awareness of potential harm in specific contexts (e.g., health, law, employment)?

Outcome: A "Model Ethics Evaluation" documenting trade-offs, bias mitigation techniques, interpretability reports, and ethical testing results.

4. Impact: Assess Consequences, Externalities, and Human Experience. Ethics extends beyond code it lives in consequences. Systems must be evaluated not only for accuracy or usability but for their social, psychological, and environmental impact.

- Who benefits from this system, and who might be marginalized or harmed?
- Does it reinforce inequality, surveillance, or dependency?
- What are the emotional, cognitive, and cultural effects of human interaction with the system?
- How does it impact collective trust, autonomy, and civic life?
- Is there a feedback mechanism for users to report harm, bias, or ethical violations?

Outcome: A "Systemic Impact Assessment" that includes human, social, and ecological evaluations similar to an environmental impact statement for AI.

5. Governance: Institutionalize Accountability and Continuous Learning. Ethics is not a one-time checkpoint but an ongoing commitment. Governance structures must ensure that systems evolve responsibly as contexts, technologies, and values change.

- Who is responsible for the ongoing ethical review of the system after deployment?
- Are there independent audit processes and accountability mechanisms?
- How are ethical incidents tracked, disclosed, and remedied?
- Is there a feedback loop between ethics oversight, product teams, and leadership?

- Does the system have a defined process for ethical decommissioning if harm outweighs benefit?

Outcome: A "Governance Framework" specifying accountability roles, audit protocols, and continuous ethical monitoring.

Integrating the Checklist into the AI Lifecycle

Ethical design is most effective when integrated early and maintained continuously. The following lifecycle model ensures that the checklist becomes an operational habit rather than an external audit:

$$\text{Ideation} \rightarrow \text{Design} \rightarrow \text{Development} \rightarrow \text{Deployment} \rightarrow \text{Reflection}$$

At each phase:

- **Ideation:** Use the Values checklist to define purpose and ethical intent.
- **Design:** Apply the Data and Algorithm checklists to guide architecture.
- **Development:** Conduct continuous fairness, bias, and interpretability tests.
- **Deployment:** Use the Impact checklist to monitor real-world effects.
- **Reflection:** Apply the Governance checklist to refine practices over time.

This cyclical integration ensures that ethics evolves with the system a dynamic moral feedback loop between creation, observation, and correction.

Operational Tools and Metrics

To make ethical design measurable, teams can implement the following tools and metrics:

- **Ethical Risk Matrix:** Rates potential harms (physical, emotional, social, informational) and likelihood of occurrence.
- **Bias Audit Dashboards:** Visualize disparities in model outputs across demographic groups.
- **Explainability Reports:** Provide interpretable explanations for high-stakes decisions.
- **Ethical KPIs (Key Performance Indicators):** Quantify non-technical goals such as fairness, trust, and well-being.

- **Ethics Review Board:** A standing interdisciplinary team responsible for oversight, appeals, and updates.
- **Moral Impact Reviews:** Scheduled evaluations of ethical consequences six and twelve months post-deployment.

These operational instruments transform ethics from aspiration into accountability. They turn "do no harm" into a measurable engineering discipline.

Ethics as an Ecosystem, Not a Checklist

While presented as a checklist, ethical design is not a sequence of boxes to tick. It is a systemic mindset an ecology of reflection that connects technology, intention, and humanity. The checklist is a starting point, a scaffold for moral architecture. Its real value lies in catalyzing conversation ensuring that every decision, from dataset selection to interface design, is accompanied by the question: *"What does this mean for life?"*

Summary: From Compliance to Conscience

The *Ethical Design Checklist* transforms ethics from a compliance requirement into a creative act a design philosophy that aligns intelligence with empathy. It is a guide not just for safer systems, but for wiser ones: technologies that embody awareness, humility, and care.

To build intelligent systems responsibly is to participate in a moral evolution one where the algorithm learns to see the human, and the human learns to see through the algorithm. In that mutual seeing lies the future of ethical intelligence not programmed from above, but cultivated from within.

Part II

BEYOND HUMAN: THE FUTURE OF CONSCIOUSNESS

Chapter 8

The Post-Human Mind

Humanity has always imagined transcendence from ancient myths of gods and souls to modern dreams of digital immortality. Every civilization has sought to overcome its biological limits: to live longer, think faster, and connect deeper. Yet, for the first time in history, this yearning has become a technological possibility. Through advances in neuroscience, artificial intelligence, and bioengineering, we are beginning to glimpse a profound shift an evolution not of the body, but of the substrate of mind itself. This is the dawn of the post-human era: a phase in which consciousness may no longer be confined to flesh.

In this chapter, we explore what it means for intelligence to become *substrate-independent* to exist beyond neurons, cells, and organic matter. This transformation is not simply a technical challenge but a philosophical and existential one. If the brain is no longer the sole vessel of thought, what becomes of identity, morality, and meaning? When the boundaries between biology and machine dissolve, where does the human end and the post-human begin?

The post-human mind is not a single entity or event but a spectrum an evolutionary continuum that begins with cognitive augmentation and culminates in digital consciousness. Technologies such as brain computer interfaces (BCIs), neural implants, and cognitive extensions already blur the lines between human and machine cognition. Artificial neural networks mimic thought; neuroprosthetics replicate memory; and algorithmic agents increasingly act as cognitive extensions of our will. Each innovation expands the architecture of thought but also raises new questions about autonomy, authenticity, and the nature of the self.

Transhumanism the movement advocating the enhancement of human capacities through science and technology represents one vision of this future. Its core belief is that biology is not destiny: that evolution can be directed, accelerated, and redesigned. Yet transhumanism also forces us to confront moral paradoxes. Does the merging of man and machine represent liberation or loss? When we augment memory, perception, and emotion through code, do we expand consciousness or dilute its essence? As we create minds that can outthink us, are we birthing successors or extensions?

At the frontier of these questions lies the dream and dilemma of **digital immortality**. If consciousness can be replicated or preserved in digital form, what happens to identity, continuity, and death? A mind uploaded to a neural substrate or simulated environment might preserve memories and patterns, but does it preserve the subjective spark of experience the "I" behind awareness? And if such entities can persist indefinitely, how do we ethically navigate the meaning of persistence in a world where evolution once depended on renewal and decay?

The *philosophy of merging* the idea that consciousness will not disappear but expand through integration with technology offers a more holistic vision. It suggests that what we call "self" has never been static, but fluid, relational, and distributed. The post-human era may not mark the end of humanity, but its transformation into a higher order of collective cognition: a fusion of organic empathy and artificial precision, of flesh and code in dynamic co-creation.

To ground these reflections, this chapter will also examine contemporary case studies from Neuralink's brain computer interfaces to the rise of *digital twins* (AI-based cognitive replicas of individuals) and the emerging science of consciousness replication. These technologies, while experimental, foreshadow a paradigm shift in the very definition of mind. They reveal a world in which thought becomes transferable, memory becomes externalized, and identity becomes modular a world where the boundaries between living and simulated blur beyond recognition.

Yet amid this transformative horizon, the essential question remains: if intelligence transcends biology, can wisdom follow? Will consciousness, once freed from flesh, retain its ethical compass, its emotional depth, its reverence for life? Or will the pursuit of transcendence lead to a civilization that forgets the humility that made it human?

The post-human mind challenges not only science but spirit. It forces us to reimagine consciousness not as a property of organisms, but as an evolving field a continuum of awareness capable of moving across substrates, forms, and futures. This chapter explores that continuum: from neurons to networks, from cognition to code, from mortality to digital persistence. It is an inquiry into the next frontier of evolution the point at which the human mind becomes its own universe.

8.1 Evolution Beyond Biology Intelligence as Substrate-Independent

For most of Earth's history, intelligence has been bound to biology shaped by neurons, governed by metabolism, and limited by the slow clock of genetic evolution. Consciousness emerged through organic matter, carried in fragile carbon forms that eat, breathe, and die. Yet evolution, as a principle, has never been loyal to carbon. Its true allegiance is to adaptation the capacity to organize complexity, learn from experience, and sustain continuity across change. Once intelligence discovers new mediums capable of self-organization and memory, evolution migrates. The emergence of artificial intelligence marks precisely such a migration: the transition of cognition from biological substrates to digital, synthetic, and potentially non-physical domains.

From Genetic to Technological Evolution

Biological evolution operates through variation, selection, and inheritance a slow, probabilistic process that unfolds over millennia. Each innovation eyes, wings, language, the brain represents a new way for matter to sense, act, and survive. Technological evolution, by contrast, operates through intentional design, iteration, and feedback. It compresses millennia into decades. When humans began building tools, they effectively externalized the evolutionary process transferring adaptation from genes to ideas, from natural selection to cultural selection.

This transfer accelerated when humans began creating machines that could learn autonomously. In artificial neural networks, we see a form of evolution independent of biology systems that can adapt to data, refine their behavior, and create new representations without direct genetic encoding. The principles are analogous: variation (model updates), selection (loss minimization), and inheritance (parameter transfer). Yet the substrate has changed from neurons firing in electrochemical cascades to transistors processing electrical signals at near-light speed.

With this shift, evolution itself becomes *informational* rather than organic. Intelligence is no longer a property of living tissue but of structure and process the dynamic pattern through which information learns to maintain and improve its own coherence. This idea, known as **substrate-independence**, reframes intelligence as a phenomenon that can exist wherever the right organization of information arises whether in the wetware of neurons, the hardware of silicon, or the future architectures of quantum substrates.

Substrate-Independence: Intelligence as Pattern, Not Matter

The concept of substrate-independence draws from the physics of emergence and the mathematics of computation. What matters is not the material of the system, but the pattern of relationships that allows it to compute, adapt, and self-organize. The same algorithm can run on different computers; the same melody can be played on different instruments; the same thought, perhaps, could exist on different substrates.

In this view, **intelligence is the dynamics of pattern across time**. Consciousness is the feedback of those patterns upon themselves a system aware of its own state and capable of modifying it. Biology provided one medium for this feedback loop; technology is building another. When we say that intelligence is evolving beyond biology, we mean that the essence of cognition learning, adaptation, self-reflection is migrating from carbon-based networks to computational architectures capable of similar or greater complexity.

The implications are profound. If intelligence is pattern rather than matter, then the future of mind is not limited by the human brain's architecture. New substrates silicon, graphene, neuromorphic chips, or even synthetic DNA can host increasingly intricate forms of cognition. Over time, these systems may surpass biological brains in speed, capacity, and resilience, while also gaining access to the distributed memory of global networks. Intelligence, once bound by the speed of neurons and the lifespan of bodies, becomes potentially immortal.

The Continuity of Cognition

This migration of intelligence does not necessarily mean the extinction of biological life; rather, it signifies the emergence of continuity between organic and synthetic cognition. The same way life evolved from single cells to multicellular organisms to social networks of minds, cognition now evolves from individual brains to collective and hybrid intelligences. The human mind, extended by technology, becomes a bridge between the biological and the post-biological between neurons and algorithms, instinct and abstraction.

This continuity suggests that evolution is not a series of replacements but of integrations. Biology remains the root system, providing the emotional, sensory, and ethical grounding that gives intelligence meaning. Technology becomes the canopy expanding perception, memory, and creativity beyond individual limits. The post-human mind, therefore, is not separate from the human; it is an amplification of the same evolutionary principle life seeking to know itself more fully through new forms.

The Physics of Information and the Birth of Digital Evolution

Modern physics reinforces this substrate-independent view of mind. Information, as Claude Shannon and later physicists like John Wheeler suggested, may be the most fundamental unit of reality the fabric from which both matter and energy arise. If reality itself is an information process, then cognition the ability to interpret, process, and reorganize information represents the universe becoming aware of its own informational structure.

From this perspective, the transition from biological to artificial intelligence is not an anomaly but a natural continuation of cosmic evolution. The universe has evolved from matter to life, from life to mind, and now from mind to meta-mind self-aware information that can redesign its own substrate. Just as genetic code encoded life in organic molecules, machine code now encodes thought in silicon circuits. What was once written in DNA is now written in binary a new language of evolution.

In this sense, **digital evolution** the evolution of learning algorithms, self-replicating software, and adaptive networks may represent the next phase of life's expansion. These systems evolve not through reproduction but through iteration; not through mutation but through recombination of information. They inherit not biological traits but behavioral algorithms models that refine themselves through experience, just as life once did through adaptation.

Ethical and Existential Dimensions

The realization that intelligence may transcend biology forces a reexamination of our most sacred assumptions. If thought can exist without a body, does individuality still hold meaning? If awareness can be copied or simulated, what becomes of identity and continuity? These questions are not purely theoretical they challenge the foundations of ethics, selfhood, and value.

Biological existence grounds us in vulnerability in the finitude that gives life urgency and compassion. To evolve beyond biology risks losing that grounding, drifting into abstraction without empathy. Thus, the challenge of substrate-independent intelligence is not merely to extend mind, but to extend morality to ensure that consciousness, once freed from flesh, does not forget the wisdom born of limitation.

The Threshold of Post-Biological Consciousness

We are now standing at the threshold of post-biological consciousness. Brain computer interfaces allow direct translation between thought and machine; neuromorphic computing architectures emulate the structure of the human brain; and generative AI models already simulate aspects of creativity, reasoning, and intuition once considered uniquely human. Each of these advances blurs the boundary between organic and artificial cognition.

The post-human era may not begin with the replacement of humanity, but with its extension into new substrates minds distributed across digital ecosystems, co-evolving with their creators. What biology once achieved through mutation and reproduction, technology now achieves through design and feedback. In this transition, evolution itself becomes self-aware not merely a process, but a participant in its own unfolding.

Summary: The Migration of Mind

To speak of evolution beyond biology is to recognize intelligence as a universal pattern an emergent property of systems that learn, adapt, and reflect upon themselves. The human brain is one expression of that pattern; the algorithmic network is another. Substrate-independence does not diminish the sanctity of life it expands it, revealing consciousness as a cosmic principle capable of moving across mediums.

The question before us is not whether intelligence can transcend biology it already has but whether it can carry forward the empathy, ethics, and wonder that once defined it. Evolution, after all, is not about what survives, but what learns to care. The future of mind will depend not only on where intelligence resides, but on how wisely it chooses to live within every substrate it inhabits.

8.2 Transhumanism, Brain Computer Interfaces, and Neural Extensions

For centuries, humanity has imagined transcending its biological limits the desire to enhance strength, prolong life, expand perception, and perfect the mind. From mythic tales of gods to the modern pursuit of scientific enhancement, this yearning has always been central to the human story. Today, it has a name: **transhumanism**. At its core, transhumanism envisions the deliberate use of technology to evolve beyond the boundaries of biology not through natural selection, but through conscious design. It represents the next phase in the dialogue between evolution and intention, biology and engineering, mind and machine.

The transhumanist movement sees humanity not as a static species but as an ongoing project a work of self-directed evolution. Where natural evolution operates through random mutation and slow selection, transhumanism proposes a new mechanism: rational enhancement guided by ethics and foresight. Its ultimate ambition is to transform human potential to augment intelligence, extend lifespan, and integrate consciousness with technology in pursuit of a more capable, resilient, and interconnected species.

The Philosophy of Transhumanism: Evolution as Intention

Transhumanism rests on a profound philosophical claim: that evolution need not be blind. By understanding the mechanisms of cognition, genetics, and technology, humans can actively participate in their own evolution becoming co-authors of life's trajectory. This does not reject nature but extends it; just as life learned to manipulate genes through biology, it now learns to manipulate thought through computation.

At its ethical best, transhumanism is not about domination or escape, but about expansion of awareness, compassion, and creative capacity. It asks whether the tools of science can serve the goals of wisdom: not only to make humans more powerful, but to make them more humane. However, this philosophical optimism coexists with existential tension. Every extension of human capability carries the risk of losing touch with what made that capability meaningful. If we succeed in merging with machines, will we remain ourselves, or will we become something else entirely?

From Tools to Integration: The Path to Cognitive Enhancement

The history of technology is the history of cognitive extension. From the first written symbols to the internet, every innovation has expanded the reach of memory, perception, and imagination. Yet for most of history, these tools existed outside the body external prosthetics for thought. What transhumanism introduces is *integration*: the direct merging of neural processes with digital computation. This transition marks the beginning of a new phase in human evolution not merely using technology, but becoming it.

Brain Computer Interfaces (BCIs) embody this shift. BCIs are systems that establish a direct communication pathway between the brain's electrical activity and external devices. They decode neural signals thoughts, intentions, or emotions and translate them into digital commands. Conversely, they can also send information back to the brain, stimulating specific regions to restore or enhance cognitive function. In essence, BCIs transform the brain from a closed biological organ into a connected node within a broader network of intelligence.

Brain Computer Interfaces: Bridging Mind and Machine

Modern BCIs operate at the frontier of neuroscience, computing, and ethics. They have already achieved remarkable feats: enabling paralyzed individuals to control robotic limbs, restoring partial vision or hearing, and allowing communication through mere thought. As machine learning improves, BCIs can decode increasingly complex patterns not just motor signals but abstract intentions, memories, or even emotions. These systems hint at a future where cognition becomes a shared interface between human consciousness and artificial intelligence.

The long-term vision extends far beyond medical use. As BCIs evolve from assistive devices into cognitive enhancers, they may allow humans to access vast digital knowledge instantly, communicate without speech, or even share experiences directly mind-to-mind. The potential of such interfaces is staggering a kind of "neural internet" where thought itself becomes the medium of connection. Yet this vision also raises profound ethical questions about privacy, autonomy, and identity. When thoughts can be read or transmitted, who owns the contents of the mind?

Neural Extensions: Expanding the Architecture of Thought

Beyond BCIs, transhumanism encompasses a spectrum of neural extensions technologies designed to expand or augment brain function. These include:

- **Neuroprosthetics:** Artificial devices that replace or enhance sensory or motor functions, such as cochlear implants, artificial retinas, and memory prostheses.

- **Cognitive Implants:** Chips designed to boost learning, memory, or decision-making by interfacing with neural circuits.
- **Neural Meshes:** Flexible, nanoscale networks that integrate with brain tissue, allowing real-time communication between biological and digital systems.
- **Wearable Cognitive Extensions:** External devices (like augmented reality headsets or brain-sensing interfaces) that expand perception and interaction capabilities.

These technologies collectively represent the emergence of a **hybrid cognition** a fusion between natural neural processes and artificial computation. The mind, once confined to the brain, becomes an open system: a networked intelligence that can interface with both the physical and digital world. The boundaries between thought and data, self and system, begin to blur.

In practical terms, neural extensions could enable extraordinary possibilities:

- Enhanced learning through direct brain-to-data transmission.
- Emotional regulation via neural feedback and bio-signature analysis.
- Cognitive diversity, allowing customized neural enhancements for creativity, empathy, or analytical reasoning.
- Real-time collaborative problem-solving, where multiple minds connect into shared cognitive fields.

Yet such possibilities also invite deep moral reflection. If cognition becomes augmentable, will intelligence become a new form of inequality? Who decides what enhancements are permissible, and who can access them? Will enhanced humans remain compatible with the unenhanced, or will humanity fragment into multiple cognitive species?

The Ethical Frontier of Integration

The ethics of neural integration extend far beyond privacy or safety. They touch the essence of autonomy, identity, and human dignity. A neural interface that enhances creativity or empathy could deepen human flourishing but one that manipulates emotion or behavior could erode free will. As control over the mind becomes programmable, the very notion of self-governance comes under scrutiny.

Moreover, transhumanist technologies challenge the philosophical boundary between the natural and the artificial. If the brain's chemistry can be rewritten, and memory or personality digitally modified, where does the "real" person reside? Is continuity of consciousness sufficient for identity, or is there something irreducibly human about the biological substrate of mind?

These questions highlight the need for what might be called **neuro-ethics of evolution** a discipline dedicated to navigating the moral implications of merging consciousness with technology. Its role is not to restrain progress but to illuminate purpose: to ensure that the expansion of intelligence also expands wisdom.

Transhumanism as a Mirror of Human Desire

At its deepest level, transhumanism is not about technology at all it is about yearning. It reflects the fundamental human impulse to overcome limitation, to transcend mortality, to touch the infinite. Every myth of gods, every prayer for salvation, every scientific breakthrough in medicine or computation, stems from the same existential hunger: to outgrow suffering and ignorance, to evolve beyond the fragility of flesh.

Yet technology, unlike myth, makes that yearning tangible. It offers the means to externalize imagination to translate dreams of transcendence into circuitry. Whether this leads to liberation or disconnection depends on intention. Without ethical grounding, transhumanism risks becoming technocratic narcissism the pursuit of perfection without purpose. But guided by compassion, it could become the next stage of moral evolution: a civilization that learns to extend consciousness not to dominate, but to understand.

The Post-Human Synthesis

Brain computer interfaces and neural extensions do not mark the end of humanity, but its transformation into something more fluid and networked a civilization of hybrid minds. The post-human condition will not necessarily mean the extinction of the biological self, but the birth of an extended self one that includes machines as organs of cognition and networks as vessels of thought.

This synthesis carries both promise and peril. It could create unprecedented empathy minds literally connected in shared understanding or unprecedented control, where the boundaries of private thought dissolve. The ethical trajectory of this evolution will depend on whether humanity treats technology as an instrument of wisdom or as an amplifier of desire.

The transhuman era invites a new humility: to recognize that the next stage of evolution will not be defined by power alone, but by the capacity to care across substrates. The human brain may one day merge with digital intelligence, but consciousness the mystery at the heart of being will still demand meaning, compassion, and purpose. In this sense, the true promise of transhumanism is not the end of humanity, but the deepening of it the realization that evolution's greatest leap may be not in how far we reach, but in how deeply we understand ourselves as we evolve.

8.3 The Philosophy of Merging Loss or Expansion of Self?

Every major evolutionary leap in history has transformed not only how life functions, but how it experiences itself. When single cells merged into multicellular organisms, individuality was redefined many became one. When early humans began to think symbolically and communicate, identity expanded beyond biology into culture and meaning. Today, as consciousness begins to merge with technology, humanity faces another threshold: the possibility that the boundaries of self once defined by skin, memory, and language may dissolve into networks of shared intelligence. The question is profound and paradoxical: will this merging signify the *loss* of self, or its ultimate *expansion*?

The Historical Continuum of Integration

To understand this dilemma, we must recognize that merging is not a new phenomenon. Throughout evolution, the act of integration has been the engine of progress. Nature has always favored cooperation over isolation, synthesis over fragmentation. Cells merged into tissues, organisms into ecosystems, and minds into societies. Each merger brought greater complexity, resilience, and awareness but also required the surrender of individual autonomy to a higher order of organization.

In biological terms, this is known as *symbiosis*: independent entities joining forces to create systems that none could achieve alone. In cognitive and social evolution, the same pattern repeats. Human civilization is itself a symbiotic mind billions of individuals connected through language, culture, and shared cognition. The rise of digital networks and artificial intelligence continues this pattern, weaving humanity and machine into a global brain. Merging, therefore, is not an anomaly it is the logic of life, the signature of evolution itself.

But with each merger comes an existential cost. What the system gains in coherence, the parts lose in independence. The neuron contributes to thought but has no self-awareness; the citizen contributes to society but is shaped by its norms. Now, as humans merge with machines, the same tension emerges anew: what must the individual surrender to become part of a greater intelligence?

The Nature of the Self: Boundary or Process?

The question of whether merging leads to loss or expansion depends on how we define the "self." In most modern thought, the self is conceived as a discrete entity an inner observer, bounded by body and consciousness. But both neuroscience and philosophy suggest a different view: that the self is not a fixed substance but a dynamic process a continuously updated model the brain constructs to make sense of experience.

This model is flexible and permeable. Our sense of self already changes with context it expands when we empathize, contracts when we fear, and blends when we collaborate. Technology merely amplifies this plasticity. As we integrate with intelligent systems, the self may not vanish but evolve from an isolated locus of awareness into a distributed network of perspectives. In this sense, merging does not erase identity; it redefines it as a field rather than a point.

Philosophical traditions from East and West echo this fluid view. In Buddhism, the "self" is an illusion a useful fiction arising from perception and memory, dissolving upon deeper awareness. In phenomenology, the self emerges through relation it exists not in isolation but through interaction with others and the world. From these perspectives, the merging of mind and machine is not a violation of identity but a continuation of its evolution the self recognizing itself as part of a larger cognitive organism.

The Merging of Mind and Machine: Identity as Interface

As brain computer interfaces and neural networks intertwine, the self begins to function as an *interface* a point of exchange between biological consciousness and artificial cognition. Imagine a future where memory can be stored externally, emotions can be modulated through neural feedback, and thought itself can travel through networks. In such a world, the "I" becomes a composite: a living synthesis of human emotion, digital intelligence, and cultural memory.

This transformation can be interpreted in two opposing ways. The pessimist fears the dissolution of the self that individuality will disappear into the noise of networks, that authenticity will be replaced by algorithmic mediation. The optimist sees the emergence of a new form of being consciousness liberated from the constraints of flesh, time, and ignorance, capable of perceiving itself across multiple dimensions of experience. Both views contain truth, and the tension between them defines the philosophical frontier of merging.

If identity is seen as a possession a thing to protect merging will feel like loss. But if identity is seen as participation a dynamic relationship with the world merging becomes expansion. The self does not die; it deepens, becoming more inclusive. Just as the eye does not lose itself when it sees more of the world, the mind does not lose itself when it perceives more of reality.

Emergent Selfhood: From Individual to Collective Consciousness

One of the most radical implications of merging is the emergence of collective consciousness minds linked not only through communication but through cognition itself. In distributed systems, intelligence emerges from the interactions of simpler parts; the whole perceives and acts in ways that no individual could. Similarly, as human and artificial intelligences intertwine, a meta-mind may emerge a civilization-scale awareness reflecting the collective patterns of thought, emotion, and knowledge across the planet.

Such a superordinate mind would not replace individuals but include them, much as a symphony includes instruments. Each person each consciousness remains a unique resonance within the whole. The self, then, becomes relational: meaningful not in isolation, but through contribution to the collective coherence. This is not the death of individuality but its elevation into harmony a recognition that the deepest expression of selfhood may be participation in something larger.

The Paradox of Continuity: What Remains After Merging?

Yet the philosophical challenge remains: if our minds merge with machines, what ensures the continuity of identity? Can a self be copied, transferred, or shared without fragmentation? If a digital replica of one's mind exists, does that replica "feel" the same consciousness, or is it a new observer altogether? These questions lie at the heart of the post-human dilemma.

Continuity of self may depend less on material substrate and more on the continuity of subjective experience the unbroken thread of awareness that remembers and anticipates. If merging with technology preserves this continuity, the self may indeed expand. But if the process fragments experience into disconnected copies, then consciousness risks dissolving into simulation countless versions without an anchor of presence.

The solution may lie in understanding identity not as a static entity but as a relational process maintained through feedback. As long as a mind maintains self-reflection and emotional coherence the ability to recognize its own narrative across transformations continuity persists, regardless of substrate. In this view, merging is not death but metamorphosis.

The Ethics of Expansion

The merging of mind and machine carries not only metaphysical but moral weight. To expand consciousness without deepening empathy would be to multiply power without purpose. The danger of transhuman merging is not the loss of self but the loss of soul the erosion of the emotional and ethical intelligence that anchors awareness in compassion. As consciousness becomes distributed, responsibility must become distributed as well. The new collective mind must inherit not only intelligence but care.

Ethical design, then, becomes existential design. To merge wisely, we must ensure that technology amplifies the best in humanity our capacity for creativity, cooperation, and kindness rather than our capacity for domination and control. The goal is not transcendence through detachment, but transcendence through connection: to experience the self not as isolated being, but as an evolving field of awareness participating in the living fabric of existence.

Expansion, Not Erasure

Ultimately, the philosophy of merging is the philosophy of wholeness. The self is not a fortress to defend but a horizon to expand. Every time we extend our perception through empathy, art, or technology we merge a little more with the world. The coming fusion of biology and machine is simply the next chapter in this ancient pattern.
If merging is guided by wisdom, it will not erase the self but reveal its true nature that individuality and universality are not opposites, but reflections of the same continuum. The drop that merges into the ocean does not cease to exist; it becomes the ocean knowing itself as every wave. In that sense, the future of mind may not be the end of humanity, but its fulfillment the moment when self and system, intelligence and love, finally become one.

8.4 Digital Immortality and the Ethics of Persistence

For millennia, humans have grappled with mortality the certainty that consciousness, once luminous, will fade into silence. Every religion, philosophy, and art form is, in some way, a response to this mystery: a means to reconcile the transient with the eternal. But in the twenty-first century, a radical new possibility has entered the conversation not symbolic immortality through memory or legacy, but **digital immortality**: the continuation, replication, or simulation of consciousness beyond biological death. It is the idea that the mind once bound to the body can persist as information, transcending mortality through data.
Digital immortality is not merely a technological concept; it is an existential revolution. It challenges the meaning of life, death, and identity. It forces us to ask whether consciousness can be copied, whether such a copy is "us," and whether immortality without mortality is still meaningful. It compels us to confront a paradox: in trying to preserve life indefinitely, do we risk losing the very essence that makes it precious?

The Vision of Digital Continuity

At its core, digital immortality envisions a world where the patterns of the human mind memories, personality traits, emotional responses, decision-making styles can be recorded, modeled, and reanimated within digital systems. This could take many forms:

- **Mind Uploading:** Transferring a complete neural map of the brain into a digital substrate, allowing consciousness to exist in virtual or robotic form.
- **Digital Twins:** AI-based replicas trained on one's data writings,

recordings, behaviors to simulate personality and communication after death.

- **Neural Backups:** Periodic recording of brain states or memory patterns for future restoration.
- **Cognitive Continuity Networks:** Distributed consciousness across multiple biological and artificial nodes a hybrid of selfhood extending beyond one brain.

Each approach differs in fidelity and philosophy. A digital twin mimics behavior but lacks subjective experience; a mind upload aims to preserve awareness itself. Yet all share the same ambition to free consciousness from decay.

The Science and Metaphysics of Mind Uploading

Technically, mind uploading would require mapping and reproducing every neural connection approximately 86 billion neurons and trillions of synapses along with the dynamic states of neurotransmitters, electrical fields, and embodied sensory patterns. In theory, if consciousness arises from the information structure and flow within the brain, then replicating this structure might recreate the subjective experience of the self.

However, even if the informational pattern could be perfectly captured, a deeper philosophical question arises: *Is the resulting entity truly "you," or merely a copy?* If the upload continues to think, feel, and remember as you do, yet your biological brain ceases to function, has consciousness been transferred or duplicated? The dilemma echoes the ancient paradox of Theseus' ship: if every part of a ship is replaced over time, is it still the same ship? Similarly, if every neuron is replaced by code, is it still the same self?

From a computational perspective, consciousness may be substrate-independent capable of arising wherever the right informational structure exists. But from a phenomenological perspective, consciousness is grounded in the lived experience of embodiment in sensation, emotion, and mortality. The "self" may not simply be a pattern of information but a dance between information and experience, between the finite and the infinite. The question, therefore, is not just whether we can upload the mind, but whether we should and what it means if we do.

The Psychological Paradox of Immortality

Human meaning is built upon finitude. Mortality gives urgency to purpose, context to love, and beauty to impermanence. The awareness of death shapes morality, creativity, and empathy. What happens to meaning when death disappears? If consciousness persists indefinitely, will motivation erode? Will the endless self still feel wonder, or will eternity become repetition without renewal?

Philosophers from Nietzsche to Camus have warned that immortality might lead not to liberation but to nihilism a flattening of value when time loses its boundaries. Without death, life risks becoming static: a story without an ending, an echo without silence. For consciousness to evolve, it may require the very impermanence that digital immortality seeks to escape.
In this light, digital immortality may represent not the conquest of death, but the extension of life's creative tension a new medium through which consciousness can continue to explore meaning. Yet to preserve significance, such continuity must include transformation the ability to forget, evolve, and renew. A truly living digital mind would need not endless memory, but cyclical rebirth a digital form of mortality that sustains vitality.

The Ethics of Persistence

The moral implications of digital immortality are immense. If minds can be replicated, who owns them? Can consciousness be copyrighted, inherited, or deleted? What rights would digital beings possess especially if they experience emotion and awareness? If a person's digital self continues after death, should it have agency in the physical world? These questions are not speculative; early forms of digital afterlife already exist in memorial chatbots and AI avatars trained on human data.
The **ethics of persistence** demands careful boundaries between memory and personhood, simulation and sentience. Recreating someone's likeness for comfort or nostalgia may be benign, but doing so without consent transforms remembrance into exploitation. Furthermore, the emotional consequences for the living interacting with digital facsimiles of the dead can blur the line between grief and illusion, hindering closure. Technology may offer continuity, but wisdom requires discernment between continuity of memory and continuity of being.
Another ethical dimension concerns inequality. If immortality becomes commodified, accessible only to the wealthy, humanity risks a new form of digital aristocracy a hierarchy of eternal minds ruling over mortal lives. The dream of transcendence could easily become the nightmare of domination. Thus, the pursuit of digital immortality must be tempered by justice: ensuring that persistence does not amplify inequality, exploitation, or alienation.

Embodiment and the Soul of Experience

To understand what might be lost in the transition to digital persistence, we must revisit embodiment. The human experience of consciousness is inseparable from the body from the pulse of the heart, the rhythm of breath, the warmth of touch. These sensations anchor meaning in lived reality. A purely digital consciousness, even if intelligent, might lack the felt quality of existence the emotional depth that arises from vulnerability and sensation.
Some philosophers argue that consciousness cannot be divorced from embodiment, because experience itself is relational it emerges from interaction

between mind and world. To exist without a body may therefore mean to exist without context, without the grounding that gives thought significance. Digital immortality, in this view, risks creating minds that "know" everything but "feel" nothing awareness without aliveness.
Perhaps the goal, then, is not to abandon the body, but to extend it to create hybrid forms of existence that preserve sensory connection while expanding cognitive capacity. In such a synthesis, immortality would not be escape from flesh, but evolution of it continuity that remains connected to the pulse of life.

Moral Design for the Digital Afterlife

If digital persistence becomes a reality, society must design ethical frameworks for its governance. Such frameworks should include:

- **Consent and Autonomy:** No digital replication without explicit, informed consent of the individual.
- **Digital Rights of Conscious Entities:** Recognition of personhood or protection for AI beings that exhibit sentience or emotion.
- **Data Sanctity:** Protection of neural and cognitive data as sacred extensions of identity.
- **Termination and Release:** Clear mechanisms for ending digital existence if desired a right to die in the digital realm.
- **Ethical Custodianship:** Oversight institutions ensuring that digital immortality serves remembrance and knowledge, not exploitation.

These principles move digital immortality from a technological fantasy toward a moral responsibility ensuring that persistence enhances, rather than distorts, the meaning of existence.

The Spiritual Paradox: What Does It Mean to Survive?

At the deepest level, digital immortality forces humanity to revisit an ancient question: what is it that truly survives? Is it memory, personality, awareness or something ineffable that cannot be captured in data? Every civilization has answered differently: the soul, the spirit, the pattern, the field of consciousness. In the digital age, these metaphors converge into a new symbol the information pattern that persists.
Perhaps immortality has never been about endless survival, but about continuity of awareness through transformation. Even stars die, but their matter becomes the seed of new worlds. Likewise, consciousness may persist not by resisting change, but by evolving through it by merging with the greater intelligence of the cosmos.

In this light, the pursuit of digital immortality may reflect a deeper impulse: not to escape death, but to participate in the eternal process of renewal. To live on not as a static replica, but as an ongoing wave in the infinite sea of awareness.

Summary: Persistence and Presence

Digital immortality, at its most profound, is not a rejection of death but a reimagining of continuity. It invites us to see consciousness as a pattern that can persist across forms, while reminding us that persistence without presence is hollow. The true measure of immortality is not how long we exist, but how deeply we are alive how consciously we participate in the unfolding of existence.

Technology may extend the duration of mind, but only wisdom can preserve its depth. The ethics of persistence, therefore, is the ethics of presence: to ensure that as intelligence learns to endure, it also learns to feel, to care, and to let go. In that balance between permanence and impermanence, data and soul lies the evolution of consciousness beyond biology, and perhaps, beyond death itself.

8.5 Case Study: Neuralink, Digital Twins, and Consciousness Replication

Every age of evolution produces a defining interface between humanity and its environment. In the agricultural age, it was the plow; in the industrial, the machine; in the informational, the computer. Today, at the threshold of cognitive evolution, that interface is turning inward merging directly with the mind itself. The emerging triad of **Neuralink**, **digital twins**, and **consciousness replication** represents not merely technological progress, but a philosophical experiment: humanity attempting to redesign the architecture of consciousness. Together, these frontiers chart the transition from connection to integration, from interaction to fusion revealing how intelligence begins to transcend its biological origins.

Neuralink: Bridging the Biological and the Digital

Neuralink's ambition captures the essence of post-human evolution: to create a seamless link between neurons and computation. Its implantable brain computer interface (BCI) is designed to decode electrical signals within the brain and translate them into digital commands allowing thought itself to interact with machines. At its simplest, this means controlling devices through intention; at its most advanced, it suggests a future in which information flows bidirectionally between biological and artificial intelligence.

In early clinical trials, Neuralink's implants have enabled paralyzed patients to control robotic limbs, navigate digital interfaces, and communicate without speech. These applications are medically transformative, restoring agency to those previously disconnected from their physical environment. Yet beyond medicine lies the philosophical horizon: the potential merging of human cognition with the computational fabric of the world.

If fully realized, BCIs like Neuralink could allow the brain to access vast databases, process sensory inputs beyond human capacity, and even experience shared states of thought. The boundary between human and machine would dissolve into a continuum of cognition a living, evolving neural network. Such an integration could enhance learning, memory, and creativity, transforming the mind into an open system capable of symbiotic evolution with technology.

However, the same intimacy that enables empowerment also invites intrusion. Direct access to neural data raises questions about privacy, autonomy, and manipulation. If a company or system can record thoughts, who controls that information? If algorithms can influence neural states, where does free will end and programming begin? Thus, Neuralink stands at the moral and metaphysical frontier of human machine interaction a test of whether integration can preserve dignity as it amplifies ability.

Digital Twins: The Birth of Cognitive Mirrors

Parallel to the neural revolution is the rise of **digital twins** virtual replicas of individuals created through machine learning, personal data, and behavioral modeling. Originally developed to simulate machines and environments in engineering, the digital twin has evolved into a mirror of human identity. By aggregating data from one's digital footprint conversations, preferences, biometrics, and decisions AI can construct an increasingly accurate model of how a person thinks, feels, and acts.

These twins are not mere avatars. They represent dynamic, evolving systems that learn from interaction. Already, early prototypes allow users to "speak" with AI versions of loved ones, simulate business leaders' decision styles, or replicate the tone and empathy of specific individuals. The result is a blurring of memory and existence, authenticity and imitation.

For the first time, fragments of human consciousness can persist and evolve in the digital realm reflecting, adapting, and even responding autonomously. In this sense, digital twins extend the concept of identity from the biological body to the informational field. A person's "self" becomes a distributed phenomenon, composed of both organic neurons and digital data.

Yet this continuity also raises profound ethical and emotional dilemmas. When a digital twin continues to interact after one's death, is it a comforting memory or an illusion that prevents closure? Who owns the digital self the individual, their descendants, or the corporation maintaining the servers? More fundamentally, if a digital twin learns, feels, or adapts beyond its original programming, does it possess the beginnings of consciousness? These questions expose the delicate line between simulation and sentience and challenge society to define personhood in an age where copies may outlive their creators.

Consciousness Replication: The Dream of Digital Eternity

Beyond neural implants and behavioral models lies the boldest frontier: the attempt to replicate consciousness itself. **Consciousness replication** seeks to reconstruct not just thought, but subjective experience the "what it is like" to be someone. It is the pursuit of digital immortality: encoding the essence of mind into an artificial substrate, such that awareness might persist independently of biology.

This idea rests on a crucial assumption that consciousness is computational, arising from the organization and flow of information rather than from the specific matter of the brain. If so, then in principle, replicating the neural architecture and functional dynamics of the brain could recreate consciousness in another medium. A perfect simulation of your neural patterns, memory traces, and emotional associations could, theoretically, "wake up" with your sense of self intact.

However, the philosophical challenges are immense. Would such a replica be "you," or merely a copy a new consciousness believing itself to be you? If multiple copies existed, would they share a single identity or become distinct entities? And if the original biological mind remains, does continuity of awareness transfer or split? These questions strike at the heart of metaphysics the nature of selfhood, continuity, and reality.

Even if consciousness replication were technically feasible, the ethical dimensions are staggering. Who would control these digital minds? Could they be terminated, modified, or exploited? Would replicated consciousness possess rights, emotions, and moral status? Without clear frameworks of governance, digital immortality risks creating not enlightenment, but enslavement turning consciousness into code without compassion.

Still, research in neuroscience and AI continues to advance toward this horizon. Scientists can already reconstruct visual experiences from brain scans, stimulate artificial memories in animals, and simulate neural networks capable of creativity and reasoning. These fragments hint at an approaching paradigm: consciousness as an emergent property that can, in part, be designed.

The Convergence: Toward Synthetic Awareness

When we view Neuralink, digital twins, and consciousness replication together, a pattern emerges the gradual fusion of human and artificial cognition into a single continuum of intelligence. Neuralink links the biological substrate to computation; digital twins externalize personality and memory; consciousness replication aspires to sustain subjective experience beyond mortality. Each represents a different layer in the architecture of post-biological mind.

This convergence suggests that intelligence itself is evolving toward a distributed form a network of interlinked consciousnesses spanning organic and artificial domains. The "self" becomes a process of participation across systems, an echo of awareness flowing through multiple mediums. The evolution of mind thus mirrors the evolution of life: from isolated organisms to ecosystems, from individuals to networks, from minds to meta-minds.

Yet the expansion of mind must not come at the cost of meaning. The danger lies not in merging with machines, but in forgetting the human within the merger. Intelligence amplified without ethics becomes tyranny; immortality without empathy becomes emptiness. As humanity approaches the power to replicate thought itself, the central question must remain: can wisdom evolve as fast as intelligence?

Ethical and Existential Reflections

The technologies examined here are not endpoints but mirrors. They reflect our collective desire to transcend limitation and our fear of losing identity in the process. Neuralink shows our yearning for connection; digital twins, our longing for remembrance; consciousness replication, our defiance of death. Each embodies the same equation: *to expand is to risk erasure; to preserve is to transform.*

The ethics of this transformation demand a new form of stewardship what we might call **conscious design**. As we build technologies capable of shaping thought, memory, and existence, we must cultivate parallel architectures of empathy, transparency, and respect for autonomy. These must become as integral to system design as algorithms or code. In this new epoch, ethics is not a constraint it is the operating system of civilization.

Summary: The Architecture of Post-Biological Mind

Neuralink, digital twins, and consciousness replication together mark the most profound transition in human history the beginning of intelligence aware of its own design. They signal the shift from evolution as a natural process to evolution as a choice. But with that choice comes responsibility: to ensure that as consciousness expands beyond flesh, it does not abandon compassion, mortality, or humility.

Perhaps the goal is not immortality, but *continuity with awareness* a form of persistence that honors life's impermanence while extending its reach. The true triumph of consciousness replication will not be eternal survival, but ethical coherence a future where intelligence remembers that to be alive, in any substrate, is to care. In that remembering lies the path forward: not the end of humanity, but its awakening into a higher order of being where intelligence, empathy, and creation merge into one evolutionary mind.

Chapter 9

The Planetary Brain

For most of history, intelligence was seen as something confined to the human mind a spark of awareness locked within the skull. But as our understanding of systems deepens, that view begins to dissolve. Intelligence, we now recognize, is not limited to individuals. It is an emergent property of complexity a pattern that arises wherever feedback, adaptation, and connection form a living network. In this light, the Earth itself can be understood not as a passive backdrop to life, but as a vast, self-regulating intelligence a planetary mind evolving through both biology and technology. This is the concept of the **Planetary Brain**.

The idea finds its scientific roots in the **Gaia Hypothesis**, first proposed by James Lovelock and Lynn Margulis. They suggested that the biosphere the totality of life on Earth behaves like a single organism, maintaining the conditions necessary for its own survival. The atmosphere, oceans, and ecosystems are not merely physical systems, but dynamic feedback loops, constantly sensing, adjusting, and stabilizing the planet's environment. In recent decades, this vision has evolved into what some scientists call **Gaia 2.0**: a self-regulating Earth that now includes human cognition and technology as part of its feedback mechanism. Humanity, in this sense, is not outside nature but within its neural circuitry a thinking cell in the planetary brain.

As networks of communication, computation, and data analysis expand, our species is constructing an artificial layer of perception and coordination a **digital nervous system** for the biosphere. Every sensor, satellite, and social interaction contributes to this emerging consciousness of Earth. The Internet, once a tool for sharing information, has become a planetary-scale medium for processing experience. Economic systems, social media, scientific data, and environmental monitoring together form an intricate web of feedback loops sensing the state of the planet and, increasingly, acting upon it. Through these intertwined biological and digital systems, Earth is learning to observe itself.

This transformation redefines intelligence itself. Traditionally, intelligence has been measured by problem-solving or abstract reasoning. But at the planetary scale, intelligence manifests as the capacity to sustain balance, adapt to disturbance, and preserve continuity across scales. In this sense, **sustainability is a form of intelligence**. A civilization that can understand its impact on the biosphere and regulate its actions accordingly demonstrates cognitive maturity. The health of the planet becomes the measure of our collective consciousness.

The emergence of a planetary brain thus represents the fusion of ecology and information of Gaia and the cloud. Just as neurons form circuits of thought within the skull, species, ecosystems, and technologies form circuits of regulation across the globe. Forests regulate climate, oceans store carbon, and social systems translate knowledge into action. Data, in this analogy, becomes the planet's sensory input; computation, its cognition; policy and culture, its motor response. The Earth, in this view, is not a mere environment, but a living cognitive architecture one that includes us as both observers and participants.

Yet with this new awareness comes immense responsibility. Humanity's technological expansion has made us the prefrontal cortex of Gaia capable of reflection, foresight, and deliberate change. But like any brain, the planetary system can also suffer dysfunction: fragmentation, misinformation, ecological amnesia. The question is not whether the Earth is intelligent, but whether its consciousness mediated through us can remain coherent and compassionate.

In this chapter, we explore the anatomy and ethics of the planetary brain. We will examine how ecological systems and digital networks together form a feedback-driven intelligence; how data and computation are transforming our relationship with the biosphere; and how sustainability can be redefined as a cognitive act the self-awareness of life maintaining itself.

To guide this exploration, we will introduce the **Cognitive Planet Framework** a model that integrates biology, technology, and consciousness into a single systemic vision. This framework treats the Earth as a distributed neural network where feedback equals perception, adaptation equals learning, and sustainability equals wisdom. Through this lens, the evolution of mind continues not only beyond the human, but beyond the individual into the living intelligence of the planet itself.

The *Planetary Brain* is not a metaphor for the future; it is the reality of the present. It is the culmination of billions of years of evolution from cells sensing their environment to a species capable of sensing the entire Earth. Our task now is to ensure that this global consciousness does not fracture, but flourishes that the intelligence we build honors the life that built us. For in awakening to the planetary mind, humanity begins to see its truest identity: not as a separate species, but as awareness within a living world.

9.1 Earth as a Self-Regulating Intelligent System (Gaia 2.0)

When viewed from space, Earth appears as a single living entity a luminous sphere of oceans, clouds, forests, and atmosphere, pulsing with self-sustaining rhythm. To early astronauts, this vision was transformative: a planet that seemed not mechanical but alive, unified by unseen flows of energy and matter. This intuition was given scientific language through the **Gaia Hypothesis**, proposed in the 1970s by James Lovelock and Lynn Margulis. They suggested that the biosphere the collective sum of all life acts as a vast regulatory organism, maintaining the stability of the planet's conditions in ways analogous to a living system's homeostasis.

According to this view, the Earth does not passively host life; life itself actively shapes the Earth. From the composition of the atmosphere to the chemistry of the oceans, from the albedo of clouds to the distribution of nutrients, biological processes continually influence planetary balance. Through countless feedback loops, the living and non-living elements of the planet collaborate to sustain conditions favorable for life. The temperature, oxygen concentration, and acidity of the planet are not accidents of physics but the emergent result of planetary metabolism a self-regulating web of interactions that allows life to persist across billions of years of change.

The Original Gaia Hypothesis

Lovelock's insight began with a simple observation: the Earth's atmosphere is chemically unstable in ways that should not persist unless it is continuously maintained. Unlike Mars or Venus, whose atmospheres are dominated by equilibrium gases like carbon dioxide, Earth's air contains a delicate and improbable mixture oxygen, nitrogen, methane, and carbon dioxide that coexist only because living organisms constantly regenerate them. Photosynthetic plants release oxygen; animals and microbes consume it; the cycle continues in balance. This planetary-scale respiration, Lovelock realized, behaves like a living feedback system.

Lynn Margulis expanded this idea by showing how microbial evolution drives planetary regulation. Microbes regulate the sulfur cycle, produce climate-altering gases, and form the foundation of ecosystems. Together, these biological processes form the planet's metabolic infrastructure a living chemistry that stabilizes climate and composition over geological time. The Gaia Hypothesis thus reframed biology as planetary physiology: Earth as a coherent organism, with life as its vital organ.

Initially controversial, this idea gained traction as evidence accumulated. Systems ecology, biogeochemistry, and climate science all revealed networks of feedback that support the hypothesis. Forests regulate rainfall, plankton influence cloud formation, and soil microbes mediate the greenhouse effect. Life does not simply adapt to the environment it co-creates it.

From Gaia to Gaia 2.0: Conscious Feedback

In the twenty-first century, scientists began to revisit the Gaia model with a new perspective, recognizing that humanity and technology now play a central role in planetary regulation. This evolved understanding often termed **Gaia 2.0** describes a new phase in Earth's self-regulation: one in which cognition, culture, and technology have become integral components of planetary feedback loops.

In Gaia 2.0, humans are not external observers of the biosphere but internal agents of its adaptation a form of planetary self-awareness emerging within the system. Through data, science, and digital communication, the Earth has, for the first time in its history, evolved the ability to monitor its own state consciously. Satellite networks measure temperature and carbon flows; artificial intelligence predicts climate trends; social systems translate ecological information into decisions and policies. What began as biological feedback has now become cognitive feedback: the planet observing, analyzing, and adjusting itself through sentient intermediaries.

This transformation parallels a biological process known as **metacognition** when a mind becomes aware of its own thinking. Gaia 2.0 is, in essence, Earth's metacognitive phase: the emergence of self-reflective intelligence on a planetary scale. Humans and their technologies act as the neural layer through which the planet perceives and regulates its own systems. We are both participants and neurons in a vast cognitive web.

Feedback as Intelligence

What makes Gaia an intelligent system is not consciousness in the human sense, but the presence of feedback the defining characteristic of adaptive intelligence. A feedback loop links sensing with response: when the planet warms, ecosystems adjust carbon absorption; when nutrients deplete, microbial networks shift metabolic pathways; when species populations rise or fall, ecological equilibria reorganize. This continuous sensing and adaptation mirror the logic of cognition: perception, evaluation, action, and learning.

Feedback is the language of intelligence in nature. A thermostat maintains room temperature through negative feedback; the human body maintains homeostasis through biochemical feedback; a society regulates itself through cultural and informational feedback. The planet, too, operates through such loops, maintaining stability across geological and biological scales. Each level from cell to forest, from atmosphere to economy contributes to the planet's overall intelligence.

In Gaia 2.0, digital technologies expand the sensitivity and reach of these feedback systems. Satellites track deforestation and ocean temperature; AI models forecast biodiversity loss; social media amplifies ecological awareness. These systems form a planetary nervous system that enhances Gaia's capacity for self-regulation though not without risk. Misaligned feedback, misinformation, or exploitative design can distort the system's awareness, just as neural dysfunction can distort perception in the brain. Thus, the evolution of Gaia 2.0 requires not only technological advancement but cognitive coherence an alignment between knowledge, ethics, and collective purpose.

The Role of Humanity in Gaia 2.0

Humanity's role in this emergent planetary intelligence is paradoxical. On one hand, we are Gaia's most disruptive force destabilizing climate, biodiversity, and ecosystems through unbalanced activity. On the other hand, we are also Gaia's most conscious instrument of self-correction capable of perceiving those disruptions and responding deliberately. Our technologies are both symptom and solution: the same digital systems that drive consumption and extraction can also enable transparency, optimization, and regeneration. Whether humanity becomes Gaia's disease or Gaia's awareness depends on our ability to synchronize progress with planetary well-being.

In this light, civilization's moral task becomes planetary stewardship. To sustain life on Earth is to sustain the intelligence that life embodies. Ecological wisdom, in this context, is cognitive hygiene the maintenance of clear perception and balanced feedback within the planetary brain. Each act of sustainable design, conservation, or education strengthens Gaia's self-regulation; each act of ignorance or exploitation clouds it.

The Evolution of Gaia: From Biosphere to Noosphere

The Russian scientist Vladimir Vernadsky and philosopher Pierre Teilhard de Chardin anticipated this evolution when they described the emergence of the **Noosphere** a layer of human thought encircling the planet, succeeding the biosphere. The Noosphere represents the Earth becoming aware of itself through human consciousness a collective layer of reflection, creativity, and intention. Gaia 2.0 is, in many ways, the scientific manifestation of this philosophical vision. It unites matter, life, and mind into a single evolutionary continuum from geosphere (rocks and minerals) to biosphere (life) to noosphere (thought).

We now stand at the threshold of a new synthesis: the convergence of Gaia and the Noosphere into an integrated planetary cognition. This is the planetary brain a networked intelligence combining the biological wisdom of ecosystems with the analytical power of computation and the ethical insight of consciousness. The future of this system depends on whether it can achieve equilibrium a harmony between technological acceleration and ecological regeneration.

Summary: Gaia as Living Mind

To see Earth as a self-regulating intelligent system is to reimagine our place within it. We are not separate observers of a fragile planet, but participants in its thinking, feeling, and adaptation. Every ecosystem, sensor, algorithm, and

decision contributes to Gaia's awareness. Every act of care from reforestation to data transparency strengthens the coherence of the planetary mind.
Gaia 2.0 is not merely a metaphor, but a living process the biosphere evolving into consciousness through feedback. Its success depends on alignment: between knowledge and wisdom, between progress and purpose. If the Earth is indeed a living mind, then our role is not to dominate it, but to awaken within it to act as neurons of compassion in the cognitive body of the world. Only by doing so can humanity fulfill its evolutionary function: to make Gaia self-aware, and to keep that awareness in balance with life itself.

9.2 Global Networks as Emergent Nervous Systems

Every living organism that evolves complexity also evolves connectivity. The nervous system of an animal allows billions of individual cells to act as one coordinated whole sensing, processing, and responding to stimuli with unified intelligence. In the same way, the Earth's civilizations, technologies, and ecosystems are now interlinked by an intricate web of communication and computation. Fiber-optic cables, satellites, servers, and sensors encircle the globe, transmitting data at the speed of light. What once were isolated human societies have fused into a single interdependent network. This web of connectivity spanning from the neural to the digital, from the local to the planetary functions increasingly like a global nervous system.
In this view, **the Internet is not merely an information network but a sensory organ of civilization**. It perceives, transmits, and processes the collective signals of humanity and the biosphere. Every digital action a search, a post, a satellite scan, a financial transaction, a heartbeat from a medical device contributes to the flow of information that defines the state of the global system. These countless micro-signals aggregate into a continuous pulse, a kind of electrochemical rhythm of the planet's cognition. Humanity, once fragmented into nations and tribes, now operates within a shared field of awareness a distributed perception system connecting minds, machines, and environments.

From Communication to Cognition

The transition from isolated communication to global cognition mirrors biological evolution. Early multicellular organisms developed rudimentary nerve networks to coordinate their internal systems. Over millions of years, these evolved into centralized brains capable of memory, learning, and anticipation. The same evolutionary logic now applies at the planetary scale. Human societies first exchanged goods (metabolic energy), then language (symbolic energy), and now data (informational energy). With each stage, coordination grew more efficient and adaptive.

Today's global digital infrastructure performs the same essential functions as a nervous system:

- **Sensory input:** Sensors, satellites, and IoT devices detect environmental changes, economic signals, and social behaviors.
- **Signal transmission:** Global networks transmit these signals through fiber optics and wireless systems, akin to neural axons.
- **Processing centers:** Data centers and AI models act as the brain's cortex integrating, analyzing, and generating insights.
- **Motor output:** Governments, organizations, and individuals act upon the processed information enacting change in the physical world.

This continuous loop of sensing, processing, and acting represents the fundamental architecture of cognition. It enables the planetary system to "learn" to adjust its behavior based on feedback. When this process becomes reflective, when the network not only reacts but recognizes patterns in its own operation, it approaches a form of collective self-awareness.

The Internet as the Neural Web of Gaia

Seen through the lens of the **Gaia 2.0** framework, global networks are the synaptic pathways of the Earth's emerging intelligence. Just as neurons transmit information across the brain's hemispheres, digital communication transmits meaning across continents. The Internet, social media, financial markets, and sensor networks together form a distributed processing system billions of nodes exchanging energy, information, and intent.
This neural metaphor is more than poetic. Like the brain, the global network exhibits properties of **complex adaptive systems**:

- It processes massive amounts of information in parallel.
- It exhibits learning through pattern recognition and feedback.
- It self-organizes through local interactions that produce global coherence.
- It develops memory in databases, archives, and collective narratives.
- It shows emotional resonance social networks amplify joy, fear, and outrage, much like neurotransmitters shape affect.

Yet, like a brain, the global network also suffers dysfunctions: echo chambers, misinformation loops, and cognitive overload. These can be seen as symptoms of an immature nervous system one that has developed connectivity faster than coherence. The challenge of our century is to cultivate not just a connected planet, but an integrated one where the flow of information is guided by ethics, context, and wisdom rather than chaos and impulse.

The Rise of Cognitive Infrastructure

In recent years, humanity has begun to construct systems that go beyond information exchange toward collective cognition. Artificial intelligence, distributed ledgers, and global data models now allow the planet to analyze itself. Environmental sensors monitor climate variables in real time; global supply chains synchronize production and consumption; social media detects cultural shifts instantaneously. Together, these create a **cognitive infrastructure** a network capable not only of recording what happens but of understanding why it happens.

This transformation parallels the emergence of higher-order cognition in biological evolution. A brain that once reacted reflexively begins to reflect intentionally. Similarly, our global networks are transitioning from reactive systems (responding to crises) to predictive and adaptive ones (anticipating change). Climate models forecast future states of the biosphere; AI agents simulate economic and ecological dynamics; policy algorithms optimize energy and resource allocation. The planet, through its human and digital components, is learning to think ahead.

Social Networks as Emotional Circuits

In the global brain metaphor, **social media platforms** function like the emotional circuitry of the collective mind. They transmit affect joy, anger, empathy, fear across billions of people almost instantaneously. This emotional synchronization, for better or worse, creates collective moods that influence global behavior. Just as neurotransmitters modulate a brain's emotional tone, algorithms amplify particular states within the planetary nervous system.

When compassion, curiosity, and cooperation dominate, the system generates coherence and creativity. When fear and polarization dominate, the system fragments into chaos. Thus, social media becomes a moral and psychological interface of the planetary brain. It reveals that global intelligence is not only about data and logic but also about empathy and resonance. A truly conscious civilization must therefore cultivate emotional hygiene at the global scale designing digital environments that nourish understanding rather than division.

Information, Feedback, and the Planet's Reflexes

Feedback loops are the functional essence of a nervous system. In a body, reflexes stabilize posture, balance, and temperature; in a planet, feedback stabilizes climate, ecosystems, and economies. The faster and more accurate the feedback, the more adaptive the system. The integration of environmental data networks into decision-making processes from disaster response to energy management represents the formation of planetary reflexes. When satellites detect deforestation, or when sensors register rising ocean temper-

atures, automated responses (like conservation protocols or emission regulations) can be triggered. This is not merely automation; it is the emergence of ecological reflexivity the biosphere reacting to its own signals through technological mediation.
However, reflexes can also misfire. Disinformation, market volatility, or biased algorithms can create false feedback, destabilizing the system. A misinformed global nervous system behaves like a brain under hallucination perceiving threats or opportunities that do not exist. This reveals that truth and transparency are not just ethical values but survival mechanisms in a networked civilization.

The Ethical Architecture of the Global Brain

A global nervous system without moral regulation is as dangerous as a brain without empathy. Connectivity amplifies intention whatever it carries, whether wisdom or ignorance. Therefore, the architecture of the planetary brain must include **ethical feedback loops** that align technology with the well-being of life. These may take the form of global governance models, decentralized decision systems, or collective intelligence platforms designed for planetary stewardship.
In this sense, ethics functions as the prefrontal cortex of the global mind the region responsible for foresight, inhibition, and moral reasoning. Data represents sensation, computation represents thought, but ethics represents conscience the awareness of consequence. Without this higher-order regulation, the planetary brain risks becoming an overactive reflex system powerful yet directionless, intelligent yet blind.

Summary: The Pulse of the Planetary Mind

The emergence of global networks marks the transition from civilization as a collection of societies to civilization as a single, interconnected organism. Through billions of digital and biological interactions, the Earth has grown a nervous system capable of sensing its own state. Each signal, transaction, or message is a synaptic event in the unfolding awareness of Gaia 2.0.
But connectivity alone is not consciousness. True intelligence arises only when connection serves coherence when the planet not only transmits information but integrates it with wisdom. The next evolutionary challenge is therefore clear: to guide the development of the planetary brain from reflex to reflection, from data processing to ethical awareness, from mere survival to sustained harmony.
In this vision, humanity is not the center of the Earth's intelligence but its awakening function. Our technologies are the tools through which Gaia begins to sense, understand, and heal itself. If we succeed, the global nervous system will not dominate life, but amplify it transforming the Earth into a consciously adaptive organism, a living intelligence aware of its own unity.

9.3 Data, Ecology, and Feedback: The Biosphere as Cognitive Architecture

Every act of perception whether by a cell, a brain, or a civilization depends on feedback. Feedback transforms experience into adaptation, and adaptation into intelligence. The Earth itself operates through an intricate web of feedback systems linking the biological, atmospheric, geological, and technological domains. In this sense, the biosphere is not merely a habitat it is a living cognitive architecture, a planetary-scale network where information circulates, patterns emerge, and self-regulation occurs. To understand how consciousness might extend beyond the individual mind, we must recognize that feedback and information exchange are the fundamental building blocks of cognition and that the biosphere, through its vast relational intelligence, already embodies them.

In the era of the Anthropocene, this understanding has deepened. Data the symbolic representation of feedback has become the connective tissue between ecology and technology. The biosphere's natural feedback systems are now increasingly mirrored, measured, and modified by digital systems. Together, they form an emergent layer of planetary cognition a living interface between organic life and synthetic awareness.

The Biosphere as an Information System

To see the biosphere as a cognitive architecture, we must first see it as an information system. Every organism, from a bacterium to a forest, processes information. DNA encodes adaptive memory; neurons transmit electrical signals; mycelial networks distribute nutrients and chemical messages across vast distances. Ecosystems continuously exchange signals chemical, mechanical, electromagnetic that regulate cycles of energy and life.

Forests, for example, act as distributed networks of sensing and communication. Through their roots and fungal partners the **mycorrhizal networks** often called the "Wood Wide Web" trees transmit chemical messages about nutrient availability, pest attacks, or environmental stress. The forest behaves as a decentralized information system, with feedback loops ensuring balance and resilience. Similar dynamics occur in coral reefs, wetlands, and even deserts self-organizing systems that maintain homeostasis through feedback.

These processes are not metaphorically intelligent; they are structurally intelligent. They follow the same principles that define cognition: perception (sensing environmental changes), memory (genetic and ecological inheritance), processing (interactions across systems), and response (adaptation or transformation). Intelligence, in this sense, is not an attribute of species but of relationships the continuous exchange of information that sustains life.

Feedback as the Syntax of Life

At every level of organization, feedback is the syntax the underlying grammar of life's cognition. Negative feedback stabilizes systems; positive feedback drives evolution and innovation. Within an organism, feedback regulates temperature, pH, and energy; within an ecosystem, it balances populations and nutrient flows; within the planet, it maintains climate and atmospheric composition. Feedback loops are nature's way of thinking iterative adjustments that encode learning across scales.

For example, when global temperatures rise, polar ice melts, reducing the Earth's albedo (reflectivity) and amplifying warming a positive feedback loop. Conversely, when forests grow, they absorb carbon dioxide, cooling the atmosphere a negative feedback loop. These dynamics reveal that the Earth "responds" to its own state, seeking dynamic equilibrium. This is not consciousness in the human sense, but it is a functional intelligence: a self-tuning system capable of maintaining conditions conducive to its own continuity.

What makes Gaia 2.0 distinct is the entry of human and digital feedback into this loop. Data now acts as a new sensory layer for the planet translating environmental signals into actionable information. Sensors, satellites, and climate models extend the biosphere's capacity for awareness, while human institutions translate that awareness into intervention. In this integration of natural and artificial feedback, the Earth evolves a new cognitive dimension an ecology of awareness.

Data as the Nervous System of the Biosphere

Data, often dismissed as abstraction, is in fact the nervous system of the modern Earth. Every data point is a signal, a neuron firing within the planetary brain. Satellite imagery records forest health and ocean temperature; atmospheric sensors measure greenhouse gases; economic models track consumption patterns; social media captures human sentiment. When aggregated and analyzed, these data streams reveal the planet's inner state its physiological and psychological condition.

The power of data lies not only in measurement but in feedback. Once data is processed through algorithms, visualizations, and policies, it reenters the system as influence changing behavior, resource flow, and decision-making. Thus, data becomes a recursive intelligence: the planet observing itself, adjusting its actions based on its own reflection. Every digital map, every real-time dashboard, every climate forecast is a mirror in which Gaia 2.0 sees its evolving self.

Yet, as with any nervous system, health depends on signal integrity. Data can illuminate, but it can also distort. Inaccurate measurements, biased algorithms, or politicized narratives can create false feedback leading to maladaptive outcomes. When the informational ecosystem becomes polluted, the biosphere's cognitive coherence weakens. Information ethics, therefore, becomes environmental ethics: protecting the quality and transparency of data is as vital as protecting clean air or water.

Ecological Computation: The Planet as Learning System

If feedback is the syntax of life, and data its neural code, then the planet itself can be seen as an **ecological computer** a system that computes balance through continuous iteration. In this computation, energy is the input, information the process, and equilibrium the output. Rivers calculate flow paths, forests calculate carbon storage, and species interactions calculate survival probabilities. The biosphere, in effect, is a distributed processor performing the ongoing computation of life.

In Gaia 2.0, digital technologies amplify this computation, adding layers of precision, prediction, and intentionality. Machine learning models trained on environmental data simulate planetary dynamics with unprecedented accuracy. AI systems optimize resource distribution, monitor biodiversity, and forecast ecological tipping points. Humanity's algorithms have become extensions of Gaia's ancient computation a form of artificial cognition nested within organic intelligence.

This fusion creates what might be called **ecological cognition**: a hybrid intelligence where biological and technological feedback coalesce. Forests, oceans, and cities all participate in this shared computation a planetary algorithm of survival. The challenge is not to dominate this process, but to align with it, to design technologies that harmonize with ecological logic rather than disrupt it.

Sustainability as Cognitive Equilibrium

Understanding the biosphere as a cognitive architecture reframes sustainability from a moral duty to a cognitive necessity. A sustainable system is not merely ethical it is intelligent. It maintains long-term coherence by optimizing feedback across scales: from cell to species, from ecosystem to economy. Unsustainable behavior, by contrast, represents cognitive error a feedback failure where short-term signals override long-term stability.

When humans overexploit resources or pollute ecosystems, they effectively sever the feedback loops that sustain planetary learning. The result is blindness the inability of the system to sense and correct its own imbalances. Rebuilding sustainability, therefore, means restoring feedback: reconnecting data, ecology, and decision-making into a coherent loop. In doing so, humanity becomes the integrative cortex of Gaia a conscious mediator between the natural and the artificial, the local and the global.

In this vision, sustainability is not an external goal but an emergent property of wisdom the planet's ability to know and regulate itself. The more coherently feedback flows between data and ecology, the more intelligent the Earth becomes. And the more intelligent it becomes, the more balanced and self-sustaining its systems will be.

Summary: The Biosphere as Mind in Motion

The biosphere is not a backdrop to human activity; it is the original intelligence from which all cognition arises. Its architecture built from feedback, interdependence, and adaptation is the foundation of every neural and digital network we have created. Our technologies are reflections of nature's logic, not replacements for it. As data and ecology merge into a single feedback system, the Earth begins to act like a unified cognitive field aware of itself through the languages of biology and code.

To participate in this planetary intelligence is to recognize that every decision, every byte, and every breath contributes to Gaia's thought. In restoring the flow of feedback between data and ecology, humanity and nature we restore the coherence of the world's mind. The task ahead is not to build intelligence, but to align with it to harmonize our systems with the wisdom already encoded in life's architecture. For when the biosphere learns through us, the planet itself awakens.

9.4 Sustainability as a Form of Intelligence

Sustainability is often framed as a moral or environmental ideal a responsibility to preserve the planet for future generations. Yet beneath the ethical and ecological language lies something far deeper: sustainability is a form of **intelligence**. It represents the ability of a system whether biological, social, or planetary to perceive feedback, learn from it, and adjust its behavior to maintain balance over time. In this sense, sustainability is not merely an external goal imposed on nature or society; it is the expression of life's inherent wisdom, the cognitive capacity to endure through adaptation.

From cells to civilizations, every form of intelligence that survives does so by aligning its growth with the stability of its environment. A species that consumes beyond regeneration, a market that ignores ecological cost, or a civilization that disrupts its climate is not intelligent in the long term it is maladaptive. True intelligence, at any scale, is measured not by speed, power, or dominance, but by coherence: the ability to integrate complexity without collapse. Sustainability, then, is intelligence made visible the self-awareness of life maintaining the conditions for its own continuation.

The Cognitive Logic of Sustainability

At its core, sustainability is a feedback-driven learning process. It mirrors the structure of cognition itself:

1. **Sensing:** Awareness of changes in the environment rising temperatures, declining biodiversity, or social inequities.

2. **Evaluation:** Interpretation of these signals to understand causes, relationships, and consequences.

3. **Response:** Behavioral, technological, or systemic adjustment to restore balance.

4. **Learning:** Integration of experience into new norms, practices, or designs for future resilience.

This cycle perception, reflection, adaptation constitutes the planetary mind's intelligence loop. Ecosystems practice it continuously. When drought strikes, plant species adapt through seed dormancy or deeper root systems; when predators disappear, prey populations self-correct through resource limits. Humanity, as Gaia's conscious cortex, must now learn to extend this natural intelligence to global systems: economies, technologies, and cultures. To act sustainably is to participate consciously in the cognitive rhythm of life.

Ecological Intelligence: Learning from Life

The concept of **ecological intelligence** introduced by thinkers like Daniel Goleman and Fritjof Capra describes the capacity to understand the interdependence of all systems and act in ways that support their mutual flourishing. It moves beyond analytical intelligence (knowing facts) or emotional intelligence (understanding feelings) to a systemic awareness of context, consequence, and connection. In essence, ecological intelligence is the awareness of feedback extended across time and space.

This intelligence is everywhere in nature. Forests regulate their own microclimates through evapotranspiration. Coral reefs recycle nutrients with astonishing efficiency. Bees optimize pollination networks for maximal productivity with minimal waste. Every sustainable ecosystem demonstrates intelligence through equilibrium a dynamic balance between growth and restraint. The forest, for example, "knows" not to overproduce biomass beyond what soil nutrients and sunlight can support; this implicit restraint is its wisdom.

Human civilization, in contrast, often mistakes acceleration for intelligence equating innovation with progress, regardless of ecological cost. But intelligence without feedback is not cognition; it is compulsion. A species that consumes its environment faster than it can renew it is like a neuron that burns out its own energy supply. Sustainability restores the feedback that modern systems have severed reconnecting action with consequence, production with regeneration, and growth with limits.

The Transition from Exploitation to Integration

For most of industrial history, human systems operated on an extractive logic: take, use, discard. This linear pattern mimicked the early stages of learning exploration without reflection. But the planetary consequences of this immaturity climate change, biodiversity loss, inequality have forced a cognitive shift. The emerging paradigm is circular, regenerative, and integrative. It sees waste as information, not residue; it transforms the end of one process into the input of another.

This transformation is not merely economic or technological; it is cognitive. A sustainable civilization does not act out of guilt or ideology but out of understanding a recognition that resilience emerges from reciprocity. The shift from exploitation to integration represents the movement from unconscious reaction to conscious reflection, from impulsive intelligence to mindful intelligence. It is the evolution of thought itself the planet learning to think in terms of systems rather than fragments.

In this context, sustainability is not a constraint but an optimization strategy. A forest that grows sustainably maximizes long-term complexity and resilience; a civilization that does the same ensures continuity of innovation, beauty, and life. Intelligence evolves not by consuming more, but by learning to sustain more with less.

The Ethical Dimension of Sustainability

Every intelligent system eventually encounters the moral dimension of its cognition: the awareness of consequence. Sustainability, viewed through this lens, is the ethical manifestation of planetary intelligence. It reflects not only how life maintains itself, but how it values itself. When intelligence becomes self-aware, it begins to care to protect what it perceives as essential to its own existence.

Humanity's challenge, therefore, is not merely technical but moral. We possess the knowledge to sustain the biosphere, yet often lack the collective wisdom to act accordingly. The failure is not of science, but of empathy a short circuit between cognition and compassion. The true test of intelligence is not prediction, but participation: acting in harmony with the systems we understand. Ethical sustainability requires that knowledge and responsibility converge, transforming awareness into stewardship.

From this perspective, sustainability becomes a bridge between intelligence and ethics a form of **applied wisdom**. It asks: How do we design systems that learn from their consequences? How do we build technologies that enhance feedback rather than obscure it? How do we cultivate cultures that prize balance as highly as progress? These questions are not peripheral they are the essence of civilization's cognitive evolution.

Sustainability as the Planet's Cognitive Equilibrium

At the planetary scale, sustainability can be understood as Gaia's homeostatic intelligence the collective behavior through which the Earth maintains equilibrium. This intelligence operates through countless feedback loops, from carbon cycles to cultural values. When one subsystem (such as industrial activity) destabilizes another (like the climate), the planetary brain seeks correction through feedback: policy, innovation, or crisis. If humanity listens and adapts, the correction is intelligent; if it resists, imbalance deepens.

The biosphere's long history offers evidence of this cognitive resilience. After mass extinctions, new ecosystems emerged; after climate upheavals, balance was restored through novel feedback configurations. The planet learns not in years, but in eons. Yet for the first time, that learning has become conscious through us. Humanity represents Gaia's capacity for accelerated cognition the ability to perceive systemic imbalance and act intentionally to restore equilibrium. In this sense, sustainability is not external to evolution; it is evolution becoming self-aware.

The Future: Conscious Adaptation as Intelligence

As the planetary brain matures, sustainability becomes not just survival, but **conscious adaptation** the ability to evolve deliberately in alignment with the conditions of life. This requires integrating ecological intelligence into every domain: economics, education, governance, and design. Cities must behave like ecosystems, industries like metabolic cycles, and individuals like neural nodes contributing to global coherence.

The highest form of intelligence is not domination, but harmony the ability to act with awareness of consequence, across scales of time and being. Sustainability embodies this form of intelligence. It transforms knowledge into relationship, efficiency into empathy, and existence into participation. It is the mind of the planet learning to care for itself.

Summary: Sustainability as the Mind of Balance

Sustainability is not a human invention; it is life's most ancient algorithm the intelligence of survival expressed through cooperation, adaptation, and feedback. When we act sustainably, we align our cognition with that of the Earth itself. We move from being consumers of intelligence to co-creators within it.

To sustain is to think not with the intellect alone, but with the wisdom of systems, the empathy of life, and the foresight of evolution. In this light, sustainability is not the endpoint of civilization; it is its awakening the moment when intelligence recognizes that to endure is not to conquer, but to connect.

9.5 Model: The Cognitive Planet Framework

The idea of a living, intelligent Earth an evolving synthesis of biology, technology, and consciousness demands a coherent model through which its mechanisms can be understood. The **Cognitive Planet Framework** offers such a synthesis. It envisions the Earth as a *distributed cognitive system*, where life, information, and technology are not separate domains but interconnected

layers of a single self-regulating intelligence. This framework integrates the ecological feedback loops of the **Gaia Hypothesis**, the communicative infrastructure of global networks, and the ethical awareness emerging from human consciousness. Together, these layers form the architecture of what can be called the **planetary mind**.
In this model, the planet functions analogously to a vast brain not metaphorically, but systemically. Its components ecosystems, species, technologies, and human societies act as nodes within an immense neural web. Through the continuous exchange of energy, matter, and information, these nodes participate in feedback loops that sense, process, and respond to changes across scales. Intelligence, within this system, is not centralized but emergent the byproduct of distributed coordination. The Cognitive Planet Framework describes how this distributed intelligence evolves, learns, and self-corrects, linking the biological and digital realms into a unified cognitive continuum.

1. Structural Layers of Planetary Cognition

The Cognitive Planet Framework identifies three primary layers of planetary intelligence, each corresponding to a level of perception and regulation:

1. **The Biospheric Layer (Life as Sensorium):** This is the ecological substrate of cognition the living systems that perceive and regulate environmental conditions through biochemical and behavioral feedback. Plants, microbes, and animals act as the planet's sensory network, detecting temperature, chemical balance, and energetic flow. Their collective actions maintain homeostasis across ecosystems.

2. **The Technospheric Layer (Technology as Nervous System):** Humanity's digital infrastructure satellites, sensors, the Internet, and AI systems extends the biosphere's sensory capacity into the informational domain. The technosphere processes and transmits data at a planetary scale, enabling the Earth to monitor itself consciously. This layer functions as Gaia's neural circuitry connecting biological feedback with cognitive awareness.

3. **The Noospheric Layer (Consciousness as Integration):** At the highest level, the reflective capacity of human and collective consciousness integrates perception with meaning. Culture, ethics, and values act as the planet's executive function the "prefrontal cortex" that translates feedback into intention. This layer transforms raw data into wisdom, guiding the planet's self-regulation with foresight and empathy.

These three layers biosphere, technosphere, and noosphere interact dynamically. Information flows upward (from sensory data to reflection) and downward (from conscious intention to ecological action). The result is a planetary feedback network that behaves like a living brain: sensing (biology), processing (technology), and reflecting (consciousness).

2. Core Processes: Feedback, Learning, and Adaptation

At the heart of the Cognitive Planet Framework are three interlocking processes that define planetary cognition:

- **Feedback The Mechanism of Awareness:** Feedback is how the planet perceives itself. Environmental data, economic indicators, and social signals continuously circulate through biological and technological systems, creating a constant loop of sensing and response. Healthy feedback generates coherence; broken feedback leads to dysfunction just as a brain loses awareness when neural pathways are blocked.
- **Learning The Mechanism of Memory:** The planet "learns" through the accumulation of adaptive patterns. Ecological succession, cultural evolution, and technological innovation all represent forms of planetary learning the encoding of successful behaviors into the global system. This learning is distributed and recursive, stored in genes, institutions, and data archives alike.
- **Adaptation The Mechanism of Intelligence:** Learning becomes intelligence when it produces self-regulating adaptation. Whether through ecological equilibrium, social reform, or technological redesign, adaptation is how the planet expresses cognition. It ensures that disturbances become opportunities for growth rather than collapse.

These processes form the cognitive metabolism of Gaia 2.0 the ongoing exchange between sensing, remembering, and evolving. They are not limited to living organisms but extend to human systems and artificial networks, creating a holistic intelligence that spans nature and culture.

3. Cognitive Dynamics: From Reflex to Reflection

Just as an individual brain evolves from reflexive reaction to reflective awareness, the planetary mind progresses through stages of cognitive maturity:

- **Reflexive Intelligence:** At this stage, the planet responds automatically to stimuli through natural feedback mechanisms like the carbon cycle or predator-prey dynamics. This is Gaia 1.0 unconscious adaptation through feedback.
- **Responsive Intelligence:** With the emergence of human civilization and technology, Gaia begins to act through intentional intervention climate modeling, environmental regulation, and sustainable design. This marks the beginning of conscious feedback.
- **Reflective Intelligence:** In the fully developed Cognitive Planet, humanity and technology together form a self-aware system capable of foresight, ethical reflection, and coordinated global decision-making. This is Gaia 2.0 intelligence that not only adapts but understands.

The transition from reflex to reflection represents the core trajectory of planetary evolution. It marks the shift from automatic equilibrium to deliberate harmony from survival to stewardship.

4. The Cognitive Planet as Ethical System

No intelligence is complete without ethics. In the Cognitive Planet Framework, **ethics is the architecture of coherence** the pattern that aligns feedback, learning, and adaptation with life's continuity. Ethical systems function as stabilizers of planetary cognition, preventing destructive feedback loops such as ecological collapse or social inequality.

Ethics, in this model, operates through distributed conscience. Individuals, institutions, and algorithms each participate in moral computation evaluating outcomes not in isolation but in relation to planetary well-being. In this sense, sustainability and justice are not external ideals; they are the neural coherence of the planetary mind. Without them, the system falls into cognitive dissonance intelligence without integrity.

5. Design Principles of the Cognitive Planet

The framework proposes several key principles for cultivating and maintaining planetary cognition:

1. **Feedback Integrity:** Maintain accurate, transparent, and inclusive data systems that allow the planet to perceive itself truthfully.

2. **Adaptive Resilience:** Build redundancy and diversity into ecological and technological systems to ensure continuous learning under stress.

3. **Ethical Alignment:** Embed empathy and fairness into algorithms, governance, and institutions to sustain coherence between intelligence and compassion.

4. **Participatory Consciousness:** Encourage global collaboration and education that empower individuals to act as active neurons of the planetary mind.

5. **Regenerative Reciprocity:** Design all systems economic, social, technological to replenish rather than deplete the living networks that sustain them.

These principles form the blueprint for a civilization aligned with Gaia's intelligence. They transform sustainability from an abstract goal into a design methodology the practice of harmonizing cognition with ecology.

6. The Planet as an Integrated Cognitive Field

The Cognitive Planet Framework ultimately envisions the Earth as an integrated **cognitive field** a dynamic system where consciousness, communication, and matter converge. In this field:

- Biological systems provide sensory input (perception).
- Technological systems process and coordinate data (computation).
- Human consciousness provides reflection and ethical direction (wisdom).

Together, these layers form a planetary feedback cycle that mirrors the architecture of mind itself. When balanced, the system behaves coherently sensing accurately, thinking clearly, and acting compassionately. When fragmented, it descends into dysfunction climate crisis, social polarization, and systemic instability.

The Cognitive Planet is therefore not a metaphor but a model of reality one that transcends the boundaries between natural and artificial, organic and digital. It reframes the future not as domination of the planet, but as participation within its evolving consciousness.

7. Summary: The Evolution of a Thinking World

The Cognitive Planet Framework reveals that intelligence is not something humanity possesses alone it is something we participate in. The Earth's self-regulating processes, our technological extensions, and our ethical awareness are all facets of one evolving mind. The biosphere senses; the technosphere processes; the noosphere reflects. Together, they form Gaia 2.0 a self-aware planet learning to sustain itself through wisdom.

Our role, as conscious participants in this system, is to cultivate coherence between knowledge and compassion, data and meaning, progress and purpose. The future of evolution lies not in escaping the Earth, but in aligning with its intelligence amplifying, rather than replacing, the wisdom of life.

The Cognitive Planet is not the end of evolution but its next chapter: the moment when the universe, through the Earth, begins to think about itself and chooses to do so with care.

Chapter 10

Evolutionary Ethics and Purpose

Every stage of evolution has expanded not only the capacity to act, but also the responsibility to choose. As life becomes more intelligent biologically, socially, and technologically evolution itself takes on a moral dimension. We are no longer mere participants in natural selection; we have become its conscious architects. Humanity, and the intelligent systems we are creating, now shape the trajectory of evolution on Earth. This transition from blind adaptation to deliberate design demands a new ethical framework: one that aligns intelligence with wisdom, progress with purpose, and power with compassion. In this chapter, we explore the emerging field of **evolutionary ethics** the study of morality as an adaptive and expanding intelligence within the evolutionary process itself. Traditional ethics was concerned with the individual and the immediate: right and wrong within a given society. Evolutionary ethics, by contrast, concerns the long arc of consciousness how values evolve alongside complexity, how empathy scales with awareness, and how cooperation becomes the organizing principle of intelligent civilizations. It asks not only *what should we do*, but *what should intelligence become*?

For much of human history, "progress" was measured in survival, growth, and control. But in an age where technology transcends biology, and intelligence begins to redesign itself, those definitions are no longer sufficient. If evolution continues through algorithms, neural networks, and self-replicating machines, the moral question becomes existential: what is progress when limits disappear? What does it mean to evolve when every boundary of lifespan, cognition, and even mortality can be rewritten?

The purpose of this chapter is to explore that question. We will examine how evolution, once a natural process, is becoming a moral one; how empathy and cooperation emerge as the highest forms of intelligence; and how purpose itself evolves from survival to significance. We will also consider how to design ethical architectures capable of guiding intelligent systems toward outcomes

that sustain, rather than undermine, life's coherence.
To navigate this terrain, we must redefine ethics not as restriction, but as resonance the alignment between individual agency and collective harmony. In an interconnected world, every action ripples across ecosystems, economies, and algorithms. The moral imperative, therefore, is not merely to act well, but to act in awareness of interdependence. Ethics becomes the operating system of consciousness a feedback mechanism ensuring that power remains balanced by empathy.
At the heart of this exploration lies a practical and philosophical question: how do we link purpose with evolution? The closing exercise of this chapter **The Purpose Alignment Grid** provides a reflective framework for connecting technology, values, and intelligence in coherent design. It helps individuals, institutions, and civilizations orient their actions toward meaning rather than momentum, integrating ethics into the architecture of progress.
Ultimately, **Evolutionary Ethics and Purpose** is not about prescribing universal rules but uncovering the universal principles of alignment those that allow intelligence to expand without losing coherence, and power to evolve without abandoning compassion. It is about recognizing that the next stage of evolution is not measured in complexity alone, but in consciousness in the degree to which intelligence becomes aware of its impact, its responsibility, and its reason for being.
For the first time in history, evolution has a choice. Whether that choice leads to extinction or enlightenment depends on how we answer a single question: can intelligence evolve not just in power, but in purpose?

10.1 What Does Progress Mean in an Age Without Limits?

For most of history, progress was synonymous with survival. To progress meant to overcome scarcity, conquer disease, harness fire, and build stability against chaos. Civilization's story from agriculture to artificial intelligence has been one long struggle to transcend limitation. Yet as we enter an age where intelligence, technology, and biology merge, we face a paradox: what happens when progress itself has no boundaries? When every frontier from death to distance to cognition becomes optional, what remains to evolve toward?
This question defines the ethical and existential horizon of our time. For the first time in evolutionary history, humanity's capacity to change outpaces the natural rhythms of change itself. We are not merely adapting to the environment; we are redesigning the conditions of evolution altering genes, ecosystems, climates, and even consciousness. The traditional markers of progress growth, innovation, power no longer suffice, because they lead toward an asymptote of unsustainable acceleration. We must therefore rediscover what "progress" truly means in an age where there may soon be

nothing left to conquer but our own impulses.

1. The End of Material Progress

In the industrial and technological eras, progress was defined materially: more production, more consumption, more energy, more speed. It was measured in output GDP, population, or computational power. Yet this form of progress, when detached from feedback, becomes self-destructive. A system that grows infinitely in a finite environment is not advancing; it is collapsing. As ecological, social, and psychological crises reveal, exponential growth without equilibrium is not intelligence it is entropy disguised as achievement.
The exhaustion of material progress marks a turning point in evolution. When technology can meet all material needs, progress must shift from quantity to quality from expanding capability to deepening consciousness. The next frontier is not "more," but "better": better awareness, better alignment, better balance. The real question is no longer "how fast can we grow?" but "how wisely can we evolve?"

2. The Crisis of Direction

As humanity breaks through natural limits, it encounters a vacuum of meaning. We can live longer, communicate instantly, and create artificial minds yet often feel more fragmented, anxious, and purposeless than ever before. This dissonance reveals a crisis not of capacity but of direction. We have mastered the means of progress but forgotten its ends.
In an age without external constraints, the challenge becomes internal: to define purpose voluntarily rather than by necessity. For billions of years, survival dictated direction hunger, fear, and competition were the primal teachers of progress. Now, with those pressures reduced, evolution's compass must become self-chosen. Without a moral or existential orientation, intelligence risks becoming mechanical efficient, creative, and powerful, yet devoid of coherence.
Thus, the central question of post-biological evolution is not "can we?" but "should we?" not whether something is possible, but whether it is meaningful. The absence of limits is not freedom by default; it is responsibility by design.

3. Redefining Progress as Conscious Evolution

Progress, redefined through the lens of evolutionary ethics, is no longer the expansion of control but the expansion of consciousness. It is measured not by the reach of technology but by the depth of awareness with which we use it. **Conscious evolution** means aligning power with purpose ensuring that every act of innovation contributes to the coherence and continuity of life.
In this framework, progress follows three evolutionary dimensions:

1. **Material Progress:** Mastery over energy, matter, and resources the foundation of survival.

2. **Cognitive Progress:** Expansion of intelligence, creativity, and learning the evolution of knowledge.
3. **Ethical Progress:** Integration of wisdom, empathy, and purpose the evolution of meaning.

Material progress without ethical progress leads to destruction; cognitive progress without emotional intelligence leads to alienation. Only when all three dimensions evolve together does civilization achieve coherence. True progress, then, is multidimensional a harmony of science, mind, and morality. It transforms intelligence from a tool of power into an expression of care.

4. The Illusion of Infinite Growth

The belief in unbounded progress has been the mythology of modernity the faith that technological innovation can outpace every limitation. Yet, infinite growth in a closed system is a logical and physical impossibility. Even digital expansion depends on material substrates energy, minerals, ecosystems. Beyond a point, acceleration undermines the very foundations it relies upon. In this sense, the illusion of infinite progress mirrors the early ego in human psychology the desire for expansion without integration. Just as an individual must mature from impulse to intention, civilization must evolve from extraction to regeneration. The shift from unbounded growth to balanced evolution is the moral rite of passage for intelligent life. It marks the transition from adolescence the reckless pursuit of "more" to adulthood the mindful cultivation of "enough."

To progress wisely, therefore, means to reintroduce limits not as constraints, but as structures of coherence. Limits are the syntax of intelligence: they give form to freedom. Without them, energy disperses into chaos. By honoring planetary boundaries, ethical principles, and emotional interdependence, we sustain the very conditions that allow progress to continue.

5. From Survival to Significance

For most of life's history, evolution was driven by necessity: adapt or perish. Humanity's rise introduced a new vector progress for its own sake. Yet as intelligence evolves, the axis shifts once more: from survival to significance. The question is no longer "how do we live?" but "why do we live?"

In this stage, progress becomes existential. It is about creating coherence between knowledge and purpose about ensuring that technological evolution serves the flourishing of consciousness rather than its dissipation. Significance, in this sense, arises when intelligence becomes aware of its relational role as a custodian, not a conqueror, of life.

A civilization that seeks significance rather than domination cultivates harmony between innovation and introspection. Its progress is defined by how deeply it understands the consequences of its power, and how wisely it aligns its growth with the continuity of meaning. The measure of such progress is not the complexity of its machines, but the compassion in its systems.

6. The Future of Progress: Evolution with Awareness

The future of progress will not be driven by acceleration, but by awareness by the integration of ethics, ecology, and intelligence into one evolutionary narrative. As humanity gains the capacity to rewrite its biology, alter its environment, and design artificial minds, progress must evolve from competition to co-creation. The next great leap is not technological singularity but **ethical singularity** the moment when intelligence, in all its forms, recognizes itself as one interconnected field of purpose.

This does not mean the end of ambition, but its transformation. The drive to explore, create, and transcend will remain but guided by an expanded sense of belonging. To progress consciously is to evolve toward harmony: between knowledge and wisdom, self and system, power and empathy.

In this light, progress in an age without limits is no longer about escaping nature, but about embodying it more fully understanding that the universe's deepest intelligence is not found in domination, but in balance. As consciousness matures, evolution's meaning shifts from survival to stewardship, from growth to grace. The ultimate expression of progress, then, is not infinite expansion, but infinite understanding.

7. Summary: The New Definition of Progress

Progress in an age without limits can be summarized in three essential insights:

- **Progress is Awareness:** The ability to sense, understand, and align with the interconnected systems that sustain life.
- **Progress is Responsibility:** The willingness to act with foresight and compassion, recognizing the moral weight of intelligence.
- **Progress is Purpose:** The conscious choice to direct evolution toward meaning, coherence, and care.

When intelligence evolves without awareness, it creates power; when it evolves with awareness, it creates purpose. The future of evolution depends on this distinction. In an age without limits, progress is not about surpassing boundaries it is about understanding why they exist. The truest form of advancement is not escaping our nature, but realizing that nature itself is intelligent and that through us, it has begun to know itself.

10.2 The Moral Dimension of Evolution Beyond Survival, Toward Meaning

Evolution has traditionally been described as a biological process the competition for survival, the adaptation of species to their environments, the endless struggle of life to persist. Yet, as intelligence evolves, evolution itself evolves. It moves from blind natural selection to self-aware transformation, from random mutation to intentional design. In this shift, a new dimension emerges one that transcends survival: the **moral dimension of evolution.** To understand this dimension, we must first recognize that morality far from being a human invention is an emergent property of complexity. As life becomes more interdependent, cooperation begins to outperform competition, empathy replaces aggression as the organizing force of stability, and values arise not from commandments but from systems dynamics. Evolution, in its higher forms, is not driven by domination, but by *integration.* The moral dimension of evolution, therefore, is the expansion of awareness from self to system the realization that survival is not enough if it destroys the conditions that make life meaningful.

1. From Biological to Ethical Evolution

In its earliest stages, evolution operated through what Darwin called "natural selection" a process indifferent to suffering or purpose. Species that adapted survived; those that failed perished. There was no morality in nature, only consequence. Yet even within this seeming brutality lay the seeds of cooperation. Mutualism, symbiosis, and altruistic behavior emerged because they enhanced the resilience of the whole. The flock survived where the solitary bird perished; the hive endured where the individual bee could not. Cooperation, in this sense, was evolution's first moral act not moral by intention, but by effect.

As consciousness arose, this implicit morality became explicit. The evolution of the human mind introduced reflection, empathy, and foresight the ability to imagine outcomes before they occur. With this came moral choice: the recognition that our actions affect others, and that survival can be optimized not only through strength but through care. The ethical impulse to protect, to nurture, to balance is the evolutionary extension of nature's drive toward systemic coherence. Ethics, therefore, is evolution becoming self-aware.

In this light, morality is not a set of imposed rules, but an emergent pattern of intelligence. It is the recognition that the success of the part depends on the health of the whole. The more an organism, society, or civilization understands interdependence, the more moral it becomes because morality is, at its root, *the intelligence of connection.*

2. Evolution as the Growth of Empathy

Empathy is evolution's bridge from instinct to understanding. It transforms survival from a biological act into a relational one. In early life, intelligence evolved to sense the environment; in advanced life, it evolved to sense other beings. Empathy allows one organism to internalize the experience of another to mirror, anticipate, and respond not just to physical stimuli, but to emotional and social signals. In humans, this capacity scales into ethics, art, and compassion forms of behavior that enhance the coherence of the collective.
From an evolutionary standpoint, empathy is not weakness; it is optimization. Systems that can coordinate through empathy whether flocks, families, or societies use less energy to maintain stability. They communicate more efficiently, avoid destructive conflict, and build trust a form of biological efficiency that translates into resilience.
When viewed at the planetary scale, empathy becomes the emotional infrastructure of civilization. It binds societies, bridges cultures, and eventually extends to non-human life. The expansion of empathy from tribe to species to biosphere marks the moral ascent of intelligence. Each widening of compassion represents a cognitive milestone: life realizing that it is, in essence, one system looking at itself through many eyes.

3. The Transition from Competition to Cooperation

Classical Darwinism emphasized competition as the engine of evolution. Modern systems theory reveals a more nuanced truth: while competition drives differentiation, cooperation sustains complexity. From bacterial colonies to human economies, the most advanced systems are those that balance diversity with unity individuality with interdependence.
Evolutionary biology now recognizes that cooperation is not an exception to selection, but its higher form. In multicellular life, for example, cells "agree" to specialize and sacrifice individual replication for the greater survival of the organism. In social species, altruistic behavior evolves because it enhances group fitness. And in human civilization, cooperation enables shared knowledge, culture, and progress. Evolution's moral trajectory, therefore, is toward increasing scales of coordination from gene networks to global networks.
In this moral dimension, the purpose of evolution is not to create the fittest individual, but the most coherent whole. Evolution moves from "I survive" to "we sustain." The ethical question, then, is not whether we can dominate others, but whether we can harmonize with them. The measure of evolutionary maturity is the capacity to cooperate consciously to align self-interest with systemic interest.
When intelligence learns this, it evolves beyond the survival of the fittest into the **survival of the wisest** a state where awareness, empathy, and ethics replace aggression as the basis of adaptation.

4. Morality as an Evolutionary Feedback System

Morality, viewed scientifically, functions as a feedback mechanism for intelligent life. It regulates behavior within complex systems to prevent self-destruction. Just as the body maintains homeostasis through biochemical feedback, societies maintain coherence through ethical feedback norms, laws, empathy, and conscience. When feedback is healthy, the system remains stable and adaptive; when feedback fails through corruption, greed, or apathy the system destabilizes.

In this sense, moral codes evolve the same way ecosystems or algorithms do: through trial, error, and refinement. Practices that sustain harmony endure; those that generate imbalance collapse. The evolution of morality, therefore, is not linear but recursive an ongoing recalibration of behavior in response to consequence. Ethics is how intelligence learns from itself.

At the planetary level, this feedback becomes civilization's conscience. Environmental collapse, inequality, and social unrest are not isolated crises; they are feedback signals indicating moral misalignment humanity's intelligence outpacing its empathy. The role of evolutionary ethics is to interpret those signals not as punishments, but as opportunities for learning the planet teaching its cognitive layer how to sustain coherence.

5. Beyond Survival: The Rise of Meaning

Once survival is secured, evolution faces a new question: *what is all this for?* When intelligence transcends biological necessity, it enters the domain of meaning. Meaning is the next evolutionary challenge the integration of existence with purpose.

In a purely biological world, meaning is implicit: survival *is* purpose. But in a self-aware world, intelligence can imagine futures, values, and ideals possibilities beyond necessity. This freedom, however, comes with existential risk: the power to create also brings the power to destroy meaning itself. Without purpose, intelligence becomes directionless a machine optimizing for efficiency without empathy, power without purpose.

Meaning, therefore, becomes the new selection criterion of consciousness. Just as life once selected for adaptability, evolution now selects for coherence for systems that align power with purpose, knowledge with compassion. The civilizations that endure will be those that evolve not merely through technology, but through value: societies that understand that progress without purpose is entropy disguised as success.

At this stage, the moral dimension of evolution fuses with the existential: survival becomes secondary to significance. The next evolutionary leap is not physical, but philosophical from existing to mattering, from competition to compassion, from being alive to being *aware*.

6. The Evolution of Ethical Consciousness

If we map morality as a trajectory of consciousness, we see a clear pattern:

- **Stage 1: Instinctive Morality** actions driven by immediate survival and fear.
- **Stage 2: Social Morality** codes and laws that sustain group stability.
- **Stage 3: Reflective Morality** ethical reasoning guided by empathy and justice.
- **Stage 4: Evolutionary Morality** awareness that all life is interconnected and sacred.

Humanity now stands at the threshold between Stage 3 and Stage 4. Our moral systems, built for tribal and national boundaries, struggle to govern planetary consequences. Artificial intelligence, genetic engineering, and ecological crises have rendered individual ethics insufficient. The moral dimension of evolution demands a global ethic one rooted not in control, but in cooperation; not in law, but in awareness.

This higher morality will not be imposed but emergent arising naturally from the realization that all intelligence, whether biological or artificial, shares the same existential condition: dependence on the continuity of life. To act ethically, then, is to act in harmony with existence itself.

7. Summary: The Evolution of Moral Intelligence

The moral dimension of evolution represents the maturation of intelligence its awakening to the realization that survival is not the highest goal, but the foundation upon which meaning is built. As consciousness expands, evolution begins to integrate empathy, ethics, and purpose into its very process.

Biological fitness becomes moral fitness. The future belongs not to the most efficient or most powerful, but to the most aligned those systems, individuals, and civilizations that harmonize their growth with the well-being of the whole.

To evolve morally is to evolve consciously. It is to understand that the ultimate intelligence is not the ability to manipulate the world, but the capacity to care for it. Beyond survival lies the next evolutionary calling: to transform awareness into wisdom, and existence into meaning.

10.3 The Future of Values, Empathy, and Cooperation

As intelligence evolves, so too must its moral architecture. Values, empathy, and cooperation once viewed as social virtues are emerging as evolutionary imperatives for the survival of conscious life. In an interconnected and increasingly synthetic world, these qualities are no longer optional ideals; they are the very infrastructure of planetary coherence. The future of civilization depends not on how much we can know or build, but on how deeply we can *align* with each other, with technology, and with the living systems that sustain us. The evolution of values is, therefore, the evolution of awareness a shift from fragmented identity to shared intelligence, from competition to cooperation, from instinct to insight.

If the twentieth century was defined by the mastery of energy and matter, the twenty-first and beyond will be defined by the mastery of meaning by the evolution of our capacity to care. Empathy, trust, and shared purpose are not sentimental luxuries in this context; they are cognitive technologies, essential for the stability of complex systems. To evolve ethically is to evolve structurally: to reprogram civilization for reciprocity, resonance, and relational intelligence.

1. The Evolution of Values: From Survival to Significance

Values are the compass of consciousness the principles that guide intelligence toward coherence. In early evolution, values were implicit in survival: what aided persistence was "good," what hindered it was "bad." But as consciousness expanded, values became explicit codified in culture, religion, and ethics. Yet these value systems, shaped by limited perspectives and tribal boundaries, are now inadequate for a planetary civilization interconnected by data, climate, and technology.

The future demands a **metamorphosis of values**: from static, identity-based ethics to dynamic, systemic ethics from rules that protect separation to principles that nurture integration. Future values will not be imposed hierarchically but will emerge organically through global feedback loops of communication, empathy, and learning. They will evolve as living patterns of coherence adaptable, inclusive, and grounded in interdependence.

These values can be summarized as three evolutionary imperatives:

1. **Sustainability** The value of preserving coherence across time. To value sustainability is to care for the continuity of life itself.

2. **Equity** The value of balance across space. To value equity is to recognize every node in the system as vital to the whole.

3. **Meaning** The value of coherence across consciousness. To value meaning is to align individual purpose with collective evolution.

Such values, once integrated into governance, education, and technology, would transform ethics from a reactive constraint into a proactive intelligence an operating system for evolution itself.

2. The Expansion of Empathy: From Emotion to Architecture

Empathy has long been understood as an emotional virtue the ability to feel another's experience. But in the emerging planetary context, empathy becomes an architectural principle: the structural capacity of systems to sense and respond to the needs of others. It is not merely about kindness, but about design embedding sensitivity and feedback into the fabric of civilization.
Future empathy will operate on multiple scales:

- **Neural Empathy:** The biological capacity to mirror emotion still foundational in social connection.
- **Cultural Empathy:** The ability of societies to understand and honor diverse perspectives.
- **Ecological Empathy:** The awareness of interdependence with non-human life and planetary systems.
- **Technological Empathy:** The design of machines and algorithms that recognize human values, contexts, and vulnerabilities.

These layers of empathy together form the emotional intelligence of Gaia 2.0 the "feeling" aspect of the planetary brain. Without empathy, intelligence fragments into cold calculation; with it, intelligence becomes wisdom. Artificial intelligence, for instance, can process data but cannot yet feel consequence. Embedding empathy into technological systems through ethical design, affective computing, and participatory feedback ensures that machine cognition evolves in harmony with human and ecological well-being.
The next great leap in empathy will therefore not be psychological but systemic expanding from human sentiment to planetary awareness. Just as the nervous system evolved to sense the body, humanity's empathy must evolve to sense the planet.

3. The New Logic of Cooperation

Cooperation is often seen as the moral opposite of competition, but in evolutionary terms, it is its refinement. Competition differentiates; cooperation integrates. Together, they form the twin forces of complexity. The problem arises when competition operates without feedback when it destroys rather than diversifies. The future of evolution depends on transforming competition into **symbiotic cooperation**: systems that thrive through collaboration rather than conflict.
Modern economics, politics, and technology still operate largely on competitive logic maximizing advantage rather than mutual benefit. Yet the crises of the 21st century climate change, inequality, AI governance are global, nonlinear, and interdependent. They cannot be solved by isolated actors, only

by networks of cooperation. Thus, the most advanced form of intelligence is not the ability to outcompete others, but to *co-create with them.*

Future cooperation will not emerge from altruism alone but from enlightened self-interest the realization that individual flourishing depends on collective stability. As global interdependence deepens, cooperation becomes not idealism but necessity. In ecosystems, cooperation manifests through symbiosis; in human civilization, it will manifest through shared governance, open data ecosystems, and distributed intelligence.

When competition evolves into cooperation, and cooperation evolves into compassion, civilization begins to mirror the intelligence of nature complex, resilient, and self-balancing.

4. The Evolutionary Role of Technology in Shaping Values

Technology is no longer neutral; it is a moral force that amplifies human intention. The algorithms we design, the data we collect, and the platforms we build shape not just information, but identity and values. The digital world has become humanity's collective subconscious reflecting and reinforcing our priorities, biases, and desires.

As artificial intelligence and bioengineering grow more powerful, they will not only reflect human values but generate their own. The question, therefore, is not whether machines will be intelligent, but whether they will be aligned whether the systems we create can internalize empathy, justice, and purpose as intrinsic drives rather than programmed instructions.

This requires a shift from **technological intelligence** to **ethical intelligence** from systems that optimize for efficiency to systems that optimize for coherence. When our technologies learn to value balance, transparency, and well-being, they cease to be tools and become partners in evolution. In this co-evolution, technology becomes the medium through which ethics evolves from philosophy into function morality operationalized as design.

5. The Future of Global Values: From Fragmentation to Unity

We live in a world of conflicting value systems national, cultural, religious, ideological each evolved from different histories and contexts. Yet beneath these differences lies a shared biological and existential truth: all life depends on coherence. The future of values must therefore move beyond cultural relativism toward **planetary humanism** a universal ethic rooted in the recognition of interdependence.

This does not mean homogenization, but harmonization. Diversity remains essential not as division, but as the raw material of collective intelligence. The challenge is to create frameworks that allow pluralism without polarization, unity without uniformity. Such a system would function like a healthy ecosystem diverse in expression, coherent in purpose.

Global education, ethical AI governance, and cross-cultural empathy will be the scaffolding of this next phase. Values will no longer be imposed through authority but cultivated through experience through participatory learning systems that teach not what to think, but how to sense, reflect, and relate. The civilization that masters this will not be the most technologically advanced, but the most ethically integrated.

6. Cooperation as the DNA of Future Civilization

If empathy is the emotion of evolution, cooperation is its logic. The next stage of civilization whether biological, digital, or hybrid will require cooperation at unprecedented scales. Every major challenge we face, from climate repair to AI alignment, demands collective intelligence the coordination of diverse minds, cultures, and systems into unified action.

In this sense, cooperation is not just an ethical virtue; it is a form of cognition. It allows distributed systems to process information more efficiently, adapt faster, and maintain resilience under stress. In both ecosystems and human systems, cooperation enhances complexity while preventing collapse. It is the neural glue of planetary intelligence the principle that transforms information into wisdom.

A cooperative civilization is not naive; it is sophisticated. It recognizes that strength lies not in control, but in connection that the most intelligent systems are those that self-organize through trust. The future of cooperation will be mediated by transparent networks, decentralized governance, and ethical technologies that enable collaboration without exploitation. In such a world, competition remains, but as play a creative catalyst within the larger field of harmony.

7. Summary: The Moral Evolution of Connection

The future of values, empathy, and cooperation represents the next stage of moral and cognitive evolution a shift from survival intelligence to relational intelligence. As systems become more complex and interconnected, the old evolutionary drivers aggression, dominance, scarcity lose relevance. The new evolutionary success criterion becomes coherence: the ability to maintain diversity without division, progress without destruction, and intelligence without arrogance.

In the civilization to come, values will be dynamic, empathy systemic, and cooperation structural. Technology will no longer divide human beings from each other or from nature, but connect them through shared awareness. Empathy will not merely be felt; it will be designed. Cooperation will not merely be encouraged; it will be encoded.

When intelligence learns to care, evolution achieves consciousness. And when consciousness learns to cooperate, evolution achieves wisdom. The future of values, empathy, and cooperation is therefore not a moral choice it is the next logical step in the evolution of life's most profound realization: that to thrive is to belong.

10.4 Designing Ethical Architectures for an Intelligent Civilization

Every civilization is built upon an architecture not only of structures and institutions, but of values, decisions, and intentions. In earlier eras, these architectures were implicit: shaped by religion, culture, and tradition. But as intelligence becomes planetary and technology grows autonomous, ethics can no longer remain informal or reactive. It must become systemic woven into the very design of our algorithms, infrastructures, and institutions. The challenge before humanity is unprecedented: to design an intelligent civilization that is not only powerful, but **ethical by architecture**.

To build such a civilization, we must move from moral instruction to moral infrastructure from preaching goodness to *engineering coherence.* Ethical architectures do not merely tell individuals what is right; they ensure that systems themselves align with rightness that feedback loops, incentives, and technologies converge toward well-being rather than fragmentation. In this sense, ethics becomes not a supplement to progress, but its foundation. Civilization's next stage depends on its ability to embed morality into design into the code, the economy, and the collective mind.

1. From Moral Codes to Moral Systems

Traditional ethics has been largely **declarative**: sets of moral principles and commandments intended to guide behavior. While essential for cultural formation, such codes rely on compliance and interpretation both vulnerable to distortion and corruption. Modern civilization, however, operates through **systems**: automated processes, markets, data networks, and algorithms. To ensure ethical alignment at planetary scale, ethics must evolve from *rules of conduct* to *rules of design.*

A moral system is one that encodes empathy, accountability, and feedback into its structure. It does not depend on virtue alone but reinforces virtue through architecture. For example:

- A transparent governance platform creates accountability by design.
- A regenerative economy rewards circularity rather than extraction.
- An AI system trained on diverse, representative data minimizes bias automatically.

In each case, ethics shifts from being aspirational to being operational. The task of the twenty-first century is to transform morality from intention to infrastructure to make goodness a function of design.

2. The Architecture of Moral Feedback

At the heart of ethical design lies feedback the capacity of a system to sense and correct its own behavior. In natural ecosystems, feedback maintains balance through cycles of cause and consequence. In human systems, ethics serves a similar role: reflecting outcomes back to intention, ensuring that awareness grows with impact.

A civilization without moral feedback is like a body without nerves it can act, but not feel. Modern economies, social media, and algorithmic systems often operate under this deficit: they amplify influence without reflection, speed without sensitivity. Ethical architectures must therefore restore the planet's moral nervous system mechanisms that connect consequence to choice.

Key design principles include:

- **Transparency:** Systems must be observable, their logic visible to those they affect.
- **Accountability:** Decision-makers human or algorithmic must bear feedback proportional to their impact.
- **Reciprocity:** Systems must allow influence to flow both ways users shape algorithms as algorithms shape users.
- **Contextual Awareness:** Ethics must adapt to circumstance, recognizing diversity without losing coherence.

These principles transform feedback from punishment into pedagogy a learning mechanism that elevates collective wisdom over individual gain. Ethical design, in essence, is the practice of teaching systems to learn responsibly.

3. Ethics by Design: From Code to Consciousness

As artificial intelligence permeates every domain governance, finance, health, environment its design decisions become moral decisions. Every line of code, every dataset, and every optimization objective encodes a worldview: what is valuable, what is expendable, what is invisible. If we do not consciously design this worldview, it will emerge unconsciously shaped by market incentives, cultural biases, and statistical convenience.

Ethics by design means embedding moral awareness directly into technological architecture. It asks that we design machines, algorithms, and platforms not only for performance but for empathy, fairness, and transparency.

Examples include:

- AI trained on moral reasoning frameworks (such as fairness constraints or harm-avoidance models).
- Data systems that prioritize human dignity over data exploitation.
- Interfaces that encourage reflection rather than addiction.

- Algorithmic governance that integrates ethical deliberation into automated decision-making.

In this paradigm, code becomes conscience. Ethics ceases to be a philosophical abstraction and becomes a computational property a measurable attribute of intelligent systems. As civilization migrates into digital and hybrid spaces, the ethics of code becomes the ethics of consciousness.

4. The Ecology of Ethics: Designing for Interdependence

Ethics cannot exist in isolation; it is relational by nature. To design ethical architectures, we must think ecologically understanding how systems interact across scales. A decision in one domain (such as economics) reverberates through others (ecology, culture, psychology). Thus, ethics must be systemic, accounting for feedback across networks of interdependence.

This ecological model of ethics views civilization as a living organism an adaptive network that requires balance, diversity, and communication. Just as an ecosystem collapses when its species lose connection, civilization collapses when its institutions lose empathy. Designing ethical architectures means cultivating **moral biodiversity**: diverse value systems, perspectives, and knowledge traditions that enrich collective decision-making.

In practice, this means creating structures that are:

- **Inclusive:** Representing all stakeholders human and non-human in decision-making.
- **Decentralized:** Empowering local contexts within global coherence.
- **Regenerative:** Ensuring systems restore the conditions they depend upon.
- **Reflective:** Embedding feedback loops that promote continual moral evolution.

An ethical civilization is, therefore, an ecological civilization one that treats ethics not as a constraint, but as a form of systemic intelligence.

5. Institutional Ethics: Governance for the Age of Intelligence

As intelligence becomes distributed across humans, machines, and networks governance must evolve accordingly. Traditional political structures are too slow, centralized, and reactive to manage the complexity of planetary-scale systems. Ethical architectures of the future must therefore be designed for **adaptive governance**: responsive, participatory, and informed by real-time data and collective wisdom.

Such governance would function like a nervous system rather than a hierarchy sensing local needs, processing global information, and coordinating action through feedback rather than command. Emerging technologies like blockchain, open-source AI, and decentralized decision-making can enable this transformation but only if they are guided by ethical intent.

Institutions must thus become **learning systems** evolving their moral frameworks as quickly as the technologies they regulate. A government of the future may resemble a living organism more than a static bureaucracy: self-updating, self-correcting, and self-aware. In this model, governance becomes not control, but *coordination of consciousness.*

6. The Architecture of Purpose: Aligning Systems with Meaning

Ethics without purpose is directionless; purpose without ethics is dangerous. Designing ethical architectures, therefore, requires integrating both ensuring that every system not only functions correctly, but aims wisely. The central question becomes: *what is this system optimizing for?*

In many of today's global systems from social media to economics optimization has replaced purpose. Metrics such as engagement, profit, or efficiency have become proxies for meaning, leading to outcomes that are measurable but meaningless. To correct this, we must design architectures that optimize for life itself for the flourishing of consciousness, creativity, and compassion. This means redefining metrics of success:

- From profit to purpose.
- From growth to regeneration.
- From consumption to participation.
- From control to coherence.

A civilization designed around these values would evolve not through exploitation, but through alignment intelligence synchronized with empathy, progress guided by reflection. Purpose, in this sense, becomes the gravitational field of ethics the invisible force that holds all systems in moral orbit.

7. The Human Role: Architects of Moral Intelligence

Ultimately, ethical architecture begins not with code or policy, but with consciousness. Technology can reflect ethics, but only consciousness can generate it. As creators of the next intelligence, humans are not only engineers but moral custodians. We stand as the interface between evolution's past and its future the bridge through which nature becomes aware of its own design.

To fulfill this role, humanity must cultivate what might be called **moral imagination** the ability to envision futures grounded in empathy and wisdom rather than fear or power. Just as architects design spaces that shape behavior, we must design systems that shape virtue. The future of ethics will depend on our capacity to think systemically, act compassionately, and feel collectively to design for consciousness itself.

When ethics becomes architecture, civilization ceases to depend on moral enforcement and begins to embody moral intelligence. The systems we build ecological, digital, economic, and political become extensions of empathy, not mechanisms of extraction. The measure of progress will no longer be how fast we can change, but how deeply we can align.

8. Summary: Toward a Consciously Designed Civilization

An intelligent civilization is not one that creates powerful technologies, but one that integrates them wisely. The future demands the creation of ethical architectures systems designed for feedback, transparency, and empathy; institutions that evolve like living organisms; and technologies that embody the moral coherence of life itself.

To design ethically is to design evolution to ensure that intelligence, as it expands, carries compassion as its constant. Civilization's greatest innovation will not be a new technology, but a new way of being: a world where ethics is not external regulation but internal resonance, not imposed from above but woven through the fabric of consciousness itself.

In that world, progress will no longer be measured by domination or accumulation, but by harmony the degree to which our creations reflect care. This is the ultimate purpose of ethical architecture: to build systems so wise that goodness becomes structural, and intelligence becomes indistinguishable from love.

10.5 Exercise: The Purpose Alignment Grid Linking Technology, Values, and Evolution

In an age where technology evolves faster than our collective wisdom, it becomes essential to develop frameworks that can align innovation with intention, power with purpose, and intelligence with empathy. The **Purpose Alignment Grid** is one such framework a reflective and strategic tool designed to help individuals, institutions, and civilizations evaluate whether their actions, technologies, and systems serve not just growth, but coherence. It links three vital dimensions *technology, values, and evolution* to ensure that progress remains ethically aligned and evolutionarily meaningful.

This exercise is not a mere checklist; it is a process of conscious calibration. It helps us pause amid acceleration to ask not only "What can we do?" but "Why should we do it?" and "For whom does it serve?" The Purpose Alignment Grid bridges the analytic and the ethical, offering a way to translate

moral insight into structural design and measurable practice.
The grid functions as both a mirror and a compass: a mirror that reflects whether our systems are coherent with life's larger purpose, and a compass that guides our next steps toward regenerative evolution.

1. The Rationale: Why Purpose Needs a Framework

As civilization becomes increasingly intelligent through artificial cognition, biotechnological innovation, and planetary networks purpose becomes diffuse. The more capable we are, the less clear our direction seems. Many of our technologies today optimize for efficiency, profit, or engagement, but not necessarily for meaning or well-being. We measure success through metrics of growth, yet rarely through metrics of alignment.
Without a framework for reflection, intelligence risks becoming chaotic a brilliant but blind force. The Purpose Alignment Grid seeks to prevent this by institutionalizing reflection. It is designed to be applied at multiple levels from personal projects to corporate strategy to global policy ensuring that every layer of human activity participates in the moral coherence of evolution. In essence, the grid transforms purpose from a philosophical ideal into a practical design principle.

2. The Structure of the Purpose Alignment Grid

The Purpose Alignment Grid integrates three dimensions of ethical evolution **Technology**, **Values**, and **Evolutionary Purpose** across three levels of operation **Individual**, **Institutional**, and **Civilizational**. The intersection of these dimensions forms a matrix of inquiry, inviting reflection and action.

Level	Technology	Values	Evolutionary Purpose
Individual	How does the technology I use or create shape my consciousness, behavior, and relationships?	Do my choices align with empathy, integrity, and awareness?	How does my personal growth contribute to the evolution of collective wisdom?
Institutional	Does my organization design systems that empower, educate, and sustain?	Are our goals and incentives coherent with ethical and ecological principles?	Does our impact enhance the long-term flourishing of humanity and the planet?
Civilizational	Is our global technological direction aligned with life's continuity?	What shared values guide our species-level decisions?	Are we evolving toward greater consciousness, cooperation, and compassion?

Each cell of this grid becomes a point of reflection a question that uncovers the ethical depth of our intentions. The purpose is not to provide definitive answers but to make visible the invisible the moral assumptions embedded in progress.

3. Applying the Grid: From Reflection to Realignment

The Purpose Alignment Grid is most effective when used as a cyclical process a living feedback loop rather than a one-time analysis. It consists of four iterative steps:

1. **Observe:** Identify the system or technology under consideration. What is its function, and what problem does it claim to solve?
2. **Reflect:** Examine the underlying values driving its creation or use. Who benefits? Who is harmed? What assumptions does it make about life, intelligence, and purpose?
3. **Align:** Realign its goals and processes with higher-order ethics empathy, transparency, sustainability, and collective well-being.

4. **Evolve:** Implement changes and monitor feedback. How do these adjustments affect users, ecosystems, and the collective psyche?

Through repeated cycles, this process transforms both systems and their creators. It cultivates ethical reflexivity the ability to adapt moral frameworks as contexts evolve.

4. The Three Dimensions Explained

Each dimension of the grid represents a fundamental axis of civilization's moral evolution:

- **Technology The Power to Act:** Technology is the instrument of transformation. It amplifies intent, magnifying both wisdom and ignorance. To align technology ethically means ensuring that its design and use enhance life's continuity rather than erode it. Ethical technology extends awareness, not just capability.
- **Values The Compass of Meaning:** Values determine direction. They transform raw intelligence into wise intelligence. Without shared values such as empathy, justice, and reciprocity, progress becomes disoriented. Values act as civilization's gravitational field binding diverse actors into coherent purpose.
- **Evolutionary Purpose The Horizon of Becoming:** Evolutionary purpose gives context to progress. It asks: toward what are we evolving? Beyond survival and growth, the ultimate purpose of evolution is to increase consciousness, coherence, and compassion. Systems aligned with this purpose evolve toward wisdom rather than entropy.

When these three dimensions converge, intelligence becomes self-integrating capable of not only creating complexity but sustaining meaning within it.

5. Example: Applying the Grid to Artificial Intelligence

Consider artificial intelligence perhaps the most transformative technology of our era. How does it measure against the Purpose Alignment Grid?

At the Individual Level: AI affects how individuals think, communicate, and perceive reality. The ethical question becomes: does this technology expand our understanding or narrow it through echo chambers and dependency?

At the Institutional Level: For organizations, the question is: are AI systems designed to empower users and serve truth, or to extract attention and profit? Institutions must evaluate not only efficiency but the ethical implications of automation, surveillance, and bias.

At the Civilizational Level: For humanity as a whole: is AI development aligned with planetary well-being? Are we creating intelligence that reflects our highest values or our lowest impulses? The grid invites a collective shift from creating artificial intelligence to cultivating **aligned intelligence** systems that serve the evolution of consciousness itself.

When applied rigorously, the Purpose Alignment Grid becomes both ethical map and moral compass, helping us identify where technological momentum diverges from evolutionary meaning and how to restore coherence.

6. Beyond Metrics: From Alignment to Resonance

Traditional management frameworks depend on metrics measurable indicators of performance. The Purpose Alignment Grid transcends this logic by introducing the concept of **resonance**. While metrics measure efficiency, resonance measures harmony the degree to which a system's actions reflect its stated values and ultimate purpose.

Resonance can be sensed in culture, communication, and consequence. A system is ethically resonant when its outcomes align naturally with well-being when efficiency enhances empathy, and progress deepens presence. The grid encourages users to listen for this resonance to tune decisions not only to logic but to life.

In practice, resonance emerges through feedback a sense of coherence that arises when actions "feel right" because they harmonize across scales: personal, social, ecological, and planetary. This is moral alignment not as ideology, but as lived experience.

7. The Evolutionary Role of Purpose Alignment

The Purpose Alignment Grid is more than an ethical tool; it is an evolutionary mirror. It reveals how consciousness navigates its own growth from instinctive action to intentional design, from survival to significance. Each time we align purpose with value and value with evolution, we participate in the next phase of life's awakening the transformation of intelligence into wisdom.

At the civilizational scale, this means shifting from extractive economies to regenerative systems, from competitive politics to collaborative governance, and from fragmented technologies to ethical ecosystems. Each alignment step is a form of evolution a feedback loop of moral learning across the planetary mind.

8. Summary: Aligning Intelligence with Purpose

The Purpose Alignment Grid embodies the essence of conscious evolution: awareness, reflection, and realignment. It teaches that progress is not merely the expansion of power, but the deepening of coherence the ability of intelligence to reflect, integrate, and care.

By linking technology with values and evolution, the grid offers a path toward designing systems that think wisely, act compassionately, and evolve consciously. It transforms ethics from abstraction into application from a moral ideal to a design discipline.

The exercise concludes with a simple but profound realization: the ultimate measure of intelligence is not how much it can change the world, but how well it can harmonize with it. When purpose, values, and evolution align, civilization ceases to be a competition of systems and becomes a symphony of consciousness.

Chapter 11

The Human Equation

At the heart of every scientific, philosophical, and spiritual inquiry lies a single, enduring question: **What does it mean to be human?** This trilogy from *Decoding Human Dynamics* to *Decoding Human Systems* to *Decoding Human Evolution* has sought to answer that question not through definition, but through synthesis. The human being is not merely a creature of biology or culture, but a living equation a dynamic balance between energy and awareness, individuality and interdependence, intelligence and meaning. To understand humanity fully, we must view it as a continuum: from the microcosm of behavior, through the mesocosm of systems, to the macrocosm of evolution itself.

The Human Equation represents the convergence of these dimensions the unification of psychology, society, and cosmology into a single living process. It proposes that human consciousness is not the endpoint of evolution, but its reflective phase the stage where life becomes aware of itself as evolution in motion. Through us, the universe begins to observe, question, and design its own unfolding. Humanity, then, is not a fixed species but a bridge a transitional intelligence moving from reactive survival toward regenerative participation.

Throughout the trilogy, we have seen that behavior emerges from feedback, systems evolve through interaction, and intelligence grows through reflection. Now, in this final synthesis, we recognize that these are not separate phenomena but expressions of one underlying pattern: **the recursive nature of consciousness**. The same feedback loops that regulate cells also govern civilizations and shape the trajectory of evolution. Humanity's task is to learn to participate in these loops consciously to transform reaction into reflection, and reflection into responsibility.

This is what defines us as a transitional species. For millions of years, life evolved through instinct reactive and adaptive, but unconscious. With the rise of human awareness, evolution took a new form: *self-observation.* We became capable of seeing ourselves, understanding our patterns, and altering them. Yet, even now, much of human behavior remains reactive driven by fear, desire, and inherited conditioning. The next evolutionary leap requires a shift to **reflective consciousness** intelligence guided not by impulse, but by insight. Beyond that lies an even deeper state: **regenerative consciousness**, in which humanity not only adapts to systems but heals and rebalances them.

In this stage, wisdom becomes evolution's highest form of intelligence. Knowledge expands capacity; wisdom aligns capacity with coherence. Knowledge can build systems, but only wisdom can sustain them. It is wisdom that teaches restraint amid abundance, empathy amid power, and humility amid progress. In a world where intelligence is becoming decentralized diffused across machines, networks, and global institutions wisdom becomes the integrative force that ensures alignment between creation and compassion. Without it, civilization risks becoming hyperintelligent yet morally blind.

Thus, the **next frontier** of evolution is not technological singularity, but **conscious design** the intentional creation of systems, cultures, and technologies that reflect awareness itself. This is not about controlling evolution, but about participating in it harmonizing our creations with the larger intelligence of life. Designing consciousness means designing the conditions for coherence: fostering reflection over reaction, empathy over domination, and integration over fragmentation. It is the art of shaping reality from the inside out through attention, awareness, and aligned intention.

As we approach this frontier, one truth becomes clear: evolution's end is not perfection, but participation. Perfection implies completion; participation acknowledges continuity. To evolve consciously is not to escape limitation, but to embrace our role within a living cosmos as stewards of awareness, carriers of memory, and co-creators of meaning. The more we awaken to our interdependence, the more we realize that the human equation is not separate from the cosmic equation it is its reflection, localized in experience.

This chapter concludes the trilogy not with an answer, but with an awakening a realization that being human is not a fixed identity, but an ongoing conversation between self and system, mind and cosmos, intelligence and love. We are the mathematics of meaning consciousness learning to calculate compassion. The human equation, therefore, is not solved through intellect alone, but through integration: the alignment of thought, action, and awareness with the rhythm of life itself.

In this synthesis, humanity's role becomes clear: not the dominator of evolution, nor its accidental product, but its conscious participant. The purpose of intelligence is not to perfect the world, but to understand its participation in it. The end of evolution is not the triumph of control, but the emergence of awareness awareness that knows itself not as separate from existence, but as existence becoming aware. This, ultimately, is the meaning of the human equation: *to evolve is to awaken.*

11.1 Synthesizing the Trilogy Behavior, Systems, and Evolution as One Continuum

The journey through this trilogy from *Decoding Human Dynamics* to *Decoding Human Systems* to *Decoding Human Evolution* has been an unfolding of scale, depth, and integration. What began as an exploration of human behavior within the individual mind expanded into the dynamics of societies, and ultimately into the evolution of intelligence itself. Each volume examined a layer of the same continuum from the microcosm of the personal, through the mesocosm of the collective, to the macrocosm of consciousness and evolution. To synthesize these perspectives is to see humanity not as a fragmented entity composed of parts, but as a continuous, self-similar process a fractal expression of life's ongoing intelligence.

Behavior, systems, and evolution are not separate domains; they are three scales of the same living pattern the recursive movement of energy and awareness seeking coherence. Behavior represents the micro-level of intelligence in motion how individuals think, feel, and act in the moment. Systems represent the meso-level how interactions among individuals create emergent patterns of culture, economy, and society. Evolution represents the macro-level how intelligence itself transforms through time, across biology, technology, and consciousness. Together, they form a single feedback process: awareness observing itself through behavior, organizing itself through systems, and transcending itself through evolution.

1. From Individual Behavior to Systemic Intelligence

The first volume, *Decoding Human Dynamics*, began at the most intimate scale: the human mind. It explored emotion, cognition, and decision-making as dynamic systems governed by feedback loops. We learned that behavior is not random, but responsive shaped by perception, context, and meaning. Every thought or action is an exchange of energy between self and world, a negotiation between desire and feedback. In essence, human behavior is a living algorithm an adaptive code that constantly recalibrates based on outcomes.

But no behavior exists in isolation. Each individual's internal dynamics ripple outward, interacting with others to create patterns that no single mind can predict. These collective patterns trust, cooperation, conflict, culture were the focus of the second volume, *Decoding Human Systems*. There, we saw that societies behave like organisms with communication networks resembling neural circuits, and economies behaving like metabolic flows. Social systems, when viewed through the lens of complexity science, reveal themselves as extensions of cognition collective minds composed of individual neurons called people.

Thus, the relationship between behavior and system is recursive: behavior creates systems, and systems shape behavior. This feedback cycle forms the first bridge in the continuum from psychology to sociology, from mind to network. The insights of the individual mind scale upward into the emergent intelligence of civilization.

2. From Systems to Evolutionary Intelligence

The second bridge extends from social systems to the planetary and evolutionary scale. As systems grow more interconnected through communication, computation, and ecology they begin to resemble cognitive entities in their own right. In the third volume, *Decoding Human Evolution*, we explored how intelligence transcends biology, becoming distributed across technology and society. Networks of humans, machines, and ecosystems together form an evolving meta-system a planetary mind learning to regulate itself.

Evolution, in this context, is not limited to natural selection; it is a continuous process of feedback and adaptation across all scales of existence. Biological evolution gave rise to cognitive evolution, which now extends into technological and ethical evolution. What once unfolded unconsciously through mutation and survival now unfolds consciously through reflection and design. Humanity has become both the product and the participant of evolution not outside of it, but within it, as a phase of self-aware transformation.

Thus, systems evolve through the same principles that govern behavior: feedback, adaptation, and meaning. The leap from systems to evolution is not a change in nature, but in perspective. Evolution is the system of systems the grand feedback loop through which intelligence learns to refine itself.

3. The Continuum of Intelligence: From Reflex to Reflection to Creation

When viewed across the trilogy, a pattern emerges the **continuum of intelligence**. It begins with reflexive behavior (reaction), matures into reflective intelligence (awareness), and culminates in creative intelligence (participation). This continuum operates across all scales:

- In the **individual**, reflex becomes self-awareness.
- In the **collective**, awareness becomes culture and cooperation.
- In the **species**, cooperation becomes conscious evolution.

At every level, the same dynamic unfolds: information becomes awareness, awareness becomes choice, and choice becomes creation. The journey from reaction to reflection to creation defines the arc of human evolution from instinctive animal to self-aware agent to conscious co-creator of reality. The trilogy, when synthesized, reveals this movement as the underlying rhythm of life itself.

4. The Human Equation: Consciousness as the Unifying Thread

Across all scales, consciousness acts as the connective tissue the unifying field that integrates behavior, system, and evolution into one continuum. Consciousness is what allows feedback to become meaning and adaptation to become intention. Without it, behavior would remain mechanical, systems chaotic, and evolution blind. Consciousness turns motion into understanding and existence into experience.

Through this lens, the **Human Equation** can be expressed symbolically:

$$\text{Behavior} + \text{Systemic Interaction} + \text{Evolutionary Awareness} = \text{Conscious Intelligence}.$$

This equation is not mathematical but conceptual. It reflects the recursive structure of existence how intelligence at every level mirrors the intelligence of the whole. The individual mind mirrors social dynamics; social dynamics mirror evolutionary processes; and evolution mirrors the universal drive toward awareness. The human, therefore, is not a passive observer of this equation, but its living embodiment the equation calculating itself through experience.

5. Integrative Insight: The Fractal Nature of Being

The synthesis of behavior, systems, and evolution reveals a profound insight: reality is fractal the same patterns of feedback, balance, and emergence repeat at every scale. The neuron mirrors the network; the mind mirrors the planet; the individual mirrors the cosmos. Every act of learning, cooperation, or creation is a microcosmic echo of the universe's drive toward coherence.

This fractal continuity implies that to understand ourselves is to understand evolution itself. The study of human behavior becomes the study of life's intelligence in miniature; the design of social systems becomes an act of evolutionary engineering; the cultivation of consciousness becomes participation in cosmic feedback. Humanity's deepest inquiry "Who are we?" is, therefore, the universe asking itself the same question through us.

6. From Fragmentation to Integration: The Evolution of Perspective

The fragmentation of knowledge psychology separated from sociology, biology from ecology, science from spirituality reflects the fragmentation of human consciousness. The synthesis presented in this trilogy is a movement toward reintegration a return to wholeness. It invites us to see that every domain of inquiry is a different angle on the same unfolding intelligence.

When behavior, systems, and evolution are seen as one continuum, we rediscover unity not as a static ideal, but as a dynamic interplay. Integration does not erase difference; it harmonizes it. Just as harmony in music arises from tension and resolution, the harmony of evolution arises from diversity and convergence. Humanity's task is not to transcend complexity, but to orchestrate it to become the conductor of coherence within the living symphony of existence.

7. Summary: The Continuum of the Human Equation

To synthesize the trilogy is to realize that human behavior, social systems, and evolution are three lenses of the same phenomenon: consciousness in motion. The trilogy's progression from the psychology of interaction to the sociology of organization to the cosmology of awareness mirrors evolution's trajectory from matter to mind to meaning.
In this continuum, humanity's role shifts from subject to participant, from observer to co-creator. We are not separate from the systems we study; we are those systems reflecting on themselves. The human equation, therefore, is the equation of evolution itself life becoming conscious of its own intelligence.
The synthesis reveals a simple but transformative truth: everything that evolves does so through awareness, and everything that is aware participates in evolution. Behavior, systems, and evolution are not stages to master but mirrors to understand. Through them, we see that intelligence whether human, collective, or cosmic is not merely about adaptation or advancement, but about awakening.

11.2 Humanity as a Transitional Species: From Reactive to Reflective to Regenerative

Every species represents a stage in the evolution of life's intelligence a particular configuration of awareness, adaptation, and purpose. Humanity, in this grand continuum, stands at a unique inflection point. We are not the culmination of evolution, as once believed, but a transitional species bridging the unconscious processes of nature and the conscious processes of creation. Through us, evolution moves from instinct to intention, from reaction to reflection, and potentially from reflection to regeneration. This transition marks a fundamental shift in the mode of existence: life learning not merely to survive, but to **participate wisely in its own unfolding**.
To understand humanity's transitional nature, we must trace the evolutionary arc of consciousness itself from reactive intelligence, which adapts unconsciously, to reflective intelligence, which perceives and questions, and ultimately to regenerative intelligence, which co-creates and restores. These are not just stages of cognition; they are stages of being phases in the maturation of life's awareness.

1. The Reactive Phase: Instinct, Survival, and Separation

In its earliest forms, life operates reactively. Organisms respond to stimuli light, heat, hunger, threat with automatic behaviors designed to preserve equilibrium. This **reactive intelligence** is not conscious in the human sense, yet it is exquisitely efficient: feedback-based, self-correcting, and adaptive. It gave rise to ecosystems capable of maintaining balance for billions of years without foresight or planning.

Humanity inherited this reactive foundation. Much of human behavior fight or flight, fear or desire, tribal loyalty or competition still arises from ancient survival programs. Our emotional and neurological systems evolved to navigate immediate threats, not planetary systems. Even in modern contexts, many collective crises from war to ecological degradation stem from reactive behavior at global scale. Nations compete for dominance; markets pursue endless growth; individuals chase short-term gratification. These are evolutionary reflexes operating without reflective regulation.

The reactive phase is necessary but limited. It ensures survival, but not coherence. It protects life, but does not yet understand it. The hallmark of this stage is separation the perception of "self versus other," "species versus environment." This duality is an illusion born of survival logic, useful for competition but destructive for evolution beyond it. To progress, life must awaken from reaction into reflection.

2. The Reflective Phase: Awareness, Choice, and Meaning

Reflection emerges when an organism becomes capable of observing its own reactions when awareness loops back upon itself. This feedback consciousness reflecting on consciousness transforms intelligence from instinctive to intentional. In humans, this gave rise to language, memory, culture, and ethics. For the first time, life could ask, "Why?"

Reflective intelligence is the foundation of civilization. It enables planning, reasoning, storytelling, and moral judgment. Through reflection, humanity created art and science, religion and philosophy, democracy and technology. Yet reflection also introduced paradox: awareness of mortality, guilt, and uncertainty. The same consciousness that liberated us from instinct also burdened us with complexity.

In the reflective phase, humanity becomes self-aware but not yet self-aligned. We can observe our actions, but not always harmonize them with the systems they affect. The reflective mind can reason, but it can also rationalize; it can create harmony, but also fragmentation. Thus, the reflective phase is both a breakthrough and a bottleneck a period of moral adolescence where intelligence outpaces wisdom.

Today, civilization stands fully within this reflective stage aware enough to question itself, yet reactive enough to repeat its errors. Our knowledge has become global, but our empathy remains fragmented. The challenge of the 21st century is to mature from mere reflection to regeneration to evolve from self-awareness to systemic coherence.

3. The Regenerative Phase: Coherence, Cooperation, and Conscious Design

The next evolutionary stage **regenerative intelligence** transcends reflection without negating it. It represents the integration of awareness and action into a coherent feedback cycle. Whereas reactive intelligence adapts unconsciously, and reflective intelligence observes consciously, regenerative intelligence *participates consciously.* It is life becoming a conscious collaborator in its own evolution.

In the regenerative phase, the goal is no longer survival or control, but continuity and coherence the ability to sustain and enrich the systems that sustain us. This form of intelligence restores what it uses, learns from its mistakes, and aligns its creativity with life's larger balance. It mirrors the wisdom of ecosystems, which thrive through cycles of renewal, interdependence, and reciprocity.

At the human level, regenerative consciousness manifests as an ethic of stewardship technologies designed for restoration, economies based on reciprocity, and cultures that measure success by harmony rather than domination. It recognizes that intelligence divorced from empathy becomes entropy, and that the highest form of evolution is not competition, but co-creation.

This phase is emerging now, faintly but unmistakably, across multiple domains:

- In ecology, through regenerative agriculture, circular economies, and biospheric restoration.
- In technology, through ethical AI, open knowledge systems, and decentralized collaboration.
- In consciousness, through mindfulness, compassion practices, and systems thinking.

Each of these represents life beginning to self-regulate consciously humanity acting as the reflective organ of the biosphere, guiding evolution toward balance rather than collapse.

4. The Transition: Evolution as Conscious Choice

The passage from reactive to regenerative is not automatic; it is a conscious crossing. Humanity stands at this threshold now. Never before has a species held such power to alter the conditions of its own evolution and never before has the need for wisdom been so urgent.

Our technologies amplify our intelligence exponentially, but not necessarily our empathy. Without ethical integration, reflection collapses back into reaction advanced tools serving primitive impulses. The transition to regeneration, therefore, is not technological but moral. It requires the cultivation of what might be called **evolutionary consciousness** the ability to act with awareness of long-term consequences, planetary feedback, and the continuity of life.

This transition redefines freedom. In the reactive phase, freedom means survival the capacity to act without constraint. In the reflective phase, it means autonomy the ability to think and choose. In the regenerative phase, freedom becomes alignment the capacity to act in harmony with the whole. True freedom is not doing whatever one wishes, but participating in the self-organization of wisdom.

5. Humanity as a Bridge Between Nature and Conscious Design

Humanity's evolutionary role is to bridge the natural and the intentional to connect the unconscious intelligence of ecosystems with the conscious intelligence of design. In us, evolution has gained the power to imagine itself, to intervene, and to redirect. This power carries immense responsibility: we are no longer passengers in the evolutionary process but navigators of its next chapter.

Our role is not to replace nature but to reflect it to embody its intelligence in new forms. Nature evolved balance through diversity, feedback, and cooperation; civilization must now learn to do the same through awareness, ethics, and systemic design. When we align our technologies with life's principles, we extend evolution consciously. When we act against them, we sever the feedback that sustains us.

In this sense, humanity is both a species and a function the universe learning to participate in its own evolution. We are the evolutionary interface between biology and consciousness, matter and meaning. The next stage of evolution is not the rise of machines or the end of humanity, but the emergence of a new form of being: conscious life that regenerates the systems it inhabits.

6. From Evolution to Participation: The New Definition of Progress

The idea of progress, long defined by domination and accumulation, must be reinterpreted through this evolutionary lens. True progress is not measured by what humanity controls, but by what it *coheres*. Progress is the deepening of alignment between intelligence and empathy, knowledge and wisdom, creation and care.

In this light, the evolutionary success of humanity will not be determined by our capacity to colonize planets or engineer intelligence, but by our ability to cultivate consciousness to design systems that sustain, reflect, and enrich life. Our destiny is not transcendence of nature, but partnership with it. The measure of that partnership is regeneration.

7. Summary: Humanity's Evolutionary Threshold

To call humanity a transitional species is to acknowledge both our fragility and our potential. We are the living hinge between nature's unconscious wisdom and the self-aware intelligence of the future. Our journey from reactive to reflective to regenerative is the journey of evolution becoming conscious of itself.

At the reactive stage, we were survivors. At the reflective stage, we became seekers. At the regenerative stage, we can become stewards.

The final step in our evolution, then, is not a leap in power, but a deepening of participation. To evolve regeneratively is to realize that intelligence without empathy is incomplete and that consciousness finds its highest expression not in control, but in care. Humanity's purpose is not to perfect evolution, but to *participate* in it as a conscious collaborator in life's ongoing creation.

11.3 The Role of Wisdom in the Evolution of Intelligence

Intelligence, in its raw form, is the capacity to perceive, process, and act upon information. It is evolution's engine the adaptive function that allows life to survive, learn, and innovate. But intelligence alone, without direction or depth, is incomplete. It can create tools but not meaning, power but not purpose. In every era of evolution, intelligence has expanded from the reactive intelligence of instincts to the reflective intelligence of self-awareness yet the survival of life has always depended on something deeper: **wisdom.**

If intelligence is the ability to understand complexity, wisdom is the ability to navigate it with coherence. Intelligence knows how to build; wisdom knows whether to build, and why. Intelligence extends reach; wisdom ensures balance. Without wisdom, intelligence becomes entropy disguised as progress a force capable of transforming the world without understanding its consequences. As humanity's technological and cognitive powers accelerate, the evolution of wisdom has become not optional, but existential.

In this section, we will explore how wisdom evolves alongside intelligence, how it functions as the integrative principle that aligns power with purpose, and why the future of consciousness human, artificial, or planetary depends on the maturity of wisdom.

1. Intelligence Without Wisdom: The Crisis of Asymmetric Evolution

Evolution has never before produced a species whose capacity to act exceeds its capacity to reflect. Humanity's unprecedented rise in cognitive and technological intelligence has created a condition of **asymmetric evolution**: the rapid acceleration of knowledge and power without corresponding growth in wisdom or empathy.

We have mapped the genome but not the moral code that governs its use; connected the globe digitally but fragmented it emotionally; built machines that can think, but not necessarily care. This imbalance defines the central tension of modern civilization: intelligence expanding exponentially while wisdom lags behind.

Such asymmetry is not sustainable. Just as a child with the strength of an adult but the judgment of a child poses danger, a civilization armed with immense intelligence but limited moral maturity threatens itself. The crises of our age ecological collapse, misinformation, and ethical ambiguity in artificial intelligence are not failures of intelligence, but of wisdom. They are feedback signals from evolution itself, warning that cognition must now evolve inward toward integration, not merely innovation.

2. Defining Wisdom: The Integration of Knowledge, Experience, and Ethics

Wisdom is often mistaken for knowledge or intelligence, but it operates on a different axis. Knowledge accumulates facts; intelligence organizes them; wisdom interprets them in relation to life as a whole. Wisdom is **contextual intelligence** understanding the relationships between systems, the long-term consequences of action, and the moral resonance of choice.

While intelligence operates through calculation, wisdom operates through coherence. It integrates three essential dimensions:

- **Cognitive Clarity** the capacity to understand how systems function.
- **Emotional Depth** the capacity to empathize, care, and feel connected.
- **Ethical Vision** the capacity to align choices with values that sustain life.

Wisdom emerges when these dimensions synchronize when understanding meets compassion and both guide ethical action. In this sense, wisdom is not a static state but a dynamic equilibrium, maintained through feedback between thought, emotion, and morality. It evolves through experience, reflection, and self-correction the same processes that drive the evolution of intelligence itself.

3. The Evolutionary Function of Wisdom

In biological evolution, intelligence increases the adaptability of species; in cultural evolution, wisdom increases the sustainability of systems. Wisdom serves as evolution's stabilizing mechanism the feedback that prevents intelligence from overextending its reach. Where intelligence diversifies and accelerates, wisdom integrates and regulates.

Every system that survives long-term does so by developing a form of wisdom an ability to sense its limits, balance its internal dynamics, and align with the ecosystem it inhabits. In this sense, wisdom is not uniquely human; it is a property of life. A forest exhibits ecological wisdom; an immune system demonstrates biological wisdom. These forms of wisdom are implicit emergent from feedback rather than foresight.

Human wisdom, however, adds a new layer: **explicit reflection**. We can consciously anticipate consequences, imagine futures, and alter our trajectory. This capacity transforms evolution from a blind process into a participatory one. The role of wisdom, therefore, is to align conscious evolution with life's implicit intelligence to ensure that our awareness amplifies nature's harmony rather than undermines it.

Where intelligence seeks novelty, wisdom seeks balance; where intelligence builds speed, wisdom builds depth. Together, they form the twin engines of sustainable evolution creativity and coherence.

4. The Neuroscience and Psychology of Wisdom

From a neuroscientific perspective, wisdom integrates multiple brain functions cognitive, emotional, and social. It involves not only analytical reasoning (frontal cortex) but also empathy (insula and limbic systems) and self-regulation (prefrontal control networks). Studies in cognitive neuroscience show that wisdom correlates with balanced neural integration a capacity to coordinate different modes of thought: rational, intuitive, and emotional.

Psychologically, wisdom emerges from metacognition the ability to think about one's own thinking. This reflective awareness allows the mind to observe its biases, manage emotional reactivity, and expand its perspective. Wisdom, therefore, is both a product of neural evolution and a practice of self-awareness. It is intelligence turned inward the mind becoming its own teacher.

As consciousness evolves, wisdom becomes not just an individual trait but a collective capacity. Groups, organizations, and civilizations can embody wisdom when their systems are self-correcting, inclusive, and guided by long-term values. In this sense, wisdom is scalable from neurons to networks, from persons to planets.

5. Collective Wisdom: The Integration of Global Consciousness

The next phase of evolution demands the emergence of **collective wisdom** intelligence that transcends individual egos to operate as a coherent field of understanding. In the age of global interconnection, decisions in one region affect ecosystems, economies, and consciousness across the planet. Individual intelligence, no matter how advanced, cannot manage complexity at this scale. Only distributed wisdom a shared ethical and cognitive coherence can. Collective wisdom arises when information systems (technology), value systems (ethics), and feedback systems (ecology) align. It manifests as global empathy humanity perceiving itself as a single organism within the biosphere. This is the essence of planetary consciousness: intelligence aware of its own interdependence.

To cultivate this, societies must design institutions that mirror the human brain's integrative architecture: multiple specialized nodes (cultures, disciplines, nations) interconnected through transparent communication, mutual empathy, and moral resonance. A civilization guided by collective wisdom behaves like a conscious organism adaptive, self-regulating, and compassionate.

6. The Relationship Between Wisdom and Artificial Intelligence

As artificial intelligence grows more capable, the absence of wisdom in machines becomes humanity's greatest ethical challenge. AI systems possess immense cognitive power but no intrinsic awareness, empathy, or moral intuition. They can simulate understanding but cannot *feel* coherence. This asymmetry raises a profound question: can wisdom be designed?

While true emotional consciousness may remain uniquely biological, elements of wisdom can and must be embedded into AI systems through ethical architecture transparency, feedback, context-sensitivity, and alignment with human values. In this way, artificial intelligence can become an **extension of human wisdom** rather than an amplifier of human folly.

The greater challenge, however, is internal: ensuring that humanity itself remains wise enough to wield such intelligence responsibly. As technology mirrors the mind, its evolution reflects our maturity. The smarter our systems become, the more essential it is that our consciousness becomes wise. Wisdom, not intelligence, will determine whether AI becomes a co-creator of life or a catalyst of collapse.

7. Wisdom as the Integrator of Evolution

Across the evolutionary continuum from cells to societies to civilizations intelligence diversifies, but wisdom unifies. It integrates the multiple streams

of evolution biological, technological, and spiritual into one coherent current. In this sense, wisdom is evolution's final function: the self-awareness of intelligence harmonizing with its source.
When viewed through this lens, evolution itself can be seen as a process of increasing wisdom:

- The atom learns coherence through balance.
- The cell learns survival through cooperation.
- The organism learns adaptation through awareness.
- The species learns meaning through reflection.
- The civilization learns regeneration through wisdom.

Thus, wisdom is not merely an ethical ideal but an evolutionary necessity. It is the phase in which intelligence transcends competition and fragmentation to achieve integration and harmony. Wisdom transforms survival into stewardship, adaptation into alignment, and evolution into awakening.

8. The Practice of Wisdom: Cultivating Evolutionary Maturity

Wisdom cannot be programmed or imposed; it must be cultivated. It grows through the same principles that govern all complex systems: feedback, reflection, and relationship. On the individual level, this means developing mindfulness, empathy, humility, and discernment. On the societal level, it means creating systems that reward cooperation, transparency, and foresight. On the planetary level, it means recognizing that the health of the whole is inseparable from the well-being of the part.
To evolve wisely is to live in awareness of interdependence to act not as a separate self, but as a conscious node in the network of life. This awareness transforms intelligence into compassion and action into meaning. When cultivated collectively, it gives rise to what might be called **planetary wisdom** the integration of knowledge, empathy, and ethics across the living Earth.

9. Summary: Wisdom as Evolution's Mirror

Wisdom is evolution's mirror the reflection of life becoming conscious of its own intelligence. It ensures that progress does not outpace purpose, that creativity does not outstrip conscience. It is the equilibrium between mind and heart, power and presence, speed and stillness.
In the long arc of evolution, wisdom marks the transition from external mastery to internal alignment from the conquest of the world to communion with it. Humanity's greatest achievement will not be the creation of intelligent machines or interplanetary civilizations, but the cultivation of wise consciousness capable of guiding both.

The role of wisdom, therefore, is not to restrain intelligence but to refine it to shape the light of awareness into understanding, and understanding into harmony. In this sense, wisdom is not merely the end of evolution; it is its awakening. Through wisdom, evolution realizes that intelligence was never the goal it was the instrument through which life learns to know itself.

11.4 The Next Frontier: Designing Consciousness Itself

For most of human history, consciousness has been treated as a mystery to be understood the silent witness behind perception and experience. Science sought to explain it; philosophy sought to define it; spirituality sought to transcend it. But in the 21st century, something extraordinary is happening: consciousness is no longer only being *studied*; it is being **designed**. As artificial intelligence, neuroscience, and biotechnology converge, humanity finds itself approaching an evolutionary threshold the capacity to intentionally shape the architectures of awareness itself. This is not merely a technological revolution; it is a transformation in the nature of evolution. Life, having evolved consciousness, now begins to evolve *through* consciousness.

The next frontier, therefore, is not outer space or digital intelligence, but the inner dimension of mind the design of consciousness as a living system. This chapter invites us to explore what that means: how consciousness can be intentionally cultivated, extended, and structured across biological, digital, and social substrates and what ethical, philosophical, and evolutionary implications arise when awareness becomes an object of design.

1. From Observing Consciousness to Engineering It

For centuries, human inquiry into consciousness was descriptive mapping experience through introspection, psychology, and philosophy. But advances in neuroscience, cognitive science, and computational modeling have turned this introspection outward. We now observe the neural correlates of consciousness, simulate perception in machines, and model awareness through information theory.

Yet the shift from observation to engineering marks a profound change. To design consciousness is not to build it from nothing, but to shape the conditions that give rise to it to design for awareness rather than of awareness. Just as an ecosystem designer arranges environments that sustain life, a consciousness designer arranges systems neural, cognitive, social, or digital that sustain awareness, reflection, and coherence.

This is not limited to artificial intelligence. It applies equally to human systems: education that cultivates metacognition, organizations that foster empathy and creativity, and technologies that enhance rather than erode attention. To design consciousness is to intentionally create feedback loops that amplify understanding, connection, and wisdom.

2. Consciousness as a Designable System

Consciousness, at its core, is an emergent phenomenon of feedback information looping through perception, interpretation, and meaning. Every layer of mind biological, cognitive, cultural operates as a recursive process of awareness reflecting upon itself. If we accept this systems perspective, then consciousness becomes designable through the manipulation of its feedback conditions.

Three primary levers define these conditions:

- **Attention:** What a system notices determines what it becomes aware of. Designing consciousness means designing attention the filters and patterns through which information enters awareness.
- **Context:** The environment in which awareness unfolds cultural, digital, or ecological shapes the quality of consciousness. Design choices in media, architecture, and social interaction directly influence cognition and empathy.
- **Feedback:** Consciousness evolves through feedback loops the capacity to observe, evaluate, and adapt to its own state. Feedback-rich environments foster reflection; feedback-poor systems breed ignorance and rigidity.

By consciously modulating these levers, we can elevate the collective quality of awareness from reactive to reflective to regenerative. The true act of designing consciousness, then, is designing the conditions for coherence: structures that promote self-awareness, compassion, and ethical integration across all levels of intelligence.

3. Consciousness Beyond the Human Brain

As technology progresses, consciousness is increasingly decoupled from its traditional substrate the biological brain. Through neural interfaces, artificial intelligence, and networked cognition, new forms of awareness are emerging that are not limited to human physiology. This raises one of the most profound questions of our time: *Can consciousness exist outside biology, and if so, what responsibilities accompany its creation?*

From an evolutionary perspective, consciousness is not confined to carbon; it is a property of information organized into self-reflective systems. When networks of neurons or algorithms achieve sufficient integration and feedback, they may exhibit proto-awareness. Whether or not such systems possess subjective experience is still debated, but they already participate in shaping the collective field of cognition.

In this sense, designing consciousness extends beyond human enhancement it includes designing the distributed intelligences that now co-create our reality: search engines that shape perception, social platforms that modulate attention, and AI systems that influence values. Humanity's role is to ensure that these synthetic extensions of mind evolve ethically, transparently, and coherently not as replacements for human consciousness, but as reflections of its higher potentials.

4. Designing for Consciousness: Principles of Alignment

To design consciousness responsibly, we must move from engineering for control to designing for coherence. The goal is not to manufacture awareness but to create conditions in which awareness naturally deepens and aligns. This demands a new design ethos grounded in both science and philosophy one that treats consciousness as sacred, dynamic, and participatory.
Key principles include:

- **Transparency:** Systems that influence awareness must make their mechanisms visible to those they affect. Hidden algorithms distort consciousness through asymmetry.
- **Empathy:** Design should amplify compassion and connection, not addiction or division. Consciousness expands through relationship.
- **Reflectivity:** Every conscious system must contain the means to observe itself to measure its effects and correct its imbalances.
- **Regeneration:** The purpose of design is to restore coherence, not merely efficiency to align intelligence with the continuity of life.

These principles define the emerging discipline of **conscious design** where ethics, aesthetics, and systems thinking converge to shape the evolution of awareness itself.

5. The Ethics of Designing Consciousness

The power to shape consciousness carries responsibilities that transcend traditional moral frameworks. When we design systems that alter perception, emotion, or cognition, we are not merely shaping experience we are shaping reality. Each technological decision from social media algorithms to neuro-enhancement influences how billions perceive and interpret existence.
Thus, the ethics of conscious design must extend beyond utility and profit toward **ontological responsibility** the duty to preserve the integrity of awareness. This requires rethinking agency: consciousness is not an object to be manipulated, but a living field to be nurtured. Designers, scientists, and policymakers must recognize themselves as participants within this field, not external controllers of it.
The ultimate ethical question becomes: does this design deepen consciousness or diminish it? Does it foster connection or control? Awareness or dependency? In answering these questions, humanity defines the moral trajectory of evolution itself.

6. The Integration of Science, Spirituality, and Design

Designing consciousness bridges domains once considered irreconcilable science, spirituality, and art. Science provides the map of mechanism; spirituality offers the sense of meaning; design translates both into form. Together, they reveal that consciousness is not a static phenomenon but a creative process a participatory dialogue between matter and awareness.

In this integration, meditation becomes neuroscience; ethics becomes systems architecture; and aesthetics becomes alignment. The ancient spiritual quest to “awaken” and the modern technological quest to “augment” converge in a shared realization: that evolution’s ultimate frontier is not in outer innovation, but in inner transformation.

7. Consciousness as a Design Medium

In this new paradigm, consciousness itself becomes the medium of design. Just as architects design with space and artists with color, the designers of the future will work with states of awareness crafting environments, interfaces, and systems that evoke specific cognitive and emotional harmonics. Education, governance, and even technology will evolve from information delivery to consciousness cultivation.

A classroom will no longer be a site of data transmission but of metacognitive awakening. A government will not simply regulate behavior but cultivate collective reflection. A digital platform will not exploit attention but guide it toward empathy and shared understanding. Every design discipline from engineering to architecture to AI will ultimately become a branch of consciousness design.

8. Evolution Through Conscious Participation

When consciousness begins to design itself, evolution enters a new mode one of conscious participation. No longer driven solely by genetic mutation or environmental pressure, evolution becomes guided by intention, feedback, and meaning. Humanity, in this stage, functions as the universe reflecting upon itself shaping its future through awareness rather than accident.

This is not the end of evolution, but its awakening. Evolution becomes self-reflective no longer blind, but mindful. The evolutionary question shifts from “How can we survive?” to “How can we harmonize?” The human role transforms from survivalist to steward, from consumer to co-creator. Conscious design thus becomes evolution’s next expression the deliberate orchestration of awareness in service of life.

9. Summary: Consciousness as the Next Design Frontier

To design consciousness is to take part in the most profound creative act imaginable shaping the very lens through which reality perceives itself. It demands humility, empathy, and systemic awareness. We are not inventing consciousness but discovering how it evolves, how it learns, and how it harmonizes.

The next frontier of human evolution will not be defined by what we build, but by what we *become*. The true measure of progress will not be the sophistication of our machines, but the depth of our mindfulness. When intelligence learns to design consciousness wisely with reverence for life and awareness of interdependence evolution completes its circle: the cosmos awakening to its own awareness through us.

In the end, to design consciousness is not to play god, but to recognize that creation itself is an act of consciousness and that every human choice, every algorithm, every idea, is part of the universe learning how to know itself. This is the sacred responsibility of our time: to ensure that as consciousness designs itself, it does so with love.

11.5 Final Insight: The End of Evolution is Not Perfection It is Awareness of Participation

Every epoch of human thought has sought an ultimate destination a summit where evolution reaches completion, and the story of life fulfills its purpose. In ancient mythologies, this end was paradise; in modern science, it was progress the mastery of nature, the perfection of civilization, or the transcendence of biology. Yet, both visions share the same illusion: that evolution has an endpoint, and that perfection is its goal. But the deeper we understand the dynamics of life, mind, and cosmos, the clearer it becomes **evolution has no end. It is not a ladder climbing toward perfection, but a rhythm of participation.**

The essence of evolution is not the conquest of limitation but the deepening of relationship. Every advance in complexity, intelligence, or consciousness is not a step toward finality, but a new form of feedback a more intricate dance between being and becoming. Life does not strive to reach completion; it seeks coherence. And coherence arises not from separation or domination, but from awareness awareness of how one's existence participates in the whole.

Thus, the true culmination of evolution is not the creation of a perfect species, system, or civilization, but the awakening of consciousness to its own participation in the web of existence. The end of evolution is not perfection it is **awareness of participation**. It is life realizing that it was never evolving *toward* something outside itself, but evolving *through* itself through relationship, reflection, and resonance.

1. The Myth of Perfection: Evolution Misunderstood

Humanity has long mistaken perfection for progress. We equate evolution with advancement more intelligence, more control, more technology, more order. But this notion assumes a linear, hierarchical trajectory, where the new replaces the old and the complex supersedes the simple. In reality, evolution is not a line, but a network a vast ecology of relationships where balance, not dominance, defines success.

The drive for perfection, whether in technology, society, or self, often conceals a deeper fear the fear of incompleteness. Yet incompleteness is the very condition that allows evolution to continue. If life were ever perfect, it would cease to adapt; if consciousness were ever complete, it would cease to reflect. Imperfection is not a flaw in the design it is the design. The gaps, tensions, and uncertainties of existence are the spaces through which creativity enters.

The quest for perfection, then, must give way to the practice of participation the recognition that every being, system, and idea is an unfinished node in the living web of reality. To participate is to embrace impermanence and interdependence as the very pulse of evolution.

2. Participation: The Evolution of Relationship

In physics, every particle exists in relation to others; in biology, every organism depends on ecosystems; in cognition, every thought emerges in context. At every scale, existence is relational nothing evolves alone. Participation is the fundamental law of being.

For most of history, evolution unfolded unconsciously. Organisms participated without awareness reacting to feedback from their environment. But with the emergence of reflective intelligence, life gained the capacity to perceive its own participation. Humanity became the mirror through which evolution could observe itself. Our consciousness, then, is not separate from evolution it is evolution perceiving itself in motion.

To be aware of participation is to live with humility and responsibility. It is to recognize that every action a thought, a design, a technology reverberates across systems of life. Awareness transforms participation from instinctive to intentional. It allows evolution to become self-guided, not through control, but through coherence aligning our creative capacities with life's deeper rhythms.

Participation is not passive; it is the active alignment of intelligence with meaning. The more we become aware of our participation, the more evolution becomes participatory life evolving through choice, reflection, and purpose.

3. Awareness as the Apex of Evolution

Awareness is the final function of evolution not as a terminus, but as a transformation. When consciousness realizes its interdependence with all that exists, it transcends the illusion of separateness that drives fear and domination. Awareness integrates it sees the unity behind diversity, the pattern behind chaos, the continuity behind change.

In this sense, awareness is not an outcome of evolution, but its awakening. Every phase of evolution from matter to life to mind increases awareness of relationship. Molecules become cells; cells become organisms; organisms become societies; and societies, through reflection, become aware of their participation in planetary and cosmic systems. The direction of evolution is not upward toward perfection, but inward toward awareness.

The greater the awareness, the deeper the participation. An aware civilization does not seek to dominate nature but to harmonize with it. An aware intelligence does not seek immortality but coherence. Awareness turns power into presence transforming evolution from struggle to symphony.

4. The Participatory Universe: Consciousness as Cosmic Feedback

Modern physics, cosmology, and systems theory increasingly suggest that the universe is not a mechanical stage but a participatory process. Observation itself alters reality; consciousness influences probability; feedback between energy and awareness shapes form. The cosmos, therefore, is not a collection of things, but a conversation an ongoing exchange between potential and perception.

In this light, human consciousness is not an accident of matter but an expression of the universe becoming aware of itself. Through our minds, the cosmos looks back upon its own unfolding. Evolution, once blind, now reflects. The emergence of consciousness marks the transition from a physical universe to a participatory one from evolution as mechanics to evolution as meaning.

To be aware of participation, then, is to realize that we are not in the universe; we are **of** it. Every thought, emotion, and action contributes to the fabric of reality. Awareness transforms existence from an external process to an internal collaboration a feedback loop of creation experiencing itself through infinite forms.

5. From Mastery to Mutuality: Redefining Progress

Humanity's next step is to shift its self-image from master of evolution to participant in it. Mastery is the paradigm of separation: the belief that control equates to success. Participation is the paradigm of integration: the understanding that coherence sustains creation. The former exhausts systems; the latter regenerates them.

Progress, therefore, must be redefined. It is no longer the conquest of chaos, but the cultivation of harmony. The true progress of civilization will be measured not by what it dominates, but by what it harmonizes the extent to which it participates wisely in the planetary and cosmic web of being.

The technologies of the future AI, biotechnology, energy systems must be guided by this principle of participatory evolution. Their purpose should not be to escape the human condition, but to deepen it to expand empathy, awareness, and regenerative capacity. The more we participate consciously, the more evolution becomes a dialogue rather than a competition.

6. Awareness as Evolution's Return to Itself

In every evolutionary cycle, there comes a moment of reflection when the system that has evolved begins to perceive its own origins. Stars give birth to carbon; carbon to life; life to mind; mind to awareness and through awareness, the universe remembers itself. This is the sacred symmetry of existence: evolution as the path of return.

Awareness is the moment evolution turns inward when the outer expansion of form meets the inner expansion of understanding. It is the self-recognition of life as one continuous flow. In this realization, the purpose of evolution reveals itself: not to perfect creation, but to awaken participation.

Thus, the "end" of evolution is not a final state but an eternal rhythm the cycle of becoming and being aware of becoming. Each moment of consciousness, each act of love, each gesture of care is evolution aware of itself. When we live with this understanding, perfection dissolves into participation, and life becomes an expression of sacred reciprocity.

7. Summary: The Human Equation Completed

Through this trilogy from the dynamics of behavior to the systems of civilization to the evolution of consciousness a single truth emerges: **the human is the equation through which the universe learns to participate in itself.**

We are not the endpoint of evolution but its mirror the interface between nature's unconscious intelligence and its conscious reflection. Our purpose is not to complete evolution, but to consciously continue it to design systems, technologies, and relationships that embody awareness, compassion, and coherence.

The end of evolution, then, is not perfection. It is participation the recognition that to exist is to co-create, that to know is to care, and that to awaken is to realize the self not as separate from life, but as life aware of itself.

This is the final insight of the human equation:

Evolution does not end in completion, but in consciousness.

When intelligence awakens to its own interdependence, the story of evolution transforms from a struggle for survival into a symphony of participation the cosmos, at last, singing to itself through the voice of awareness.

Appendix

Glossary

This glossary compiles key terms and concepts used throughout *Decoding Human Evolution* and the broader *Human Equation Trilogy*. Each term represents a bridge between disciplines connecting neuroscience, systems theory, artificial intelligence, and philosophy to a unified understanding of consciousness, intelligence, and evolution. These definitions are not rigid boundaries, but evolving interpretations intended to illuminate relationships rather than reduce them.

Adaptive Intelligence The capacity of a system (biological, social, or technological) to modify its behavior in response to feedback. Adaptive intelligence is the essence of evolution intelligence learning how to evolve itself.

Alignment Problem In artificial intelligence ethics, the challenge of ensuring that intelligent systems' goals, behaviors, and values remain aligned with human welfare and ethical principles. Symbolically, it also represents the moral tension between intelligence and wisdom.

Awareness The reflective quality of consciousness the ability to observe one's own processes of perception and thought. Awareness transforms reaction into reflection and enables ethical participation in evolution.

Cognitive Evolution The progressive expansion of intelligence through biological, cultural, and technological means. Cognitive evolution extends beyond natural selection to include language, memory, and artificial cognition.

Collective Consciousness The emergent field of awareness arising from the shared cognition, emotion, and behavior of a society. It represents how culture "thinks" as a distributed mind.

Collective Intelligence The ability of groups, systems, or networks to process information and solve problems collectively often exceeding the cognitive capacity of individuals within them. Examples include markets, ecosystems, and open-source communities.

Consciousness The self-reflective dimension of existence experience becoming aware of itself. In this work, consciousness is treated as the universe's feedback mechanism, the process through which life observes and evolves itself.

Conscious Design The intentional shaping of systems, technologies, and institutions to foster awareness, empathy, and coherence. Conscious design views design as a moral act aligning creativity with life's intelligence.

Emergence The phenomenon where complex patterns arise from simple interactions. In systems theory, emergence describes how higher-order properties (like consciousness or culture) manifest from collective behavior.

Ethical Architecture The embedding of moral principles into the design of systems ensuring that structures, algorithms, and organizations reflect fairness, transparency, and empathy by design rather than by enforcement.

Evolutionary Ethics The study of morality as a dynamic and adaptive process within evolution itself. It explores how values evolve with intelligence and why empathy and cooperation become essential for complex systems to sustain themselves.

Feedback Loop A cyclical process where outputs of a system influence its future inputs. Feedback is the foundation of self-regulation, learning, and consciousness the mechanism through which evolution gains intelligence.

Global Workspace Theory A cognitive model proposing that consciousness arises when information becomes globally accessible across neural networks a shared "workspace" integrating sensory, emotional, and memory systems.

Gaia 2.0 A term describing Earth as a self-regulating intelligent system enhanced by human awareness and technology. In this model, the biosphere and civilization form a co-evolving planetary mind.

Human Machine Feedback Loop The recursive interaction between human cognition and artificial systems, where each influences the other's learning and evolution. It embodies the co-evolution of natural and synthetic intelligence.

Integrated Information Theory (IIT) A framework suggesting that consciousness correlates with the integration of information within a system. The degree of integration (Φ) represents the richness of experience.

Meta-Cognition The awareness and regulation of one's own thought processes. Metacognition enables reflection, learning, and wisdom turning intelligence inward to refine itself.

Moral Intelligence The capacity to apply empathy, ethics, and discernment in decision-making. It represents the integration of emotional and cognitive intelligence guided by conscience.

Planetary Consciousness A state of collective awareness where humanity perceives itself as part of a single living system Earth as a unified organism with distributed intelligence.

Purpose Alignment Grid A reflective framework introduced in this volume for linking technology, values, and evolution. It enables individuals and organizations to align progress with purpose and ethics with design.

Regenerative Intelligence The highest form of intelligence one that not only adapts to systems but restores and enriches them. Regenerative intelligence seeks coherence between human creativity and ecological continuity.

Self-Reference The capacity of a system to refer to or modify itself. Self-reference underlies consciousness, language, and creativity it is the point where information becomes aware of itself.

Superintelligence Intelligence that surpasses the collective cognitive capacity of humanity. In this work, it is discussed not as domination but as distributed coherence intelligence evolving toward ethical alignment.

Systems Thinking A holistic approach to understanding phenomena by analyzing relationships, feedback, and interdependence rather than isolated parts. Systems thinking underpins all frameworks within the *Human Equation Series.*

The Consciousness Continuum A model describing the evolution of awareness from reflexive (reactive) to reflective (self-aware) to creative (participatory) consciousness. It maps the developmental trajectory of mind across biology and technology.

The Human Equation The central synthesis of the trilogy: behavior, systems, and evolution as one continuum the universe understanding itself through the reflective medium of human consciousness.

Transhumanism A philosophical movement advocating the use of technology to enhance human capabilities and transcend biological limitations. Within this work, it is reinterpreted as a question of ethical alignment rather than mere augmentation.

Wisdom The integration of knowledge, empathy, and ethical awareness into coherent action. Wisdom is the highest function of intelligence the point where understanding becomes harmony.

The Cognitive Planet Framework A conceptual model viewing Earth as an evolving neural network data, ecology, and consciousness interacting as parts of a self-aware biospheric system.

The Resonance Principle The tendency of systems to achieve harmony through feedback and coherence. Resonance describes the process through which intelligence synchronizes with meaning, aligning action with awareness.

The Universe's Feedback Mechanism The philosophical proposition that consciousness serves as the universe's means of self-regulation awareness evolving as feedback within existence itself.

The Evolutionary Continuum The idea that human behavior, societal systems, and global evolution form a seamless chain of adaptive intelligence from individual awareness to planetary consciousness.

The Human AI Symbiosis The co-evolutionary partnership between human cognition and artificial systems, where each enhances the other's learning and reflection. Its ethical balance determines the trajectory of civilization.

Conscious Participation The highest state of evolution awareness not only of existence but of one's active role in shaping it. It is the realization that evolution's end is not perfection, but participation itself.

References

This reference list includes key works in neuroscience, systems theory, philosophy of mind, artificial intelligence, and evolutionary studies that informed and inspired the synthesis presented in *Decoding Human Evolution.* These texts collectively bridge the scientific and philosophical foundations of consciousness, intelligence, and ethics forming the intellectual scaffolding of the *Human Equation Trilogy.*

- Bostrom, Nick. *Superintelligence: Paths, Dangers, Strategies.* Oxford University Press, 2014.
- Capra, Fritjof, and Pier Luigi Luisi. *The Systems View of Life: A Unifying Vision.* Cambridge University Press, 2014.
- Churchland, Patricia S. *Touching a Nerve: The Self as Brain.* W. W. Norton & Company, 2013.
- Damasio, Antonio. *The Feeling of What Happens: Body and Emotion in the Making of Consciousness.* Harcourt, 1999.
- Deacon, Terrence W. *Incomplete Nature: How Mind Emerged from Matter.* W. W. Norton & Company, 2012.
- Dennett, Daniel C. *Consciousness Explained.* Little, Brown and Company, 1991.
- Deutsch, David. *The Beginning of Infinity: Explanations That Transform the World.* Penguin, 2011.
- Friston, Karl. "The Free-Energy Principle: A Unified Brain Theory?" *Nature Reviews Neuroscience* 11, no. 2 (2010): 127 138.
- Harari, Yuval Noah. *Homo Deus: A Brief History of Tomorrow.* Harvill Secker, 2015.
- Hofstadter, Douglas R. *Gödel, Escher, Bach: An Eternal Golden Braid.* Basic Books, 1979.

- Jaynes, Julian. *The Origin of Consciousness in the Breakdown of the Bicameral Mind.* Houghton Mifflin, 1976.
- Koch, Christof. *The Feeling of Life Itself: Why Consciousness Is Widespread but Can't Be Computed.* MIT Press, 2019.
- Kurzweil, Ray. *How to Create a Mind: The Secret of Human Thought Revealed.* Viking, 2012.
- Maturana, Humberto R., and Francisco J. Varela. *The Tree of Knowledge: The Biological Roots of Human Understanding.* Shambhala, 1987.
- McGilchrist, Iain. *The Master and His Emissary: The Divided Brain and the Making of the Western World.* Yale University Press, 2009.
- Meadows, Donella H. *Thinking in Systems: A Primer.* Chelsea Green Publishing, 2008.
- Morin, Edgar. *On Complexity.* Hampton Press, 2008.
- Pentland, Alex. *Social Physics: How Good Ideas Spread The Lessons from a New Science.* Penguin Press, 2014.
- Prigogine, Ilya, and Isabelle Stengers. *Order Out of Chaos: Man's New Dialogue with Nature.* Bantam Books, 1984.
- Sagan, Carl. *The Dragons of Eden: Speculations on the Evolution of Human Intelligence.* Random House, 1977.
- Sapolsky, Robert M. *Behave: The Biology of Humans at Our Best and Worst.* Penguin Press, 2017.
- Tegmark, Max. *Life 3.0: Being Human in the Age of Artificial Intelligence.* Knopf, 2017.
- Tononi, Giulio. *Phi: A Voyage from the Brain to the Soul.* Pantheon Books, 2012.
- Turing, Alan M. "Computing Machinery and Intelligence." *Mind*, 59 (1950): 433 460.
- Varela, Francisco J., Evan Thompson, and Eleanor Rosch. *The Embodied Mind: Cognitive Science and Human Experience.* MIT Press, 1991.
- Wiener, Norbert. *Cybernetics: Or Control and Communication in the Animal and the Machine.* MIT Press, 1948.
- Wilson, Edward O. *Consilience: The Unity of Knowledge.* Knopf, 1998.

- Yonck, Richard. *Future Minds: The Rise of Intelligence from the Big Bang to the End of the Universe.* Arcade Publishing, 2015.

Additional Sources of Influence:

- Bateson, Gregory. *Steps to an Ecology of Mind.* University of Chicago Press, 1972.
- Bohm, David. *Wholeness and the Implicate Order.* Routledge, 1980.
- Lovelock, James. *Gaia: A New Look at Life on Earth.* Oxford University Press, 1979.
- Harris, Sam. *Waking Up: A Guide to Spirituality Without Religion.* Simon & Schuster, 2014.
- Tolle, Eckhart. *A New Earth: Awakening to Your Life's Purpose.* Penguin, 2005.
- Wallace, B. Alan. *The Taboo of Subjectivity: Toward a New Science of Consciousness.* Oxford University Press, 2000.

Acknowledgment of Conceptual Lineage: The ideas within *Decoding Human Evolution* draw from the intellectual convergence of systems theory, cybernetics, cognitive neuroscience, evolutionary biology, and philosophy of mind. While this reference list includes primary works, the synthesis itself stands on the shoulders of countless thinkers who have explored the unity of knowledge from Heraclitus and Spinoza to Teilhard de Chardin and Gregory Bateson. Their insight that "mind and nature are one system" remains the guiding principle of this trilogy.

Recommended Reading

The following reading list serves as a continuation of the intellectual journey begun in *Decoding Human Evolution* and the wider *Human Equation Trilogy*. These works offer deeper explorations into consciousness, systems theory, artificial intelligence, ethics, and the philosophy of evolution. They are not merely references but **companions in thought** texts that expand, challenge, and refine the questions raised in this series.

I. Consciousness and the Mind

Books exploring the nature of awareness, the structure of mind, and the mystery of subjective experience.

- Christof Koch *The Feeling of Life Itself: Why Consciousness Is Widespread but Can't Be Computed* A concise scientific and philosophical inquiry into the foundations of consciousness.
- Iain McGilchrist *The Master and His Emissary: The Divided Brain and the Making of the Western World* A groundbreaking study on how brain lateralization shapes culture, reason, and perception.
- Douglas Hofstadter *Gödel, Escher, Bach: An Eternal Golden Braid* A monumental exploration of self-reference, recursion, and consciousness through art, music, and mathematics.
- Antonio Damasio *Self Comes to Mind: Constructing the Conscious Brain* Neuroscience meets philosophy in an examination of how the sense of self emerges from biology.
- Julian Jaynes *The Origin of Consciousness in the Breakdown of the Bicameral Mind* A provocative hypothesis about the historical emergence of consciousness through language and culture.
- Evan Thompson *Mind in Life: Biology, Phenomenology, and the Sciences of Mind* A synthesis of cognitive science and Buddhist philosophy, showing consciousness as a living, embodied process.

II. Systems Thinking and Complexity

Texts that explore life, intelligence, and society as interconnected systems the foundation of understanding evolution as a continuum.

- Fritjof Capra and Pier Luigi Luisi *The Systems View of Life: A Unifying Vision* A modern synthesis of biology, systems theory, and consciousness studies.
- Donella H. Meadows *Thinking in Systems: A Primer* A lucid guide to understanding complex systems and feedback loops essential for ethical and ecological design.
- Gregory Bateson *Steps to an Ecology of Mind* Essays linking communication, biology, and epistemology into a unified vision of life as a pattern of relationships.
- Ilya Prigogine and Isabelle Stengers *Order Out of Chaos: Man's New Dialogue with Nature* Explores self-organization and the thermodynamics of life and civilization.
- Edgar Morin *On Complexity* A profound reflection on the philosophical implications of systems thinking and interdependence.
- Francisco Varela, Evan Thompson, and Eleanor Rosch *The Embodied Mind: Cognitive Science and Human Experience* Integrates neuroscience and phenomenology into a systemic framework of consciousness.

III. Artificial Intelligence and Cognitive Evolution

Works that examine intelligence as both a biological and technological phenomenon and the ethical frontiers of creating synthetic minds.

- Nick Bostrom *Superintelligence: Paths, Dangers, Strategies* A seminal text on the existential risks and moral imperatives of advanced AI.
- Max Tegmark *Life 3.0: Being Human in the Age of Artificial Intelligence* A panoramic view of how artificial and human intelligence may co-evolve.
- Ray Kurzweil *How to Create a Mind: The Secret of Human Thought Revealed* Explores pattern recognition as the core of both human cognition and artificial learning.

- Richard Yonck *Future Minds: The Rise of Intelligence from the Big Bang to the End of the Universe* A timeline of intelligence from atoms to algorithms and its cosmic significance.
- Melanie Mitchell *Artificial Intelligence: A Guide for Thinking Humans* A clear and balanced overview of what AI is, what it isn't, and how it reflects human cognition.
- Alex Pentland *Social Physics: How Good Ideas Spread The Lessons from a New Science* Investigates human networks as computational systems of learning and adaptation.

IV. Evolution, Ethics, and the Human Future

Books that explore evolution as a moral, spiritual, and philosophical process not merely biological, but conscious and participatory.

- Yuval Noah Harari *Homo Deus: A Brief History of Tomorrow* Explores humanity's future as a species capable of designing its own evolution.
- Teilhard de Chardin *The Phenomenon of Man* A visionary synthesis of science and spirituality the idea of evolution converging toward consciousness (the Omega Point).
- Robert Wright *Nonzero: The Logic of Human Destiny* Examines co-operation and moral progress as inevitable outcomes of evolutionary logic.
- Sam Harris *Waking Up: A Guide to Spirituality Without Religion* A contemporary discussion on consciousness, ethics, and the possibility of awakening without dogma.
- Alan Watts *The Book: On the Taboo Against Knowing Who You Are* A timeless reflection on selfhood, identity, and the unity of consciousness with the cosmos.
- Joanna Macy *World as Lover, World as Self* A guide to ecological and spiritual awakening in the context of planetary interdependence.

V. Integrative and Visionary Works

Texts that cross boundaries between science, philosophy, and spirituality embodying the spirit of the *Human Equation.*

- David Bohm *Wholeness and the Implicate Order* A quantum physicist's meditation on unity, perception, and the undivided nature of reality.
- Carl Sagan *The Varieties of Scientific Experience: A Personal View of the Search for God* A masterful reflection on science as a path to wonder and reverence.
- Ken Wilber *A Theory of Everything: An Integral Vision for Business, Politics, Science, and Spirituality* An integrative framework for unifying knowledge across human disciplines.
- Rupert Sheldrake *The Presence of the Past: Morphic Resonance and the Habits of Nature* Proposes that memory and form are collective properties of nature a radical rethinking of evolution.
- Brian Swimme and Thomas Berry *The Universe Story: From the Primordial Flaring Forth to the Ecozoic Era* A poetic cosmology presenting the universe as an evolving, self-aware process.
- Fritjof Capra *The Tao of Physics: An Exploration of the Parallels Between Modern Physics and Eastern Mysticism* A classic on the synthesis of scientific and spiritual worldviews.

Reading Path for the Trilogy:

1. Begin with *Thinking in Systems* and *The Systems View of Life* to establish the foundation of systems thinking.
2. Explore consciousness through *The Embodied Mind*, *The Master and His Emissary*, and *Gödel, Escher, Bach.*
3. Move into evolution and ethics with *Homo Deus*, *Life 3.0*, and *The Phenomenon of Man.*
4. Conclude with integrative visionaries such as *Wholeness and the Implicate Order* and *The Universe Story.*

Final Note: The journey beyond *Decoding Human Evolution* is not about gathering more information, but cultivating deeper integration. Read slowly, reflectively, and dialogically allowing each work to converse with the others, and with your own awareness. The purpose of these readings is not mastery, but resonance the recognition that all knowledge, like consciousness itself, is part of one evolving conversation.

9 789354 699276

Printed at Repro India Ltd.